About the author

Award-winning investigative journalist Andrew Fowler began his career in England, where he covered the 1970s IRA bombing campaign for the *London Evening News*. His past roles include chief of staff and acting foreign editor of *The Australian* newspaper, and reporter with SBS *Dateline* and Channel 7. For the last 20 years he was a reporter with the ABC's *Four Corners* and *Foreign Correspondent* programs. He also headed the ABC's Investigative Unit.

Fowler first interviewed Julian Assange for *Foreign Correspondent* in early 2010 and went on to write *The Most Dangerous Man in the World*, which has been translated and published in countries as diverse as USA, China, South Korea, Russia, Indonesia, Romania and Taiwan. It was described by Daniel Ellsberg, whistleblower of the Pentagon Papers, as 'A gripping thriller. By far the best account of Julian Assange's motives and the talents that make him so dangerous', and by Geoffrey Robertson QC as 'the most balanced, fair and factual account yet published of a saga much misrepresented in the media'. Andrew's original ABC program about Assange and WikiLeaks won the New York Festival Gold Medal.

Andrew Fowler spends his time between Paris and Sydney.

The War on Journalism

****

MEDIA MOGULS, WHISTLEBLOWERS AND THE PRICE OF FREEDOM

****

ANDREW FOWLER

WILLIAM HEINEMANN: AUSTRALIA

For my courageous mother, Dorothy

A William Heinemann book
Published by Random House Australia Pty Ltd
Level 3, 100 Pacific Highway, North Sydney NSW 2060
www.randomhouse.com.au

Penguin
Random House
Australia

First published by William Heinemann in 2015

Random House Books is part of the Penguin Random House group of companies whose addresses can be found at global.penguinrandomhouse.com.

National Library of Australia
Cataloguing-in-Publication Entry

Fowler, Andrew John, author.
The war on journalism/Andrew Fowler.

ISBN 978 0 85798 684 9 (paperback)

Journalism.
Newspapers.
Freedom of the press.
Whistle blowing.

070.4

Cover image © STILLFX/Shutterstock
Cover design by Luke Causby, Blue Cork Design
Internal design by Midland Typesetters, Australia
Typeset in Janson Text 12-15.5pt by Midland Typesetters, Australia
Printed in Australia by Griffin Press, an accredited ISO AS/NZS 14001:2004 Environmental Management System printer

Contents

CHAPTER I

Reaching Out

In the early Northern Hemisphere summer of 2010 a 26-year-old computer analyst, Edward J. Snowden, drove into the US military base at Yokota, Japan, to begin work in what is officially described as a forward defensive military complex, home of the fighter-bomber wing of the United States Air Force (USAF). While the air base is important, its real significance has nothing to do with aircraft. It is the Japanese control centre of one of Washington's most secret operations.

A few hundred kilometres away, perched on the hills near the ancient township of Misawa, are a series of satellite dishes directly linked to Yokota. The covers that shroud them, giving them the appearance of gigantic golf balls supposedly protect the dishes from the weather. But like much of what is here, they are not what they seem. The covers shield prying eyes and foreign satellites from seeing exactly where they are pointing. They are part of the USA's global surveillance program, operated by the ultra-secretive National Security Agency (NSA). The NSA is part of an international information-gathering system employing 30,000 staff, including cryptographers who are code-breakers and electronics experts who build systems to intercept information by the truckload.

Here they use the satellite uplinks to spy on the whole area of northern Asia, from China to Russia and across to India, intercepting telephone calls, emails and all forms of electronic data.

1

In the shadow of the huge dishes lies Lake Ogawara. It was where, in 1940, the Imperial Japanese Naval Air Force practised its bombing runs for the attack on Pearl Harbor the following year. The plan Snowden had conceived was every bit as audacious.

Snowden was no innocent to the world of espionage. He'd worked for the CIA in Geneva and fully understood the way the system operated, how it compromised diplomats and business executives and spied on targets for the benefit of the United States. But the activities he discovered at Yokota, Snowden suspected, weren't simply top secret – they were illegal. Over the course of his time at Yokota Air Base – employed by one of the contractors to the NSA – Snowden got his first glimpse of the immense power of the agency. He watched drones in real time as they surveilled people they might kill. He had the ability to view entire villages and see what everyone was doing. Chillingly Snowden saw the NSA tracking people's internet activities as they typed. The more time Snowden spent in Japan the more he realised he couldn't keep 'it all to myself'. He felt it would be wrong to help 'conceal all of this from the public'.[1]

By 2012 Snowden had moved to Hawaii and began working for the head office of the NSA contractor Booz Allen Hamilton. The weather was certainly better than in Japan but the work was very much the same. Over the next few months though, Snowden's fears would be confirmed: the NSA now had a power vastly superior to anything he had ever seen before. He lay awake at night worrying about the consequences – and whether he wanted to be part of it: the NSA was spying on everyone on Earth. Every detail scooped up from emails, phone calls and social media archived forever, providing a huge searchable database on every individual on the planet. The NSA shared the load with its sister organisations in other English-speaking countries. They had built massive complexes around the globe where the colossal volumes of data could be stored and analysed – in Canada, the United Kingdom, New Zealand and Australia, where a former sheep farm near the nation's capital, Canberra, had become home to mega-computers in buildings the size of aircraft hangars: the southern wing of the NSA's vast digital archive. By now Snowden had downloaded thousands of documents he thought the world should see, including information on the NSA's secret monitoring of the entire telecommunications infrastructure of the United States.

In May 2013 Snowden phoned in sick at his US$120,000 a year job and caught a taxi to the airport on Honolulu Island. There, as he made his way past the low-rise buildings and the decorative palm trees, he looked no different to the thousands of other young people milling through the airport on that spring day, glued to their iPhones or desperately searching for a wi-fi connection. A keen observer might have noticed that Snowden carried an exorbitant amount of internet hardware – stuffed in his bags were four laptops and countless thumb drives. The information they contained would later reveal extraordinary details of 'Big Brother' surveillance by the NSA: top-secret programs called PRISM and Boundless Inform-ant, which sucked up whatever was accessible, categorised it according to keywords used in communications and then stored it for possible future retrieval. The NSA's primary role is to protect the USA from terrorism, but Snowden discov-ered the agency was targeting millions of ordinary people and world leaders who had nothing to do with terrorist threats to the United States or its citizens.

The importance of what the files contained could not be overstated. They gave a view into the heart of the most secre-tive organisation in the world. The NSA had paid millions of dollars from a special operations fund to nine US internet companies for access to their material, including email, mobile phone and instant messaging information from Google, Yahoo, Microsoft and Skype.

The NSA tracked any mobile phone anywhere in the world, allowing it to discover who was meeting whom, where and when. So powerful were the tracking tools, there was nowhere to hide – unless the user disconnected from the internet.

Snowden was now in possession of potentially the biggest intelligence leak in history, even overshadowing the extra-ordinary WikiLeaks Cablegate revelations by Bradley, now Chelsea, Manning. There were many parallels between the actions taken by Manning and Snowden, and the latter would draw useful lessons from Manning's stark experiences. As he boarded a plane for Hong Kong, Snowden had already made up his mind about how best to make this treasure-trove of information public, and he was determined not to suffer the same fate as Manning: Amnesty International had denounced Manning's treatment in custody;[2] the matter was also raised by the Human Rights Council of the United Nations;[3] one of the charges Manning faced carried a life sentence.

For a US citizen *The New York Times* would have been the obvious first place to go. But he was unimpressed at the way the newspaper had dealt with a huge story involving the NSA after the 9/11 attacks on New York and Washington. In mid-2004 the newspaper learned that the NSA had used its vast powers to eavesdrop on US citizens at the explicit direction of then President George W. Bush. With Bush running for re-election, such revelations may well have damaged his chances. *The New York Times*, citing national security concerns, decided not to publish. Yet several months later, with Bush's tenure in the White House assured, those security concerns seemingly disappeared and *The New York Times* broke the story. It went on to win a Pulitzer Prize. Snowden was not persuaded that *The New York Times* had acted honourably.

Instead he had made contact with a little-known New York filmmaker. Laura Poitras had been nominated for an Oscar for one of her productions but what had caught Snowden's interest was the movie she was making at the time involving WikiLeaks founder Julian Assange. Entitled *Citizenfour*, it was about government surveillance. The film's stand against what she believed was a dangerous and unnecessary intrusion into the lives of ordinary citizens had already seen Poitras stopped and searched many times when she reentered the United States. Her life was about to get a whole lot more complicated.

Impressed by her work, Snowden had approached her to act as the go-between to contact a then obscure blogger, Glenn Greenwald. From her eastside New York apartment Poitras sent encrypted messages to Greenwald, whom she had met while making the film, alerting him that Snowden wanted to make contact. Though Greenwald, a former lawyer and human rights advocate, also wrote informed pieces from his home in Brazil's São Paulo for the London *Guardian*, he was more widely known for his work for the online news and information site salon.com, aka Salon.

That Snowden was about to give his story to two relative unknowns said much about the public's crisis of confidence in the modern mass media. Despite offering the biggest leak since the 1971 release of the Pentagon Papers, Chelsea Manning had been rebuffed by the two biggest dailies in the United States, *The New York Times* and *The Washington Post* – Snowden had simply decided to bypass them. Whichever way it was viewed, the insiders of the fourth estate – with their cosy and often self-serving relationships with powerful institutions – were being overtaken by the outsiders: those who did not conform to the usual journalistic reliance on information drip-fed to them from the government.

As Snowden flew into Hong Kong – choosing the former British colony because, as he saw it, it had a 'spirited democracy' but importantly it also put him outside the clutches of both US and British security services – half a world away, Greenwald and Poitras boarded a plane in New York to join up with him.

Snowden ensconced himself in one of the best hotels in
Hong Kong. The Mira on busy Nathan Road might be expensive at AU$400 a night but the attraction for Snowden included
reasonable security, a free smartphone to use while he was a
guest and high-speed internet wi-fi in every room.

Up the road was the US embassy with its CIA station,
and Snowden was only too aware of how vulnerable he
was. Worried there might be spy cameras in the walls,
he wore a hood which covered both his head and his laptop –
a somewhat clumsy but effective protection from prying eyes
when he typed passwords on the keyboard. He also barricaded
the door with pillows to prevent eavesdropping devices from
picking up sounds of conversations from outside. Snowden
was convinced his life and those of any journalists who dealt
with him were in danger. 'The US intelligence community,'
he wrote later, 'will certainly kill you if they think you are the
single point of failure that could stop this disclosure and make
them the sole owner of this information.'[4]

When he met Greenwald and Poitras, he told them he was
willing to 'sacrifice all' because he couldn't in 'good conscience'
allow the US government to 'destroy privacy, internet freedom
and basic liberties for people around the world with this
massive surveillance machine they're secretly building'.[5]

—

In London, *The Guardian*'s utilitarian offices sit in stark
contrast to the neo-gothic architecture of the nearby
St Pancras railway station, built in the 1860s – a time when
the printed word travelled at the speed of the fastest loco-
motive. Back in those days editors had time to ponder on what
to publish. For *The Guardian*'s editor, Alan Rusbridger, there
was no such luxury. Yet the story from Greenwald – written
after just one day with Snowden in Hong Kong and which
would eventually become part of the biggest journalistic
scoop in the history of journalism – sat in the editor's inbox

for three long days. Rusbridger – who had made a name for himself and his newspaper publishing the WikiLeaks cables – was holding back.

At that stage Snowden had not revealed his identity; it's possible Rusbridger was haunted by the case of a whistleblower from the Government Communications Headquarters (GCHQ), the United Kingdom's equivalent of the NSA, who leaked a devastating memo from the NSA before the 2003 invasion of Iraq that revealed the United States was trying to manipulate the UN Security Council vote. The story was published in *The Observer*, *The Guardian*'s sister paper. Katharine Gun, a Chinese-language specialist, was later arrested and charged under the Official Secrets Act. Rusbridger had seen the lengths the government was prepared to go to prosecute her before finally deciding not to proceed and was clearly rattled. It's believed what saved Gun from prosecution was the fear that any court hearing might expose the fact the British government knew the argument for going to war was based on dubious legal grounds.

Greenwald credits his partner, David Miranda, with pushing him to hold *The Guardian*'s feet to the fire and not delay on this bombshell publication. 'I had my chat box open on my laptop while talking to *Guardian* editors, and I had David on the phone in my ear, and he's dictating what to write to them word by word. It was something like, "Please consider this my resignation if the article is not published by 5 p.m. today", and I was like, "Oh my god, David, I cannot say that!"'[6]

Eventually the first NSA story was published on *The Guardian*'s website. It was hardly an auspicious beginning to a series of startling revelations but it was further evidence that even newspapers like *The Guardian* could waver under pressure. Interestingly it had not been Rusbridger who had given the go-ahead to publish. A deputy editor had made the final decision.

What it did say about *The Guardian* was that it had taken an outsider – Greenwald was not on the staff payroll – to stand up to the pressure; even to issue threats of his own. *The Guardian* had been faced with a stark choice: publish the story or someone else will. *The Guardian* did not have exclusive access to the Snowden files.

On the other side of the Atlantic, *The Washington Post* – the newspaper that broke Watergate, an extraordinary investigation which led to the first resignation of a US president – was gearing up to publish its version of the NSA revelations. Unlike *The Guardian*, it would not face grave sanctions for doing so, such as the prospect of prosecution under the Official Secrets Act. US journalists are in a more privileged position to report on national security than any other journalists in the world. The US Constitution's First Amendment guarantees freedom of speech, acting as a shield from prosecution no matter how damaging the leak may be, unless it can be proved the journalists were working as spies.

It's only fair to point out that neither the WikiLeaks exposés nor any of the material released by Snowden have resulted in anyone's death. Though governments and sections of the press have hysterically condemned the leaks as endangering national security, they have failed to produce any evidence.

Despite its status as the newspaper with one of the greatest reputations for investigative reporting, based in a country where journalists can write with impunity about national security, *The Washington Post*'s publication of the NSA revelations was not as gutsy as it perhaps seemed. The *Post* asked an outside contributor to write the report based on Snowden's leaks – not a staff member – echoing *The Guardian*'s arrangement with Greenwald. When Snowden asked the *Post* to publish within 72 hours the full text of a PowerPoint presentation describing PRISM, a sophisticated interception system, not only did the *Post* fail to do that, the newspaper later openly admitted it 'sought the views of government officials about the potential harm to national security prior to publication and decided to reproduce only four of the 41 slides' given to them by Snowden.[7]

Snowden was naive if he believed *The Washington Post* would publish everything. The editor has the right to decide when to publish and what to publish. But in boasting – in a puzzling background report – that it 'broke' the story, the *Post* unwittingly drew attention to a major failing: it only published after *The Guardian* went to press with Greenwald's report. By delaying publication, if the intelligence community, or the government, raised any hostile questions, the *Post* could safely argue it was merely playing catch-up with *The Guardian*. It had forgone being first with the Snowden stories in exchange for an easier life. It was not exactly the kind of hard-nosed journalism that had made the *Post* famous and it pointed to a serious problem which had begun to infect much of US journalism. On 6 June, while many at the *Post* quietly celebrated that the story had finally made it into the paper, there was also a worrying suspicion that the *Post* was far closer to the Washington Establishment than was good for its journalism.

Maybe Snowden should have expected it. It's one of the reasons he had decided to go with Greenwald and Poitras. *The Washington Post*'s handling of the WikiLeaks *Collateral Murder* exposé – which showed US helicopter gunships killing unarmed civilians, and two journalists, in a town square in Baghdad in 2007 – had posed many questions about what had happened to the once mighty media institution.

David Finkel, a Pulitzer Prize-winning journalist with the newspaper, was embedded with the US troops in Baghdad, writing a book called *The Good Soldiers*. In it, he gives a vivid description of the killings, and quotes much of the dialogue that would feature in the *Collateral Murder* video. When Finkel's book came out, *The Washington Post* carried a story about the killings but that's where it ended. There was no follow-up investigation by the paper. It was not until

WikiLeaks published the *Collateral Murder* video three years later that the horrific truth was exposed.

The Snowden case revealed once again the timidity of newspapers on both sides of the Atlantic when offered an astonishing story. *The Guardian* prevaricated until it decided that losing the story was worse than not publishing it; *The Washington Post* only published after *The Guardian* had taken the lead. Having previously chosen not to deal with *The New York Times* after they had kept secret the NSA's illegal bugging of US citizens, Snowden's carefully considered better bet for publication on US soil had not lived up to expectations.

After the initial flurry of stories Snowden waited in Hong Kong, deciding what to do next. If Snowden had expected to encounter what the doyen of investigative journalism Seymour Hersh calls 'courageous editors' who would publish and be damned, he was sadly disappointed.

It was Hersh who revealed over 40 years ago the massacre at My Lai in Vietnam where hundreds of men, women and children in a village were slaughtered by US troops. Even then it was a difficult story to get published but today it would be virtually impossible, without a box full of documents. 'These chickenshit editors will only publish with documents,' he said. 'They're a travesty of journalism.'[8] Even detailed documentation wasn't helping Snowden.

In the more than 40 years that have elapsed since Seymour Hersh and *The Washington Post* exposed the US military atrocities in Vietnam, journalists appear to have become positively obedient: more inclined to regurgitate government spin than to query it.

—

It was in Iraq that Manning witnessed US deception – and a compliant media reporting first-hand – and was motivated to begin leaking about it. Snowden, who before he began working for US intelligence joined the US military to fight for what he saw as freedom in Iraq, was similarly angered by what he discovered. What Snowden unearthed was not deceptive US conduct in some far-flung corner of the world; he stumbled across a war against the American people: a surveillance state where no one could have a private life. It was the ultimate betrayal of what he believed he was working for: a more just world, where tyrants were brought to account. What he discovered was deception, lying and cheating on a grand scale, all carried out by the US government. But it wasn't just the US government that was culpable. It had supplicant supporters.

The five Anglo-Saxon nations that share in the NSA's spying – the United States, Canada, the United Kingdom, New Zealand and Australia – essentially the Second World War intelligence alliance, are known collectively as Five Eyes. They see the world in a similar way. Though the United States provides a large amount of the technical hardware the other four countries do their own spying too, much of it on behalf of the NSA. It's their way of paying back the United States for access to its global spy network. But there is a bigger price the United States charges: obedience to its foreign policy.

With the exception of Canada the other countries, particularly the United Kingdom and Australia, were in lock-step with the United States as Washington tried to establish the case for sending in the troops. Though millions took to the streets in opposition the United States tentatively won the propaganda war – the path for invasion in March 2003 was now clear. During the early part of the war, the media was kept carefully in check. Anxious to be vindicated, a few days later the US President, speaking in Poland, announced that weapons of mass destruction (WMDs) had been found. The CIA issued a six-page document detailing the discovery. But Bush and the CIA were wrong. The mobile chemical labs were nothing of the sort. In fact they didn't exist.

This massive failure, which dented the already fragile public support for the war, did not go unanswered by the media. And like in a children's story, or an Old Testament eye-for-an-eye narrative, retribution was swift. Two of the governments involved in George W. Bush's 'Coalition of the Willing' launched a near simultaneous attack on their influential public broadcasters. On 28 May 2003 in Australia the government's Communications Minister, Senator Richard Alston, sent a blistering complaint to the Australian Broadcasting Corporation (ABC), detailing what it said were 68 separate occasions of bias, mainly on the part of its flagship morning current affairs radio program, *AM*, in its coverage of the war. There was not one single complaint about factual errors; what angered the minister was the way questions were framed and the overly skeptical nature of the reporting of 'US victories'.

On the other side of the world, 24 hours later, Thursday 29 May 2003 was starting as an unseasonably warm morning. BBC defence reporter Andrew Gilligan placed a phone call from his apartment in south-west London, using his special broadcast-quality line, into Broadcast House in central London. A few seconds later, at 6.07 am, he was live on the breakfast radio program *Today*. Gilligan reported that he understood the British government had 'sexed up' a dossier on WMDs to support its case for war and that Tony Blair, the Prime Minister, probably knew that an assertion that Britain would only have a 45-minute warning of a possible attack against what he termed 'UK sovereign base' areas in Cyprus was false.[9]

From that moment on Gilligan became the target of the British government. After a vitriolic campaign, he was forced to resign. He faced criticism from inside the BBC from editors who originally congratulated him on a great story but then became critical of his journalism and character when the government complained. Now, a decade after the war and three major inquiries later, it is known that Gilligan was correct in his central assertion: the Iraq dossier which the Blair Government was using to argue its case for war was

severely flawed. These incessant attacks on public broadcasters are the public face of what Five-Eyes governments do to
silence critics; the inviolability of the fourth estate has been
sacrificed in the pursuit of their goals or to cover themselves
from political fallout from failed policies. What happens in
areas where governments operate in the shadows, hidden from
view and any public accountability is even more dangerous
for democracy.

What occurred at *The Guardian* offices in London late
one night might never have been known but for the unexpected sequence of events that followed. On 19 August 2013
Snowden collaborator Glenn Greenwald's partner, David
Miranda, flew from Berlin to Heathrow en route to his home
in Brazil. As he entered the transit area he was taken to one
side by two men. They led him into a nearby room and forced
him to hand over his computers, phones and flash drives.
What they were searching for was not a surprise: they were
right in believing that he was carrying a significant dossier
of documents from Edward Snowden. They confiscated the
heavily encrypted material and sent it to GCHQ in an attempt
to open the files. For the next nine hours Miranda was inter-
rogated by people who did not give their names, but identified
themselves only by a number.

Although stopping and interrogating Miranda as he couri-
ered material to be used in the journalistic investigation
of the NSA was scarcely cricket – and it did draw the ire of
some European newspaper editors – comparatively speaking,
it was nothing . . .

Later Rusbridger would be hauled before a parliamentary
inquiry and grilled on his patriotism.

———

What perplexed Rusbridger more than his rap on the
knuckles for challenging the government was the reaction to
his story from other journalists. Many continued to condemn

The Guardian's reporting of the Snowden revelations even as those revelations pointed to acts of illegality by the intelligence agencies, particularly the NSA. The most strident attacks on *The Guardian* came from the Murdoch press, and *The Sun* newspaper in particular. One article described the publishing of the Snowden documents as a treasonable offence, an irony missed by the Murdoch press, which had just been castigated for its criminal acts involving phone-hacking.

In the wake of the Murdoch revelations and as the public called for greater control of the press, the British media fell into two camps. Murdoch's newspapers, *The Sun* and *The Times*, perhaps self-servingly, launched strong campaigns against any restrictions. But less obviously the Murdoch press was joined by the *Daily Mail* and *The Daily Telegraph*, which supported strong campaigns against any control, invoking the role of the media in exposing the excesses of government. The *Daily Mail* had the most negative coverage. For every article it published that contained a positive-only outlook of the proposed legal changes, there were 'more than 33' that presented only critical views.[10]

The Sun followed in second place – for every article that had a positive view, 29 negative ones were published. Others, like *The Guardian* and *The Independent*, were more balanced in their reporting of the proposed new laws to protect the rights of the individual from phone-hacking or other forms of invasion of privacy.

The Snowden revelations changed all that. The press was once again divided but this time, those who stood against any control of the print media – in particular the Murdoch press, *The Daily Telegraph* and the *Daily Mail* – now wanted the media not only controlled but prosecuted.

'Prosecute *The Guardian* for Aiding Terrorists Via Leaks', screamed *The Sun*,[11] 'Leftwing Paper's Leaks Caused "Greatest Damage to Western Security in History", say Whitehall Insiders', exclaimed the *Daily Mail*.[12]

This was more than a petty spat. It revealed a fault line at the heart of mass newspaper journalism. The editors of some of Britain's most influential newspapers had turned the journalistic shibboleth of arguing truth to power on its head. The individual did not have a right to privacy – but the state did!

In wartime newspapers have nearly always toed the government line by not reporting sensitive information that might be against what is generally known as the national interest. The Iraq War's growing list of misdemeanours, to put it mildly, by western powers is the most recent example. We would know of few of the atrocities and lies had WikiLeaks not documented them. Manning, for example, revealed not only how many civilians had died, but just why the United States did not want the number known. Yet in 2013 – with no war and no one suggesting that anyone had lost their lives because of the Snowden revelations – sections of the British media took a jingoistic view, closing their eyes and embracing the flag. By doing so, they compromised the primary role of journalism in disclosing inconvenient truths and, more importantly, failed in their role as a counterweight to the excesses of executive government.

Their actions in shutting down this legitimate journalistic endeavour is the price journalism is paying for slavishly adhering to the argument that the world is now engaged in a never-ending War on Terror.

—

Revelatory and investigative journalism in the west is in a state of crisis. Attacked from without, it is also attacked from within by journalists who long ago abandoned the core journalistic principle to question those in power.

And those who brought the public the truth – Edward Snowden, Julian Assange, Chelsea Manning and Glenn Greenwald – have been vilified by governments and other journalists in the process.

Across London, at the Ecuadorian embassy, Julian Assange understands only too well how those who supposedly champion freedom of information jealously guard the power to control it. He's been holed up claiming asylum there since 2012, arguing that Swedish prosecutors should travel to London if they want to interview him about allegations of sexual misconduct and rape. In 2014 he appeared to be making headway. The Swedes were increasingly embarrassed and, as is often the case, money was a factor too. Keeping tabs on the person who first alerted us to the perils of the surveillance state is costing the Metropolitan Police £11,000 a day; the embassy is under 24-hour surveillance. As he walks the corridor of the ground-floor embassy Assange laughs at the role many believe he played in Snowden's decision to expose the NSA spying scandal.

It's true that earlier in 2013, just a few weeks before Snowden left his job in Hawaii, Assange had called for anyone in the NSA to come forward and reveal the extent of their spying operations. But what pleases Assange most is that his 'big bang' theory has been vindicated. A drip-feed of stories is merely an irritation, he argues. The data drop from Manning that produced the Afghan War Diary, the Iraq War Logs and Cablegate helped overthrow governments and changed perceptions of US foreign policy. Snowden's NSA leaks, even more significant than Manning's, have already had major repercussions and the world is only now beginning to understand the magnitude of what the NSA has unleashed upon us all.

Paradoxically, at a time when information flows around the world more freely than ever before, the controls are tightening. The digital window, which revealed to the world gigabytes of truth about the way that governments operate, is in danger of closing shut. It is one of the great ironies that the person who has done more than most to waken the world to the perils of unchecked government power is secreted away in a dacha near Moscow – frequently in contact with Assange, who in turn is holed up in the Ecuadorian embassy in London. Revealing the secret actions of governments comes at a high cost. It has made Assange and Snowden virtually stateless. Manning will be over 60 by the time she has served her time in prison.

With governments desperate to control information, we are witnessing a war both on journalism and the public's right to be well informed. Though the internet has made it easier to disseminate information and for all of us to access libraries of knowledge at the click of a mouse, it has also handed governments a weapon of extraordinary power – systems of mass surveillance, with all their attendant horrors. The internet has produced the most profound challenge to journalism and society since the invention of the printing press first made it possible for the ordinary individual to confront the power of the state.

CHAPTER 2

Star Chamber

On 1 February 2012 the Middlesex–London Health Unit issued a cold weather alert, warning of plunging temperatures. Standing opposite Westminster Abbey and the Houses of Parliament in Central London, the Supreme Court looked particularly grey in the morning gloom. It was hardly a good omen for Julian Assange as the United Kingdom's most powerful court began examining his final appeal to the British judicial system against extradition to Sweden on allegations of sexual molestation and rape. What played out there in the ensuing days would determine whether Assange was free to return to his work holding governments to account or, to put it in his words, 'shining light in dark places'. But just as importantly, the proceedings would showcase the intricate relationship between the British judiciary and those who write the laws, members of the House of Commons, a short walk across the square.

As the Queen's Counsels faced off in the ornately wood-panelled courtroom, there was a sense of history being played out. Not only was the court itself a new creation – hewn out of the House of Lords, which had recently lost its role as the final court of appeal – but the legislation before it was also untested. At issue: the legality of the European arrest warrant by which Swedish prosecutors wanted to extradite Assange.

The arguments centred on the true intent of parliament as it framed the law in the chaotic and neurotic time following the Twin Towers attacks. The European arrest warrant was designed to scoop up terrorists with the minimum amount of fuss – and whisk them off for trial. It was a badly framed law which years later the British parliament would sort out and change. But in the meantime Assange was faced with the law that existed. His barrister struggled with the argument about what the MPs had really meant when they introduced the law, against the Crown's literal interpretation. As often happens in courts of law, the literalists won the day and once again Julian Assange found himself sandwiched between the law and politics. His legal proceedings had not been about freedom of speech, but hanging in the air was the suspicion that the British government was attempting to silence one of its enemies, to make the pain Assange had been causing with WikiLeaks go away. Notwithstanding the intricate arguments of QCs at 10 paces, the judiciary appeared to have delivered the desired outcome.

History is dotted with examples of enmity between the state and disseminators of uncomfortable information, stretching back 300 years and beyond to the birth of the modern press and later what Edmund Burke dubbed the fourth estate. It says much that the other bastions of the modern realm – the legislature, the church and the judiciary, represented by London's House of Commons, Westminster Abbey and the Supreme Court – are crowded together around Parliament Square. Britain's newspapers used to be huddled nearby in Fleet Street but in the 1980s they shifted to cheaper accommodation, far down the river in the former docklands at Wapping; a less salubrious address, although some may have felt more at home there. Wapping is famous as the 19th-century home of 'Execution Dock', where pirates and other seafaring criminals were hanged close to the low-water mark, their bodies left dangling until they had been submerged three times by the tide. It's where Rupert Murdoch had the British headquarters of his publishing empire.

It may have been only a short trip up the Thames from Wapping to Portcullis House, an ugly mock gothic-style building opposite Big Ben, but there's no doubt Murdoch deeply resented being forced to face his inquisitors there: a committee of British MPs probing what became known as the phone-hacking scandal. They determined to discover exactly what had gone on inside Murdoch's newspaper offices, whose phones had been bugged and, more to the point, who knew about it in senior management; the stakes were high. The phone-hacking investigation threatened to undermine the entire News Corp empire and even jail its leadership. As a spectacle it would captivate a nation which smelled blood, and wanted revenge; little has changed since the days of the hangings at Execution Dock.

Novelist Frederick Forsyth, who made his name as a writer of political thrillers, was aghast that journalists and even Murdoch himself would be called to give evidence. He launched an attack on the investigation in his column in the *Daily Express*, a right-wing newspaper targeted at those who longed for Britain to be great again but didn't quite have the stamina to wade their way through *The Daily Telegraph*. Forsyth savaged the committee as being a 'Star Chamber' – a reference to hearings dating back centuries whereby kings and queens of England used their imperial power to silence their critics.

Forsyth, a stickler for accuracy and authenticity in his works of fiction, somewhat missed the mark with this thinly veiled accusation of abuse of power. In the original Star Chamber, wealthy press barons like Murdoch would have been more likely sitting next to the regent – as part of the select group chosen to help make judgements – rather than in the dock. When the members of the fledgling press eventually ran into trouble with the Star Chamber, it was the struggling publisher of pamphlets who got dragged into the intricately painted courtroom – its ceiling adorned with stars, thus its name – to confess their sins. In what may appeal to those who have grown distrustful of their media, errant journalists found guilty of defamation were branded with a hot iron, the letters 'FA' for false accuser, burned into their faces.

Nevertheless some commonality can be found between the Star Chamber and parliamentary investigations. For instance both had to grapple with the disruptive effects of new technology. The Caxton printing press challenged the power of the Star Chamber by making books and pamphlets – the forerunners of newspapers – fast and cheap to print. The internet, able to move gigabytes of information in seconds, is posing the same threat to power that William Caxton's printing presses did five centuries ago. The Star Chamber recognised the threat: the presses were duly licensed and those who rejected the conditions of censorship lost the right to publish; coincidentally many presses either mysteriously burned down in the night or were smashed by mobs. As now, the state could claim biased reporting then muzzle the media in the 'national interest'.

Paralleling the official response to WikiLeaks after its Cablegate revelations so inflamed US politicians, in 1632 the Star Chamber banned all 'news books'.[1] The reason? Complaints from Spanish and Austrian diplomats that English journalists were unfair in their reporting of the Thirty Years' War, which was ravaging their countries at the time.

The dismantling of the Star Chamber came on the eve of the English Civil War: in 1641 King Charles I, cutting deals to hold on to power, allowed parliament to put an end to it. The loosening of controls created a flourishing industry overnight. Between 1640 and 1660, at least 300 news publications were produced. In this new environment parliament placed itself above the monarch and even God to make laws. The rise of parliamentary power, apart from a few hiccups along the way, had become unstoppable.

Although the Star Chamber's censorship and licensing powers had ended, the defamation laws remained – the one last obstacle to total freedom of speech. In a move that shows the agelessness of self-interest, parliament decided to retain the laws for the general population, but to exempt themselves. Under what is known to this day as parliamentary privilege, MPs could say more or less what they liked in the House of Commons without being held to account for defamation or libel. It is one of the ironies of history that the parliament that did so much to create a modern democracy did so little to uphold freedom of speech for others. The rich and powerful, notably the monarch, nobility and the church – a good many of whom were parliamentarians anyway – artfully preserved the ability to sue for defamation; whenever newspaper proprietors or journalists raised issues they wanted kept secret, they could claim that their good names had been impugned.

Across the Atlantic, those kings and queens of England have become historical allies of Arnie 'The Terminator' Schwarzenegger, who advocated for a restriction on what the United States holds most dear, the principle of free speech. In 2005, in a bizarre twist, as the Governor of California, Schwarzenegger – whose macho onscreen persona killed thousands in cold blood – signed legislation to ban the sale of violent video games to young children. The legislators wanted a huge '18' – for the minimum age – stamped on the outside of the game box and a legal obligation that they would not be sold to underage children. Californians were particularly concerned about video games that included 'killing, maiming, dismembering, or sexually assaulting an image of a human being' in a way that is 'patently offensive', appeals to a 'deviant or morbid interest' and lacks 'serious, literary, artistic, political, or scientific value'.[2] When the video game manufacturers and retailers argued any restriction on selling their games – a US$10 billion-a-year business – was in breach of the First Amendment to the US Constitution, protecting freedom of speech, California took its argument to the US Supreme Court. The court found that video games qualify for First Amendment protection. Like protected books, plays and movies, they communicate ideas through familiar literary devices and features distinctive to the medium. And 'the basic principles of freedom of speech . . . do not vary' with a new and different communication medium.[3]

Thus the First Amendment guards its provision of free speech so carefully that it allows the 'publication' of the most vicious bloodthirsty video games. The case does show why US journalists enjoy the best 'free speech' protection in the world. It's why, in theory at least, newspapers in the United States are free to publish government secrets without fear of prosecution. Unlike their counterparts in the United Kingdom they face no Official Secrets Act; a law that restricts freedom of speech would be in breach of the First Amendment.

What the United States does have is the Espionage Act of 1917. Used to prosecute Daniel Ellsberg, who leaked the Pentagon Papers to *The New York Times* in 1971, it is a permanent threat to intimidate, silence and prosecute whistleblowers. It was used to jail Chelsea Manning, and unfortunately for Edward Snowden it is hanging over his head with its provision for 'closed courts' – secret grand jury hearings that would 'indict a ham sandwich, if that's what you wanted', to quote a New York state chief judge.[4] It's one of the numerous reasons that Julian Assange feels safer in his Knightsbridge sanctuary than facing the perils of the judicial system in Sweden with the possibility of extradition to the United States.

However on balance the British legal system is far more dangerous to navigate for outspoken journalists.

—

It's widely accepted that the polemicist and poet John Milton, who struggled so long and hard against censorship, planted the intellectual seeds for the French and American revolutions with his eloquent arguments for freedom. Published in 1644 during the English Civil War, his essay 'Areopagitica' is arguably the most famous defence of freedom of speech ever written. Milton implored parliament to 'give me the liberty to know, to utter, and to argue freely according to conscience, above all liberties'. Quashing a publication simply because it was unlicensed, because it was not in keeping with state law and morality, 'kills reason itself'. Though Milton spoke from a religious perspective, his arguments strongly resonated with the secular view of libertarian freedom: censors would always have biases and be partial; much better for intellectual rigour to let ideas flourish and then have them challenged or dismissed in debate. For Milton it was a cruel act that saw the laws which argued for greater freedom being rejected at home only to be embraced by America after it freed itself from Britain.

As recently as the 1960s Milton was being quoted in a US case that had its genesis in the back pages of *The New York Times*. Taking up a whole page between a story about the power wielded by notorious Teamsters union official Jimmy Hoffa and an advertisement for Philadelphia Cold Beer was an extraordinary advertisement. Headlined 'Heed Their Rising Voices', it called for donations to support Dr Martin Luther King Jnr's civil rights movement in the southern US states. Dozens of notable US citizens and stars of the time, including singers Harry Belafonte, Sammy Davis Jnr, Nat King Cole and actor Marlon Brando, put their names to the advertisement.

The basic facts of the matter were clear. The newspaper had published the advertisement, the aim of which was to raise money for Dr King and other civil rights activists who strongly opposed Alabama's plan to obstruct their civil rights campaign – especially the right to vote.

Among the specific allegations the advertisement made were that:
- Students from the black Alabama State College in Montgomery had marched to the State Capitol building and sung 'My Country, 'Tis of Thee', a song extolling the virtues of a free United States;
- Their payback was expulsion from the school at which the entire school body protested;

- Police, armed with shotguns and tear gas, then surrounded the campus;
- College officials locked the dining hall in an effort to 'starve out' the protesting students into submission;
- Dr King had been arrested seven times for frivolous or specious charges such as 'loitering'.

The trouble was, none of the statements was true. The Montgomery City Commissioner, L.B. Sullivan, who had the specific responsibility for overseeing the police force, sued the newspaper for defamation. Sullivan was awarded half a million dollars – more than US$ 4 million by today's value.

The New York Times appealed to the Supreme Court in Washington. It was here in early 1964 that the court brought down its decision, the most important First Amendment ruling to this day. As a wipe-out, it was complete. The judges decided 9–0 that the defamation action brought against *The New York Times* was in breach of the Constitutional right to freedom of speech. Their ruling echoed the very argument that Milton had put to the English House of Commons three centuries earlier. The judges even mentioned Milton: 'A rule compelling the critic of official conduct to guarantee the truth of all his factual assertions – and to do so on pain of libel judgments virtually unlimited in amount – leads to a comparable "self-censorship",' they said. 'Allowance of the defense of truth, with the burden of proving it on the defendant, does not mean that only false speech will be deterred.'⁵ It would also mean that accurate speech would be impeded. In other words open discussion would be stifled. *The New York Times* had done nothing wrong in publishing the advertisement, even if the details were incorrect, because it acted in good faith, the court decided.

Significantly the judges added that even a false statement may be deemed to make a valuable contribution to public debate.

Newspapers in Britain's other great colony, Australia, had no such luck with free speech. They were even worse off than their counterparts in the motherland. The international Australian human rights barrister Geoffrey Robertson QC, who is part of Julian Assange's legal team, understands only too well. He represented a young journalist who found a document among his belongings – put there by an old girlfriend, Robertson suspects. When the journalist telephoned to ask the company mentioned in the document for a comment, 'the next thing he knew he was hauled into court and ordered to name the source'.[6] Things were looking grim for the journalist until the case ended up in the European Court of Human Rights. The judgement supported the 'protection of journalistic sources as one of the basic conditions of press freedom . . . without such protection . . . the vital public watchdog role of the press may be undermined.'

Britain's entry into the European Community gave its journalists a level of protection denied to the former colonies like Australia, who were largely left to follow the old British legal system. Recently, there have been attempts by the Australian government to create whistleblower protection laws – and journalist shield laws – but essentially defendants are forced to rely on the good will of the court rather than any guaranteed rights, and foreshadowed security laws could see journalists jailed.

In terms of freedom of speech, all has not been completely lost on the southern front. Just as Australia produced Rupert Murdoch, a non-conformist publisher who dominated the world when print ruled, it also created Julian Assange, a revolutionary of the internet age. What Assange did in July 2014 didn't quite measure up to the defining moment of the US Constitution, but it certainly challenged the restrictions on free speech in a way that would have made Milton proud.

The state of Victoria likes to see itself as legislatively progressive. Victorians proudly drive around with their car numberplates carrying the motto 'Victoria: The Place To Be'. If you've got something to hide that might well be right because Victoria's justice is often carried out in the shadows. Not much disinfecting sunshine for the people of Australia's second largest state by population. Instead the courts are fond of issuing what are known as super-injunctions – gag orders so tight that even reporting their existence is a breach of the court order and thus a crime. They handed out 1502 of them in one five-year period.

In the Australian winter of 2014 WikiLeaks gained access to one of the super-injunctions issued by the Victorian Supreme Court and published it on its website. It was a juicy story that, without doubt, the public had a right to know about. The super-injunction concerned possible criminal charges against senior people connected to a company partly owned by the Australian Federal Reserve Bank. In one of the biggest bribery cases in Australian history, they were alleged to have paid millions of dollars to foreign governments and their officials to win lucrative banknote-printing contracts. Among those named in the gag order were the President of Vietnam, Truong Tan Sang; the former Prime Minister of Malaysia, Mahathir Mohamad; and two former presidents of Indonesia, Megawati Soekarnoputri and Susilo Bambang Yudhoyono (SBY).

The Australian government went to enormous lengths to protect the names, arguing that publishing them might harm Australia's national security. As is often the case, the cover-up was worse than the possible crime. Susilo Bambang Yudhoyono, for one, made it plain he would have preferred his name to have been raised in open court rather than kept secret – which, he said, suggested he had something to hide.

In the borderless world of the internet the story was unstoppable. It received extensive coverage online, with reports linked directly to the documents on the WikiLeaks website.

What is curious is the way the mass media reported the super-injunction. In Australia all the main outlets were cowed by the 'national security' threat. They revealed some details of the super-injunction but none of them named any of the people involved or the positions they held in government.

In Britain it was unsurprisingly a similar story, with the media and populace labouring under defamation and libel laws little changed since 'Mad' King George III was on the throne. The notion espoused by Milton and embraced by the United States that democracy is best served by no pre-censorship of published material has been destroyed in the nation which gave birth to it. *The Guardian* went as far as it safely could, revealing that there was a suppression order but blacking out the names on the document.

The most courageous of the global mainstream media appeared to be the French daily newspaper *Le Monde*, which revealed both details of the case and the identities of some of the parties involved.

Strangely missing was any mention of the story in either *The New York Times* or *The Washington Post*. Even though the First Amendment protects them from prosecution, like many media outlets in the United States, both newspapers are close to the Washington Establishment, often checking stories with the government before running them, particularly when there are issues of so-called national security with a closely allied country like Australia. The freedom of speech provision of the US Constitution is only as strong as the editors who exercise it.

—

As News International and the *News of the World* faced their accusers in the parliamentary select committee, they were acutely aware they had no US-style free speech provisions to fall back on. The best they could expect was that the evidence they gave could not be used against them in any criminal investigation. But they had other concerns. They were under attack from inside their own industry. Journalists who supported transparency and accountability relished seeing long-time

enemy Rupert Murdoch discomfited under hostile questioning. MP Tom Watson asked Rupert Murdoch had he read
the committee's last report, which referred to the 'collective
amnesia' of his company's executives when they gave evidence
to the committee:

> *Murdoch:* I haven't heard that. I don't know who made that
>   particular charge.
> *Watson:*   A parliamentary inquiry found your senior
>   executives in the UK guilty of collective amnesia
>   and nobody brought it to your attention. I do not
>   see why you do not think that that is very serious.
> *Murdoch:* But you're not really saying amnesia, you're really
>   saying lying.
> *Watson:*   We found your executives guilty of collective
>   amnesia. I would have thought that someone would
>   like to bring that to your attention – that it would
>   concern you. Did they forget?
> *Murdoch:* No.[7]

Forget all the protestations at being in favour of free speech;
when it came down to scoring a political or commercial advantage over an opponent, newspapers and their editors were in
the gutter with the rest of them.

It did not bode well for the future of free speech reform in
the United Kingdom. There would be more stoushes between
government and media to come and the victories over the
Murdoch press would be seen for what they were: ammunition
for those who wanted to muzzle the media.

And there were many interested parties who not only
wanted to do that but to silence their informants too. Edward
Snowden, unable to return to his own country because his
passport has been cancelled, is marooned in a state where free
speech does not exist. His three closest supporters all ended
up far from the clutches of Washington: Glenn Greenwald
in Brazil and Laura Poitras and Sarah Harrison in exile in

Germany, a country where free speech now flourishes after its suppression under fascism and communism.

According to Harrison, there is support for WikiLeaks and Snowden in the German community because 'the surveillance revelations have struck a chord in Germany more than other countries'. There is a 'critical mass' of politicians and the media which are 'generally onside'.[8] In 2012 Germany passed legislation which 'prohibited the prosecution of journalists for reporting classified information obtained from government informants'.[9] It also tightened the circumstances in which a journalist's materials could be confiscated.

News International appears to be a defender of free speech on matters of royal tittle-tattle and the private lives of celebrities. Is it safe to presume they would invoke the same principle concerning matters of national security? History suggests not. For centuries press barons have followed their personal interests and taken little notice of what was in the public interest.

The press is perfectly capable of abandoning its essential role as the fourth estate – a countervailing force to those who possess often unquestioned power in the community – even to the point of joining an organised push to remove a democratically elected government from office. It is achievable under the right circumstances: with the involvement of intelligence agencies, journalists who know what is happening but keep silent, and an egotistical tyrant – Cecil King – running the most popular newspaper in the world.

CHAPTER 3

The Power of One –
Plot and Plunder

The tiny village of Orsay, surrounded by rolling green hills just 20 kilometres south-west of Paris, seems an unlikely place for a British press baron to plot the downfall of the UK government. Its neat rows of single-storey terracotta-roofed homes call to mind conformity rather than France's revolutionary history. The town hall proudly lists the local inhabitants who put Orsay on the map, from sports stars to mathematicians. It's an impressive group, but among them are two people the town would probably rather forget.

Sir Oswald Mosley and his wife, Diana Mitford, both spent most of the Second World War interned in British prisons or under house arrest, deemed to be a threat to the country's national security; they moved to France after the war. Sir Oswald, a political maverick, had started as a Conservative MP, then switched to Labour before abandoning the mainstream to establish the British Union of Fascists, popularly known as the Blackshirts. Diana, Lady Mosley, had a virulent hatred of Jews and publicly expressed a love of Hitler; she and Sir Oswald were married in the Berlin home of the Third Reich's propaganda chief, Joseph Goebbels.

The Mosleys remained well connected: they had become friends with the Duke and Duchess of Windsor – the former King Edward VIII and his wife, Wallis Simpson, both Nazi sympathisers – who lived just six kilometres away.[1]

In early 1968 Sir Oswald and Lady Mosley received an unexpected request: a meeting with Cecil King, the publisher of Britain's *Daily Mirror*, by far the biggest selling newspaper in the country, with more than five million readers in 1967. As the publisher of a Labour-supporting newspaper, it might have seemed odd that King was keen to meet Mosley but King was not what he appeared to be, asserting his power amid the turmoil of postwar Europe.

As King made his way across the Channel the first stirrings of a revolt against the French government had already started. Eventually the violent and destructive upheaval would force the French President, Charles de Gaulle, to call elections, facing down the demonstrators with a 'sack me or back me' demand.[2] Meanwhile in Eastern Europe the Czechs were gearing up for their 'Prague Spring', standing up to the Soviet Union with demands for free elections. But as the patrician newspaperman and his wife, Ruth, drove past the ornate black wrought-iron gates at the entrance of the Mosleys' lakeside mansion, 'Le Temple de la Gloire', democracy could not have been further from King's mind. He believed that the British Labour Prime Minister, Harold Wilson, re-elected two years earlier, should be ousted from power.

The Swinging Sixties which ushered in the first Labour government for 13 years also heralded immense social change. The sexual revolution and the unstoppable rise of British pop music were markers of what King saw as political and social decay. In King's view Wilson was 'a liar and the economy was in an appalling state'.[3] Stagnating industry, a weak currency and increasing unemployment were just a few of the reasons King wanted Wilson out.

Why did Cecil King go to such lengths to pick Oswald Mosley's brains? On the surface it might have seemed highly unlikely that, apart from detesting Harold Wilson, the Mosleys had much in common with King and his wife. The *Daily Mirror* under King boasted it had been Labour from its founding in 1903. Yet that hadn't been exactly true. The *Daily Mirror* seldom mentions the fact that it had enthusiastically supported Mosley's fascist Blackshirts.

As Britain suffered in the Great Depression of the 1930s, with unemployment at 25 per cent, Mosley promised answers based on protectionism and government spending. His mass rallies in London – which attracted over 100,000 people on at least one occasion; the charismatic Mosley was adept at galvanising public opinion – warning of the perils of communism and railing against what we now know as multiculturalism terrified the nation as much as his Blackshirt thugs terrified the Jews of London's East End. Charging through the streets chanting, 'The Yids, the Yids, we've got to get rid of the Yids', they beat up anyone who stood in their way, smashing property and attacking synagogues. Mosley became so taken with this form of national socialism, he travelled to Italy, meeting with the fascist leader Benito Mussolini to discuss how his policies might work in Britain.

The *Daily Mirror* was owned then by Viscount Lord Rothermere, who was anything but a supporter of socialism. He was, for a time at least, an enthusiastic advocate of fascism. He even gained Hitler's admiration as someone who gave the Third Reich a fair hearing. In return Rothermere thought Oswald Mosley and his fascists were sensible and patriotic. 'HURRAH FOR THE BLACKSHIRTS!' trumpeted one of his newspapers, the *Daily Mail*, in January 1934; 'GIVE THE BLACKSHIRTS A HELPING HAND', demanded Rothermere in the *Daily Mirror*. Rothermere sold the *Daily Mirror* shortly afterwards but it seems the fascist affection lingered on with its new owner, the International Publishing Corporation (IPC), led by his nephew Cecil King.

Though King courted Labour's postwar leaders, he held them in low regard, describing Clement Attlee as 'a complete drip' and Hugh Gaitskell as 'a vain man without substance or principle'.[4] He warmed at first to Harold Wilson, mainly because Wilson had promised to take the United Kingdom into the European Common Market.

The theme of a united Europe standing between what the Mosleyites saw as a Mongolian–Asiatic Russia and a Jewish–Negro America had become an obsession with the exiled Mosley and also with King. Dumbfounded hacks at the *Daily Mirror* were required to write article after article setting out the plan for 'Nation Europa', which were then foisted on a mostly baffled *Mirror* readership.[5]

As he left the idyllic setting of 'Le Temple de la Gloire', built in 1800 for a French general who believed he might one day succeed Napoleon, King had succession plans for Mosley too: a high place in Cabinet in the new government he was planning to install in Britain.

Later, over lunch in Paris, King told a stunned *Daily Mirror* correspondent Peter Stephens of his plans for Mosley and Britain once Wilson was ousted, something he considered a given. King said he believed that Sir Oswald Mosley was 'by far the cleverest English politician of the 1930s', adding that 'he is an extremely brilliant man and he could still make a useful contribution'. Asked if he was thinking of including him 'in your replacement government', King replied, 'Why not? People have forgotten about his past.' King said he had to 'time everything with great care'.[6] In what must have been a difficult conversation for Stephens, he asked his boss, 'Do you see yourself as a minister without portfolio going around sorting out each ministry and putting it on its feet?' King replied, 'There is an awful lot that needs sorting out and that might be a very good idea. I'm not quite sure yet.'[7]

Born into Fleet Street's 'royal family', the Harmsworths and Northcliffes, Cecil King was brought up in an environment of wealth, privilege and eminent social connections. His school was Winchester College and from there he took the natural escalator to Christ Church, Oxford. As *Daily Mirror* senior journalist Geoffrey Goodman observed, 'He believed he was born to rule, an image of himself which never departed.'[8]

It was not a view entirely shared by Harold Wilson. As recognition for the *Daily Mirror*'s support in getting Labour elected in 1964, Wilson offered King a life peerage, but that wasn't enough. King wanted to be an earl – a hereditary peer, able to pass his title to his children – possibly to outshine his uncle, Lord Northcliffe. Wilson refused, pointing out it was Labour policy not to grant hereditary peerages.

Wilson found a compromise, appointing King to the board of the Bank of England. Although he accepted the appointment, the grandiose King was not consoled; quite the contrary. The governor of the bank, Lord Cromer, was a hereditary peer. Consequently King would daily be reminded that he hadn't received a peerage he could pass on to his children. It proved a foolish political move on Wilson's part. Not only had he embarrassed King, he had thrown him into the arms of a man opposed to everything Wilson stood for. Cromer, who saw nothing wrong with inherited wealth and privilege, had several heated confrontations with Wilson about how best to handle the economic crisis. At one time Wilson asked Cromer, 'Who is the Prime Minister of this country, Mr Governor, you or me?'[9]

Lord Cromer knew exactly where the real power lay; one need only look to his pedigree. His wealth can be traced back to the 19th century, with the founding by his ancestors of the banking company Baring Brothers & Co., a bastion of the City of London. In 1817, the Duc de Richelieu, King Louis XVIII's Prime Minister, is reputed to have listed the six great powers in Europe as follows: 'England, France, Prussia, Austria, Russia and Baring Brothers'.[10] High praise from the poster boy for exercising political power. Barings was the bank where everyone who was anyone in Britain kept their money; bankers not only to large numbers of Britain's aristocracy and the senior military, Barings was also the Queen's banker. Then there were the all-important familial and social connections. With Lord Cromer married to Esmé Harmsworth, North-cliffe's niece and a personal assistant to the Queen, Cecil King, Northcliffe's nephew, was drawing himself further into a deeply conservative world of money, power and extreme right-wing politics.

King continued his 1968 tour of France, wining and dining with the politically powerful and the commercially influential and explaining what was wrong with Britain and how to fix it. Being a member of the Bank of England board, people paid close attention to King, particularly when he told them Wilson had been fudging the figures on Britain's gold and convertible currency reserves, which underpinned the value of the currency. Coming from such a highly placed source as King, the news hit the financial markets like an earthquake, heralding a huge run on the pound as overseas investors began gambling on a possible devaluation. Wilson blamed what he called 'the gnomes of Zurich'[11] – Swiss bankers – for sterling's ills as the weakened pound created havoc in the British economy, causing a surge in inflation. He had no idea of the extent of the treachery which had been unleashed across the English Channel as King tried to make sure his prophecy of disaster for Britain came true.

But on 19 February 1968 Wilson got a very good idea of what King was up to. Page one of *The Guardian* carried the headline 'Making a New Start with a Coalition Government MR CECIL KING LEADING THE SOUNDINGS'.

King was doing more than that. He was scheming to involve the British military in a plan to take over government.

—

In May, having swapped the cold weather of France for a dreary start to an English spring, Cecil King walked up the front steps of an Edwardian residence in Belgravia – situated halfway between Buckingham Palace and Harrods – and was welcomed into the sumptuous home of Louis Mountbatten, a cousin of the Queen. Mountbatten had recently retired as the head of the British Armed Forces. He also held the distinction of being the last viceroy of India.

Another visitor that late afternoon was a friend of Mountbatten's, the British chief scientist Sir Solly Zuckerman. Accompanying King was Hugh Cudlipp, King's appointee as the *Daily Mirror* editor – the man who had helped shape the paper's style, tuning it to a niche market aimed at the working class. Where most papers on the left were either heavily political or worthily dull, Cudlipp – a journalist from a humble family in Wales who had worked his way to the top – created bold headlines and straightforward text: a mixture of sex, crime and outrage with a heavy political message, the first tabloid journalism.

Though they came from opposite ends of the British social classes, Mountbatten and Cudlipp had a strong friendship. Mountbatten had earlier confided in Cudlipp his concerns about the state of the country: 'Important people, leaders of industry and others approach me increasingly saying something must be done. Of course I agree that we can't go on like this. But I am 67 and I'm a relative of the Queen: my usefulness is limited. This is a job for younger men, and obviously talent and administrative ability which does not exist in parliament must be harnessed.'[12]

According to Cudlipp, Mountbatten then suggested the formation of 'something like the Emergency Committee I ran in India'.[13] He would have been hard-pressed to find a worse example, for Mountbatten's Emergency Committee presided over the death of up to one million people as it sought to control India in the dying days of empire before independence.

Mountbatten also suggested, Cudlipp said, 'a private meeting of some sort. What did I think?'[14]

Cudlipp says he told Mountbatten, 'I think it is important you take no personal initiative of any sort. You should wait until you are approached.'[15] Mountbatten said he certainly didn't 'want to appear to be advocating or supporting any notion of a Right Wing dictatorship – or any nonsense of that sort. Nor do I want to be involved at my age. But like some other people I am deeply concerned about the future of the country.'[16] In a memo Cudlipp informed King that Mount-batten had told him earlier that 'nothing much could be done about the developing situation anyway, unless the [*Daily*] *Mirror* was behind a move in a particular direction'.[17]

In his memoir, Cudlipp recalled the conversation that took place in Belgravia as darkness began to fall:

> King explained that in the crisis he foresaw as being just around the corner the government would disintegrate, there would be bloodshed in the streets, the armed forces would be involved. People would be looking for somebody like Lord Mountbat-ten as the titular head of a new administration, somebody renowned as a leader of men who would be capable, backed by the best brains and administrators in the land to restore public confidence. He ended with a question to Mountbatten – would he agree to be the titular head of a new administration in such circumstances?
>
> Mountbatten turned to his friend Solly, 'You haven't said a word so far. What do you think of all this?'
>
> Sir Solly rose, walked to the door, opened it, and then made this statement: 'This is rank treachery. All this talk of machine guns at street corners is appalling. I am a public servant and will have nothing to do with it. Nor should you, Dickie.' Mountbat-ten expressed his agreement and Sir Solly departed.[18]

King, who took a contemporaneous note, maintained that Mountbatten was far keener than Cudlipp remembers. After Zuckerman had left Mountbatten revealed he had just had lunch at The Horseguards, an elegant Victorian hotel off Whitehall. Next door to the Ministry of Defence, The Horseguards, with its sweeping terrace views of the Thames, is a favourite haunt of the military Establishment. 'Mount-batten said that morale in the armed forces had never been so low. He said that the Queen was receiving an unprecedented number of petitions, all of which have been passed on to the Home Office.'[19] In his notes King also records that, 'According to "Dickie" [Mountbatten's nickname among friends and family]', the Queen was 'desperately worried over the whole situation. Mountbatten is obviously close to her . . . she is spending this weekend at Broadlands [Mountbatten's country home in Hampshire].'[20]

King said that Mountbatten asked 'if I thought there was anything he should do. My theme was that there might be a stage in the future when the Crown would have to intervene: there might be a stage when the armed forces were important. Dickie should keep himself from public view so as to have clean hands if either emergency should arise in the future. He has no wish to intervene anyway.'[21]

Following this tête-à-tête King set out on a course to change the government, using the most potent weapon he had, the *Daily Mirror*.

Two days later, on 10 May, the *Daily Mirror* ran a front-page editorial under the headline 'Enough Is Enough'. The condemnatory article was published under the byline 'Cecil H. King'. King wrote that Wilson had 'lost all credibility and all authority'.[22]

Within days the board of IPC decided it wasn't Wilson, but King who should go. He received a hand-delivered letter while he was shaving telling him the board wanted him to resign. When King resisted, the board fired him. In his place the board appointed as its chairman King's protégé, Hugh Cudlipp.

King's attempt to manipulate public opinion and engineer the politics of a nation might have failed but what is important to appreciate is that he got that far. His actions underscore just how much power press barons can exercise, particularly

when vested interests are threatened by a reforming government. The coup conspiracy also unmasked the role of insiders,
acting as little more than megaphones for their confidential
sources – leaking biased and uncorroborated stories to mislead
the public. It was a process that would be refined by another
press baron.

One of the first decisions Cudlipp made was to sell the
loss-making *Daily Herald*, a joint operation between IPC
and the Trades Union Congress. The former editor of *The
Times*, Harold Evans, described the *Herald* as the offspring
of an unlikely marriage between a race-horse and a cart-
horse. The buyer was a then little-known Australian, Rupert
Murdoch. Ironically IPC's sale of the *Daily Herald* would
create a monster that would devour the *Daily Mirror* and end
the serious popular journalism it had fostered: intelligent
and clear writing about complex subjects, told in a bright and
entertaining way. Murdoch rebranded the *Herald*, naming it
The Sun, but the politics stayed the same as Murdoch sought
to retain its trade union readership in the run-up to the 1970
election. For Murdoch it was simply a commercial decision. In
the future this kind of behaviour would help him become one
of the most successful media barons of the 20th century.

—

Intertwined with accounts of Harold Wilson's time in high
office are myriad stories of skullduggery and intrigue that
go beyond Cecil King's involvement, though King's clumsy
actions appear to have had far-reaching consequences. Wilson
went into the 1970 election as favourite. Ranged against
Labour, however, were the bulk of the press, including *The
Times*, which carried centre-page articles attacking the
Wilson Government's economic record. They revealed an
extraordinary amount of detailed knowledge – but the identity
of the writer was a mystery; the author had used an alias. It
is now revealed that the secret writer was none other than

Lord Cromer, an ally of King's, drawing on much of the inside information he had gleaned while acting as governor of the Bank of England. The fact that *The Times* was happy to hide Cromer's identity from its readers says much about the conspiracy that was building around Wilson to destroy his chances of victory, despite King's public disgrace. In 1970 Wilson lost what many thought was an unlosable election to the Conservative Party led by Edward Heath. For Wilson equally as problematic was the interest intelligence agencies had been taking in his private life. Once again King played a role. It had been happening since Wilson first came to power in 1964.

The CIA London Station had been busily reporting on rumours of a possible romance between Wilson and his assistant, Marcia Williams. Wilson had gone so far as to sue pop group The Move for a saucy postcard promoting their latest single 'Flowers in the Rain' which featured a naked Prime Minister and Marcia Williams in bed. Now CIA Director Richard Helms reported to President Lyndon Johnson that Williams might be getting a divorce.

Exactly where this information originally came from is not clear, but we now know that during the 1960s MI5 installed listening devices in 10 Downing Street, the Prime Minister's official residence. They were placed in the Cabinet room, the waiting room and the Prime Minister's study on the instructions of the then Prime Minister Harold McMillan after his Conservative government was rocked by a national security crisis – Secretary of State for War, John Profumo, had been having an affair with Christine Keeler, a model, who in turn had been sharing a bed with the Soviet Naval attaché. The bugs remained in No. 10 from July 1963 until Labor Prime Minister Jim Callaghan discovered their existence and ordered them to be removed around 1977. For the entirety of Wilson's tenure MI5 had been been privy to many of his most private conversations.

What role, if any, these bugged conversations played in the undermining of Wilson is unknown, but Cecil King – still trying to sabotage Wilson behind the scenes – had regular meetings with Helms. In his memoirs King catalogues one of the earlier ones, on 16 September 1966. He tells of how he was driven to the CIA headquarters in Langley, where he met Helms, about whom he wrote: 'a professional intelligence man, is very pleasant to meet and highly intelligent, couldn't have been more friendly and at my departure asked me to come again'.[23]

Nearly 50 years later, the details of those meetings remain a tightly guarded secret. In September 2014 the CIA responded to my freedom of information (FOI) request about the meetings that Helms had with King. The response stated bluntly that 'the fact of the existence or non-existence of requested records is currently and properly classified'. The refusal was covered by FOI exemptions covering 'intelligence sources and methods, information that is protected from disclosure'.[24]

As the years passed the intelligence agencies came out with unkinder 'revelations' about Wilson and Williams, including allegations which questioned their loyalty to Britain. This story – which would cause the Labour government enormous political pain – had its genesis in the heady days after the Second World War.

Labour had swept to power in a landslide, unexpectedly throwing Winston Churchill out of office. They were times of a happier relationship between the *Daily Mirror* and Labour: the paper's strong backing had helped them win. Prime Minister Clement Attlee personally thanked Cecil King for his support.

As a party of the left, Labour was particularly concerned about any perception it was soft on communist and Soviet penetration. When rumours began circulating about the deputy head of MI5, the United Kingdom's security service, possibly having been compromised by the NKVD – the main security agency for the Soviet Union, superseded by the KGB in 1954 – the Home Secretary, Herbert Morrison, immediately sidelined him. Years later, the hunch about Guy Liddell would be proved right. In 1940 he had employed Anthony Blunt as his personal assistant, become a close friend of Guy Burgess and often lunched with Kim Philby: three members of the infamous Cambridge spy ring. But for now, the well-connected Liddell – he had been married to Calypso Baring, one of the daughters of Barings Bank senior executive Cecil Baring – received an unconventional reprimand of sorts. Whereas he had been due to take over as director general of MI5, despite the concerns about his loyalty, Liddell was instead made head of counter-intelligence, spying on the very NKVD operatives in Britain he was suspected of working for.

Liddell was upset at not getting the top job at MI5 and felt he'd been unfairly treated by the Labour Party. In 1947 the counter-intelligence section he headed up decided to do something remarkable, even in the world of espionage. After a communist civil servant spoke approvingly about Harold Wilson on a tapped phone line, the section created a special MI5 file on Harold Wilson. The file was so secret MI5 gave it a special coded name: Wilson was to be known as Norman Worthington.

To Peter Wright, a senior MI5 counter-intelligence officer who was a member of a committee codenamed Fluency, tasked with investigating Soviet penetration of British intelligence agencies, there was no doubt that Wilson was a KGB spy. It seems that Wright felt everyone was a double agent or a traitor in British intelligence. He even suspected the head of MI5, Sir Roger Hollis. Such was Wright's power that he decided to take action against Wilson, recruiting a group of disaffected intelligence officers in MI5. Dispirited by the defection of Kim Philby – the MI6 head of counter-intelligence – to the Soviet Union in 1963, they began what can only be described as a witch-hunt.

Wright and his cohorts had been spurred on by the claims from high-profile Soviet defector and KGB operative

Anatoli Golitsyn in 1961 that Wilson was a 'KGB informer' and an 'agent of influence'.[25] Golitsyn asserted that during his time as President of the Board of Trade in the late 1940s, Wilson had been on trade missions to Russia and struck up a friendship with Anastas Mikoyan, probably most famous for his role during the Cuban Missile Crisis – breaking the news to Fidel Castro that Moscow was going to pull its nuclear weapons out of his country. Wilson also formed a close relationship with Russian Foreign Minister Vyacheslav Molotov. Those connections might have done wonders for British trade, but now they did nothing for Wilson's reputation with the intelligence agencies.

According to material revealed in the KGB archives, Wilson's insights into British politics were highly rated by the Soviet administration. Inside its imposing headquarters in Red Square, the KGB opened an 'agent development file' on Wilson in the hope of recruiting him. Wilson was given the codename 'OLDING'. Interestingly the KGB file also recorded the comment that 'the development did not come to fruition'.[26]

When former Labour leader Hugh Gaitskell died suddenly in 1963, Golitsyn developed a story that he had been poisoned by the KGB to enable Wilson to succeed him as Labour leader. It was a dubious theory, but it was consistent with what Golitsyn told MI5.

One of the few people to have had access to MI5's secrets is Christopher Andrew, professor of Modern and Contemporary History at Corpus Christi College, Cambridge. He has also sifted through what are known as the Mitrokhin files, the records assiduously copied from top-secret KGB files by a KGB dissident named Vasili Mitrokhin, who fled the Soviet Union in 1992 and brought them to England. Andrew, who is also the official MI5 biographer, found that Wilson had never been a KGB spy, all but branding Golitsyn a liar and pointing an accusing finger at MI5: 'Sadly, a minority of British and

American intelligence officers . . . were seduced by Golitsyn's fantasies.'[27]

Andrew identifies two of those 'seduced' – both powerful forces in western intelligence – as James Jesus Angleton, the chief of CIA counter-intelligence, and his British opposite number in MI5 at the time, Peter Wright.

Whether Golitsyn's statements were fantasy or not, Wright and up to 30 other officers took them as permission to begin a major war of destabilisation against the Wilson Government. Wright began working closely with Cecil King, whom he described as 'a longtime agent of ours'.[28]

Whether or not King was himself an MI5 agent or the creation of another Wright fantasy, he appeared to be in full agreement with the coterie of malcontents festering in the domestic spy agency who wanted Wilson out and were gathering their forces. The Conservative-dominated MI5 was in a state of mental dyspepsia: struggling to deal with how easily it had been deceived by those considered their own, the impeccably well-connected Cambridge Four: Guy Burgess and Donald Maclean, Kim Philby and finally, confessing in 1964, the Keeper of the Queen's pictures, Sir Anthony Blunt.

Wright began a vicious campaign against the incoming Labour government. Over the following years MI5 didn't simply spy on Wilson, they dogged him every step of the way. Stories appeared in the press about the time he had spent in Eastern Europe as President of the Board of Trade – an organisation to help Britain's postwar export effort. Wilson did meet people MI5 legitimately had under surveillance, though there's no evidence he knew they were working for the Russians.

In Wright's zest to find a traitor, he discovered what he thought was a soft target in Labour MP Bernard Floud, whom Wilson had lined up for a ministerial job. MI5 told Wilson they were concerned about Floud and wanted to tap his phone. Wilson resisted but allowed the organisation to call him in for

an interview. On 4 August 1966 MI5 began their questioning – codenamed Operation Roast Potato – at a special flat in
Audley Street, Mayfair. Just under a kilometre away in MI5
headquarters, at the time in Curzon Street, Wright listened in
via a hidden microphone. It was Wright's job to play the 'bad
cop' when the time was right. He did it well, walking into the
room to confront Floud with the fact that MI5 knew he had
been friends with many communists at Oxford University.

Wright explained that, without any further clarification on
the matter, MI5 would be forced to deny him the clearance for
the ministerial appointment. Floud, already coping with the
death of his wife, and his career now in ruins, killed himself
the next day, 10 October 1967, at his St Pancras home. He was
52 years old.

In MI5's official history no responsibility is taken for his
death, even though it tacitly accepted that Floud had been a
victim of what the tabloid press is often accused of – a beat-up.
According to Professor Christopher Andrew, who wrote MI5's
authorised history, *The Defence of the Realm*, MI5 found 'the
investigation of Floud was of less importance than it seemed
to the Security Service at the time'. There was – and is – no
evidence that he had any communist contacts after 1952. It
added, 'His prewar contacts with Soviet intelligence are also
unlikely to have been of great significance.'[29]

As *The Guardian*'s former investigations editor David
Leigh, author of *The Wilson Plot*, points out, 'Bernard Floud
was indeed bullied with false allegations that he was a communist while in a state of grief after his wife's death. Thanks to
the files, [Christopher] Andrew exonerates him and confirms
that Peter Wright lied about the relevant dates of interroga-
tions to try to make Floud look guilty.'[30]

Though Floud's death was reported, his interrogation by
MI5 did not make the papers. There was another suicide
caused by MI5's incompetence in the Floud case[31] and the
agency was concerned about its image. The MI5 plotters

were able to choose which stories they leaked, and which they kept secret. It was a game Cecil King understood only too well.

He apparently told Wright that the *Daily Mirror* 'would publish anything MI5 might care to leak in his direction'.[32] But what King didn't know is that he had stiff competition. Wright had already teamed up with Fleet Street journalist Chapman Pincher of the *Daily Express*.

Chapman Pincher – his real name was Henry Chapman Pincher but his first editor at the *Express* told him to use his middle name because it sounded more authoritative – built a formidable reputation as a news breaker who repeatedly 'scooped' the rest of Fleet Street. Pincher, from a military family, took a strange course to journalism, starting his working life as a technical officer in the rocket division of the Ministry of Supply during the war and eventually becoming a reporter on the *Daily Express*.

Peter Wright was not Pincher's sole source. He developed an extremely close relationship with Lord Mountbatten. Mountbatten even invited Pincher to his £100 million estate, Broadlands, an honour restricted mostly to the highest echelons of the royal family; the Queen and Prince Philip are believed to shoot on the estate three times a year. The homestead is a 60-room Palladian mansion set in 5000 acres of woodlands and lakes in Hampshire. The estate's fishing and shooting is reputedly the best in the area. No doubt Pincher, who grew up in the West Yorkshire country town of Pontefract, best known for manufacturing liquorice sweets, would have been impressed.

Pincher disclosed that the First Sea Lord and Chief of the Defence Staff would become chattier than usual while out shooting. 'He invited me to shoot at Broadlands and even dictated a story to me once when I was travelling in his Land Rover, which went straight into the newspaper . . . but under my name, not his.'[33]

Exactly what the story was is not known, but on past performance it would not have been favourable to Labour. The *Daily Express* bombarded its readership with stories which reinforced the hope that the 'Great' could be put back into 'Britain'. It delighted its often xenophobic readers with stories criticising Wilson's attempts to gain Britain membership of the European Community, forerunner of the European Union, and anything which showed how the Brits outsmarted foreigners.

Pincher fitted in well. He specialised in writing stories about how clever the intelligence agencies were – trapping Soviet spy Gordon Lonsdale; arranging an elaborate spy exchange deal to free Greville Wynne, an MI6 officer the Russians had caught spying for Britain – or related themes, such as the expulsion of 100 Soviet staff from its London embassy on suspicion of espionage. He was the master of the official leak.

The historian E.P. Thompson was unimpressed: 'The columns of the *Daily Express* are a kind of official urinal where high officials of MI5 and MI6 stand side by side patiently leaking . . . Mr Pincher is too self-important and light-witted to realise how often he is being used.'[34]

But it never worried Pincher that he was being used by senior figures with ideas to promote or scores to settle: 'I'm up for use any time. If someone wants to come and tell me some news that nobody else knows and I make a lovely scoop of it, come on, use me!'[35] But at the heart of Pincher's work – what animated him philosophically and politically – lay the greatest conspiracy of all. Like his source Peter Wright, he believed that Harold Wilson was a KGB spy.

When Wilson and Labour were re-elected in 1974, the forces that had gathered to dispose of the government six years earlier, and which had been quiet during the Conservative government of Edward Heath, swung back into action. The Swinging Sixties, when London lit up the world stage with The Beatles and the Rolling Stones, hippies and sexual freedom, were a fading memory. The economy had not improved. Strikes were rampant. And in the midst of all that another threat appeared on the streets – agitating to establish a united Ireland the Provisional Irish Republican Army (IRA) began a massive bombing campaign.

—

In early 1974 the British Army temporarily sealed off Heathrow airport. Newspapers widely reported that the exercise was aimed at terrorists – late the previous year the Palestine Liberation Organization (PLO) had killed 30 people at Rome's Leonardo da Vinci airport – but Wilson's assistant Marcia Williams was not convinced: 'That wasn't an operation to deal with terrorists,' she said in a 2006 BBC documentary called *The Plot Against Harold Wilson*, based on interviews with herself and Wilson. Williams believed it was a rehearsal for something far more sinister – a military coup. Significantly, many people had been briefed in advance but not the Prime Minister or his assistant. In the interviews Wilson pointed the finger directly at MI5, accusing the intelligence organisation of operating a disinformation program – black propaganda – against him and other Labour politicians.

There was strong evidence that Wilson was right. MI5 had been working closely with an organisation called the Information Policy Unit – part of the British Army press office in Northern Ireland. Its work included routine public relations but its primary objective was to place disinformation stories in the press as part of a psychological warfare operation. The black propaganda operation called 'Clockwork Orange' had been set up ostensibly to spread lies about the Provisional IRA.

No one would have known anything about Clockwork Orange if it hadn't been for Colin Wallace, a quietly spoken Ulster Protestant who worked in the Northern Ireland Army press office and who later went public about its activities.

As a youth the highly intelligent and hardworking Wallace was infatuated with the symbols of the union – the flag, the crown, the Presbyterian Church and the army. By the age of 29 he had become the youngest man in the British Army to attain the rank of lieutenant colonel. Recruited into the Information Policy Unit, Wallace was soon put in charge of black propaganda operations. One of the journalists Wallace used to spread his fake stories was Chapman Pincher of the *Daily Express.*

Under the headline 'Chapman Pincher: The Man Who Gives You Tomorrow's News – Today', Pincher reported that the IRA was recruiting ex-Vietnam veterans in the United States to fight in Ireland. With the Vietnam War unpopular in the United Kingdom it was an attempt to blacken the name of the IRA. If the Vietnam vets ever ended up in Northern Ireland they were the quietest Americans in history. No one has ever heard of them since.

Another planted fake story given to Pincher portrayed the IRA as incompetent buffoons. It involved claims in a supposed internal IRA memo that the British had intercepted weapons and bombs being imported by the IRA and had tinkered with them to make them misfire or prematurely explode.

Pincher explained that the IRA had deliberately concocted this document and then leaked this 'false information' in the hope of 'showing that the British will stoop to any devilry'. Breathlessly Pincher explained to his readers that it was all a hoax. 'My inquiries have established this memo is a fake,' he wrote.[36]

Pincher was absolutely right about that: it was a fake. What he didn't understand was who had faked it.

The document had not been written by the IRA, but by the Clockwork Orange group. They had concocted the fake IRA document and 'leaked' it in an attempt to sow doubt and confusion in the IRA's ranks. Whether it achieved its purpose is unclear but it certainly confused Pincher. Willingly or not, he had been used.[37]

Aware of how successfully their disinformation program was working, the Clockwork Orange group lifted their sights: they began attacking members of Harold Wilson's government. Journalist briefings by Wallace and his colleagues included distributing forged documents showing members of the government were either communists or republican sympathisers involved in a campaign to destabilise Northern Ireland. Or they were simply taking bribes.[38] The stories ran in a broad range of outlets, as diverse as the satirical magazine *Private Eye* and the *Daily Express*. No one seemed concerned about whether the reports could be verified. The right-wing press in particular was simply happy to use the information to attack Labour. In the BBC documentary *The Plot Against Harold Wilson*, Wallace tellingly revealed that the Information Policy Unit briefed the press with false information linking Wilson and other Labour MPs to Soviet intelligence and the IRA. 'The intelligence community,' Wallace explained, 'believed that the government of the day was unable or unwilling to take the necessary measures to deal with the threat – with the scale of the threat. They believed they were the guardians of the United Kingdom. They felt that the political machinery was incapable of giving them support or introducing the policies that would enable them to deal with that threat.'

He went on, 'The information that I received was related to political unreliability. It was quite clear that this information was designed not just to discredit [Wilson] in a general sense, but bearing in mind that we were in a period running up to a general election, that that information would, most likely, have had a fairly major impact on how the public viewed him.'

Wallace became disillusioned, not just with Clockwork Orange operations, but his discovery MI5 was turning a blind eye to the sexual abuse of children at a local orphanage home. Shortly after attempting to make public statements about both the problems at the home and the existence of Clockwork Orange he was bundled out of the military, but worse retribution followed. Wallace was arrested and subsequently convicted of the manslaughter of the husband of one of his work colleagues. It was alleged he had beaten an antiques dealer to death before attending a dinner party with the dead man's wife.

It wasn't until nearly 10 years later, in 1996, in the light of new forensic and other evidence that the guilty verdict was overturned. Wallace, who had spent six years in jail, received compensation from the British government. But by then the damage done to Wilson's credibility was irreparable.

—

Back when Clockwork Orange was in full swing, it wasn't only newspapers, radio and television that swallowed the fabricated material being pumped out. It fed the anger of an increasing number of officers in the British military.

General Sir Walter Walker had retired from the post of NATO Commander of Northern Europe in 1972. Two years later, with miners striking and the country working a four-day week because of power shortages, Walker doubted the police and army would be able to maintain order without help. Along with another retired senior military figure, Major Alexander Greenwood, he began to organise a private army.

Greenwood, a caricature upper-crust British military figure, spoke on *The Plot Against Harold Wilson* about how he had returned from a cruise down the river Rhine to discover to his horror England was 'no longer a green and pleasant land . . . I thought the BBC would break down for one thing. I thought the trains would fail to run. London airport would not function anymore. The ports would be stagnant. There would be complete chaos in the land.'

Major Greenwood added that what he could not understand was why Wilson had not been removed already. 'You know the people who work in the City of London were not liking it and people who work as stockbrokers usually come from the best schools and a lot of them have titles and they weren't liking it at all.'

Another interviewee on the BBC documentary *The Plot Against Harold Wilson*, former intelligence officer Brian Crozier, admitted to having been engaged in a covert campaign to eject Wilson from power. Some of the officers he lobbied, he said, 'seriously considered the possibility of a military takeover'.

Asked, 'Were they top brass?' – from the top drawer of the military – Crozier replied, 'At the risk of making myself unpopular – yes.' Once again the former head of the British Armed Forces, Lord Mountbatten, became involved, he said.

According to Major Alexander Greenwood, Lord Mountbatten rang up Sir Walter Walker one evening and said, 'If you want any help from me, will you let me know?'[39] Furthermore Sir Walter Walker had prepared a sort of speech which the Queen might read out on the BBC that asked the people to stand behind the armed forces as there was a break-down of law and order and the government could not keep the unions in control.

But the preparations went further even than that. Harold Wilson would later tell Barrie Penrose and Roger Courtiour, the two journalists in whom he confided following his resignation, that senior members of the Establishment, including the Earl of Cromartie, a distant relative of the Queen, had been to see the Queen Mother to seek her blessing for the coup. Penrose and Courtiour secretly recorded their conversations with the former PM and the tapes they made formed the primary material for the BBC documentary *The Plot Against Harold Wilson*. Wilson maintained that the plans were for the Queen Mother to be made titular head of an interim administration. Wilson said he knew that the Queen Mother had been 'privately critical' of the government.

Meanwhile Chapman Pincher was playing his role with gusto. He hit the after-dinner talk circuit to spread the news about Wilson and Williams – and why they had to go. One evening, when no doubt Pincher assumed he was speaking confidentially to the amazed guests in an elegant country mansion, in the audience was someone who was listening more closely than most: Martin Gilbert, Winston Church-ill's legendary biographer. Pincher says he had been invited to reveal 'all the Fleet Street rumours'. But Gilbert was adamant that Pincher volunteered more than just a few colourful anec-dotes; he remembered him revealing 'the most terrifying facts about the Prime Minister and Marcia Williams, the prime minister's secretary'.[40] Pincher told the dinner guests Wilson and Williams were KGB.

Yet Chapman Pincher, who boasted that he was so close to Mountbatten and his friend Sir Solly Zuckerman that he coined a joint nickname for them, the Zuckbatten Axis, was very quiet about the biggest story of all – the conspiracy to remove Harold Wilson.[41]

It would be kind to say Pincher was simply a journalist who had fallen into the old trap: 'captured' by sources who had provided him with decades of stories, he was compromised. All this would be plausible but for the fact that earlier in the 1970s Pincher had already written stories about MI5 spread-ing malicious material about Wilson. Pincher's main source back then had been the head of the UK's foreign intelligence agency MI6, which was fighting a turf war with its domestic counterpart MI5.

Now Pincher had switched sides, and when MI5 became his source, he kept their dirty work secret. Embarrassingly for Pincher, in 1987 Peter Wright began spilling the beans in detail in his book *Spycatcher*, a sensational account of the attempt to oust Wilson. Audaciously Pincher accused Wright of fabricating the Wilson plot to sell his book. In a poetic twist of justice Pincher, the ace insider, had been scooped by one of his former sources.

A secret investigation by Lord Hunt, a former cabinet secretary, confirmed the central allegation about the MI5 destabilisation campaign. Lord Hunt said in August 1996, 'There is absolutely no doubt at all that a few, a very few, malcontents in MI5 . . . a lot of them like Peter Wright who were rightwing, malicious and had serious personal grudges – gave vent to these and spread damaging malicious stories about that Labour government.'[42]

Nobody in MI5 has ever been charged for the plot to bring down Wilson. Even those who publicly revealed their roles in planning a coup d'état have never been officially questioned about their involvement in the case. For their part, with the exception of one or two newspapers, the media treated the whole affair as simply political theatre.

—

While Britain was convulsing with an attempt to remove the Wilson Government, on the other side of the world in Australia another Labor government – this one headed by Gough Whitlam, the charismatic former barrister – was struggling to stay in office. Like Wilson, Whitlam had been elected with a strong reforming agenda after years of conservative government. Like Wilson, he attempted to create a fairer society, introducing free university education, increasing minimum wages and establishing the universal health care insurance scheme, Medicare.

Like Wilson, he too had received the support of Rupert Murdoch's newspapers. 'It's Time' was the slogan of the Australian Labor Party (ALP) in 1972, and after 23 years of conservative rule most Australians were indeed ready for change. *The Australian* marked Labor's victory with supportive front-page headlines. But by 1974 the Murdoch papers had turned on Whitlam. As the world economy slumped with the tripling of oil prices overnight, Whitlam and his government could do nothing right, according to the Murdoch newspapers. *The Australian* reported the country was 'Spinning Out of Control' and later it was on a 'Slippery Path to the Cliff'.

There's no doubt that Labor was in trouble, trying to finance shortfalls with foreign funds of questionable provenance. But it seems even before that Murdoch had made up his mind. And he was briefing the new US Ambassador to Australia, Marshall Green, recently appointed by US President Richard Nixon.

Nixon had drafted Green in from Chile, where the CIA had helped topple the democratically elected President Salvador Allende the previous year, 1973. In 1966 Green had been US Ambassador to Indonesia, where US intelligence played a significant role in aiding the killing of up to 500,000 Indonesians in an anti-communist purge. What followed was the ousting of Indonesia's first democratically elected president, Sukarno. Now as he lunched with Rupert Murdoch in November 1974, Green heard that the Whitlam Government was on the way out too.

US State Department documents reveal that during a 'wide-ranging and apparently very candid conversation' the 'well informed and extremely influential'[43] Murdoch spoke freely on the fortunes of the Whitlam Government.

In a classified cable Marshall Green reported to Washington that Murdoch privately predicted that 'Australian elections are likely to take place in about one year' and that Murdoch 'expects to support the opposition in the next election'.[44]

Within a month the language got much tougher. Entitled 'Australian Publisher Privately Turns on Prime Minister', a telegram from US Consul-General in Melbourne, Robert Brand, reported to the State Department that 'Rupert Murdoch has issued [a] confidential instruction to editors of newspapers he controls to "Kill Whitlam".'[45] He described Murdoch as 'the l'enfant terrible of Australian journalism'.

The tabloid Sydney *Daily Mirror* led the none-too-subtle charge against Whitlam. It carried a headline on 26 November 1974, 'Gough's Promise: Cheap Rents'. For the second edition the headline changed to 'Gough Panics: Cheap Rents'.

Just as the rumours swirled around Wilson and Marcia Williams, the ALP suffered similar attacks. In February 1975 *The Daily Telegraph* published a photograph of Deputy Prime Minister Jim Cairns and his assistant, Junie Morosi, having breakfast on a hotel balcony, but it did not show his wife, Gwen, who was also present. The *Telegraph* ran the headline 'Breakfast with Junie'.

A few months later, Murdoch appointed right-wing ideologue Bruce Rothwell as editor-in-chief of *The Australian*. Rothwell, who according to friends described the CIA as the 'cornerstone of democracy',[46] began an unrelenting assault on the Whitlam Government. Stories were being rewritten and slanted.

On 28 October 1975, 76 members of the Australian Journalists Association who worked at *The Australian* expressed concern that the paper had become a laughing-stock. They protested against the 'blind, biased, tunnel-visioned, ad-hoc, logically confused and relentless' way policy was affecting news coverage and added, 'We can be loyal to *The Australian* no matter how much its style thrust and readership changes, as long as it retains the traditions, principles and integrity of a responsible newspaper. We cannot be loyal to a propaganda sheet.'[47]

As with the plot against Wilson, it wasn't simply the press; Whitlam had the intelligence agencies gunning for him too. In the far north-west of Australia, the Naval Communication Station Harold E. Holt – supposedly a joint facility operated by the United States and Australia – has an antenna so high it can be seen for kilometres around. But its activities were hidden from the Australian government. The United States secretly used it to help Israel during the Six Day War of 1967 and to aid its B-52 bombers during their saturation attacks on Cambodia during the Vietnam War. It was one of the most important communications stations anywhere in the world for Washington.

Its work linked closely with another Australian-based US asset several thousand kilometres to the south-east. Not far from Alice Springs in the heart of Australia, along a narrow road, lies Pine Gap, originally described as a Joint Defence Space Research Facility. But what Whitlam discovered was that the research that Pine Gap was doing had nothing to do with space and a lot to do with what was happening on Earth. It was one of the most important spy bases the United States operated anywhere in the world, sucking up everything from electronic details of rocket launches to private telephone calls. What's more, it was joint in name only. The United States controlled everything that happened at the base and the Australian presence there was merely token.

As members of the Whitlam Government began to question the role of Pine Gap, the administration became victim of a destabilisation campaign which closely mirrored what was happening in London.

Even before the Whitlam Government was elected in 1972, the CIA's chief of counter-intelligence, James Jesus Angleton, reportedly 'shuddered when he was told [Australia was] about to fall into the arms of a "party that has extensive historical contacts with Eastern Europe", a party whose constitution commits it to socialism'.[48] The hostility became palpable as Whitlam shifted Australia towards the Non-Aligned Movement of nations, opposed nuclear weapons and ordered that his staff should not be 'vetted or harassed' by the Australian Security Intelligence Organisation (ASIO).[49] When government ministers publicly condemned the US bombing of Vietnam as 'corrupt and barbaric', a CIA station officer in Saigon said, 'We were told the Australians might as well be regarded as North Vietnamese collaborators.'[50]

Theodore Shackley, who had run the CIA's Saigon office at the height of the Vietnam War and was about to become chief of the CIA's East Asia Division, which included protecting the North West Cape and particularly Pine Gap, was also gravely concerned when Whitlam indicated that his government might not renew the lease on the US bases when they fell due in a few years. On 4 November 1975, Shackley sent a message to ASIO: 'The CIA cannot see how this dialogue with continual reference to the CIA can do other than blow the lid off those installations ... particularly the installation in Alice Springs.' It added, 'The CIA feel that if this problem cannot be solved they do not see how our mutually beneficial relations are going to continue.'[51]

Victor Marchetti, the CIA officer who had helped set up Pine Gap, was blunt: 'This threat to close Pine Gap caused apoplexy in the White House ... a kind of Chile [coup] was set in motion.'[52]

With the intelligence agencies and the Murdoch press now firmly opposed to the Whitlam Government, they gained an extraordinarily powerful ally, Australia's Governor-General, Sir John Kerr.

The son of a boilermaker, Kerr embraced his royal role – and all the pomp that accompanies it – with extraordinary passion. He was an ill fit for a government that had decided to drop royal patronage and end royal honours. Kerr was not only the Queen's man, he had strong ties to Anglo-American intelligence. He was a member of the Australian Association for Cultural Freedom, described by author Jonathan Kwitny – a former *Wall Street Journal* reporter – in his book *The Crimes of Patriots*, as, 'an elite, invitation-only group ... exposed in Congress as being founded, funded and generally run by the CIA'. The CIA 'paid for Kerr's travel, built his prestige ... Kerr continued to go to the CIA for money'.[53] Christopher Boyce, who worked as a CIA contractor operating part of the Pine Gap satellite surveillance system, said the CIA referred to Kerr as 'our man Kerr'.[54]

With the Opposition Coalition parties blocking government finance bills in the Senate and the Murdoch press whipping up hysteria that the country was in a crisis of Whitlam's making, Kerr began sounding out Buckingham Palace's view that he might dismiss the government.

At a celebration to mark the independence of Papua New Guinea, Australia's sole colonial dependency, on 16 September 1975, Kerr took the extreme step of raising with Prince Charles the possible dismissal of the Whitlam Government and 'his grave fear that he would himself be dismissed by Whitlam should he do so'.[55]

Charles replied, according to Kerr's notes of their exchange, 'But surely, Sir John, the Queen should not have to accept advice that you should be recalled at the very time, should this happen, when you were having to dismiss the government.'

On his return to England Charles took up Kerr's concern with the Queen's private secretary, Sir Martin Charteris. Unknown to Australian Prime Minister Gough Whitlam, Charteris then wrote to the governor-general. Charteris told Kerr that, should what he euphemistically termed 'the contingency to which you refer' arise, the Queen would 'try to delay things',[56] although Charteris acknowledged that, in the end, the Queen would have to take the advice of the Prime Minister.

For Kerr it was a green light: if Whitlam moved against him, the Queen would slow down the process. And only later take the advice of the Prime Minister.[57]

Eight weeks later, on 11 November 1975, Kerr sacked the Whitlam Government. Kerr had done to Whitlam what press baron Cecil King, and sections of the UK's intelligence agencies and the military, wanted the Queen's permission to do to Wilson – remove him from office.

In the United Kingdom, the truth about the Wilson plot was known to at least one journalist, Chapman Pincher. But Pincher, the ultimate insider and a journalist whom much of the British media, including the BBC, exalted at his death in 2014 as an exemplary newspaper reporter, failed to raise the alarm.

Others too were seduced by leaks against the Wilson Government from MI5's propaganda machine, Clockwork

Orange, taking the insiders' easy road to stories that would please their newspaper proprietors – and the established order.

In Australia the journalists knew something was amiss but had scant evidence of the then deeply hidden opposition to the Whitlam Government by US intelligence agencies. As laid down by Whitlam in his account of his time in office, *The Whitlam Government 1972–1975* (Penguin Books, Melbourne, 1985), their role was all but confirmed by an emissary sent to Australia in 1977 by then US President Jimmy Carter. Whitlam described a breakfast meeting with Warren Christopher, the US Assistant Secretary of State for Asia and the Pacific, at the Qantas VIP Lounge at Sydney Airport on Wednesday 27 July 1977; other officials were present. Christopher made it clear to Whitlam that he had 'made a special detour in his itinerary for the sole purpose of speaking to me'. Christopher told him that the 'US Administration would never again interfere in the domestic political processes of Australia'. He added that President Carter would 'work with whatever government the people of Australia elected'.

If the US intelligence action had been covert, one thing was out in the open for all to see – the blatantly anti-government journalism being produced by *The Australian*.

Many of the journalists were so outraged they went on strike, took to the streets, and burned copies of *The Australian* outside the company's Sydney headquarters. They had become journalistic whistleblowers.

Murdoch boasts that he helped remove Whitlam from office. That was almost certainly the case, but what is of greater significance is that – as in the United Kingdom – intelligence agencies and the royal family also became involved. Together they formed a destructive and corrosive force against democracy. Newspapers – and their owners – had not only abrogated their responsibility to act without fear or favour, they had become the propaganda arm against democratically elected governments.

In the past they held most of the levers of power. The internet would change all that.

CHAPTER 4

Rise of the Internet

Daniel Ellsberg's home isn't far from the shifting geological plates of the San Francisco fault line that caused the earthquake which devastated the city in 1906. In a way Ellsberg himself straddles a division: the world's most famous whistleblower of a pre-internet world is a hero to those who have followed him in a very different digital age.

His allure is perhaps easy to understand. Ellsberg wasn't a typical dissenter: Harvard-educated, he had served two years in Vietnam as a marine corps lieutenant and later worked for the Pentagon on nuclear war-fighting policy. His conversion to whistleblowing came after he stumbled across a brutal truth that would challenge the beliefs of any rational person: commissioned by US Defense Secretary Robert McNamara to contribute to a review of Vietnam War history, he discovered a report that carefully documented what successive administrations secretly thought of the conflict. In essence, they all recognised that the war was unwinnable. The report later became known as the Pentagon Papers.

In March 1969, when Ellsberg was working on another Defense Department project for the RAND Corporation think tank, he used his security clearance and asked the Pentagon for a full copy of the highly classified report to be sent to him. When it arrived he placed it in a high-security safe in his office.

Haunted by the thought that Nixon could use nuclear weapons in Vietnam, Ellsberg began to think seriously about what he could do to stop the war's escalation. Having earlier advised the US government on nuclear warfare strategies, Ellsberg understood more than any other civilian what kind of horror could be unleashed by US weapons far more powerful than those that devastated the Japanese cities of Nagasaki and Hiroshima at the end of the Second World War. While wrestling with his conscience and weighing up what to do, Ellsberg came into contact with draft resisters who told him they were prepared to go to jail rather than fight in Vietnam. Those interactions helped concentrate Ellsberg's thinking.

A little over six months later, in October 1969, he walked out of the RAND office, got into his car and drove a few blocks to the workplace of a friend. Availing themselves of that company's Xerox photocopying machine, for several days Ellsberg and his friend photocopied all 47 volumes of the 7000-page report. It was time-consuming and tedious work and when it was finished Ellsberg must have wondered if it had all been worthwhile. Now with a copy of the report he planned his next move. Several times Ellsberg tried to persuade senior politicians to take action to reveal the truth about the Vietnam War, but no one would listen. He even offered them copies of the report. Blocked by the political system, in frustration he turned to *The New York Times* to get the story out. On 13 June 1971, when the newspaper published the Pentagon Papers, it was not only the biggest leak ever, but the last great leak of the pre-digital analogue age. Ellsberg defended his actions as upholding the highest principles of the US Constitution.

Amid the clamour for his prosecution from the White House, Ellsberg handed himself over to US law enforcement agencies, saying he was prepared to accept the consequences of his actions and face charges under the Espionage Act of 1917. In the end, the case against Ellsberg was thrown out of court, not because – as is popularly believed – he was protected by the Constitution's First Amendment, which guarantees free speech, but because the prosecution botched the case by illegally wiretapping Ellsberg's phone and breaking into his doctor's office in the hope of gathering evidence to smear his name. Ellsberg's leak is largely credited with bringing the Vietnam War to an end.

In 1969, while Ellsberg and his friend slaved over an overheating photocopier, a bunch of scientists were making history of a different kind in a nondescript cream brick building at Stanford University. They were taking the first steps to create a system giving whistleblowers the kind of power Ellsberg never dreamed of – the ability to access and copy secrets at the click of an icon. The Stanford scientists were working on a program called the Advanced Research Projects Agency, or ARPANET. Its project manager, Bob Taylor, had three computer terminals in his office, each one connected to a different computer in a different part of the country. The problem was, each computer had a different connection. As Taylor explained, 'To get in touch with someone in Santa Monica through the computer, I would sit in front of one terminal, but to do the same thing with someone in Massachusetts, I would have to get up and move over to another terminal. I mean, you don't have to look at this very long to realize this is silly. It is stupid. So I decided, okay, I want to build a network that connects all of these.'[1]

The challenge Bob Taylor and his team set for themselves was to see if every computer could connect to each other from any one terminal. As the project evolved, down the coast at the University of California, Los Angeles (UCLA), student computer programmer Charley Kline prepared for the big moment. At just after 10 pm on 29 October 1969, he tried to make contact by remotely logging in to the computer over 500 kilometres away in Stanford. Kline typed in the first letter of the word login, 'L'. The Stanford team told him over the phone, yes they had received 'L' on their screens. He typed the second letter, 'O'. 'Okay,' came the response. Then in the middle of the historic start of the internet age, the system crashed. Only after an hour of feverish activity did the team solve the problem and the computers connected. It would be true to say that at that moment, if not the internet itself, the child of the internet was born.

Taylor, for one, had a very sound idea of what he had created. Back in 1968, with a colleague, he had predicted the extraordinary impact computerised networks could have on everyday life. Facebook, Google Earth and Twitter were years away – waiting for the invention of the World-Wide Web by British scientist Tim Berners-Lee, which would allow mass interconnections between individual users – but Taylor obviously understood what was possible. He spoke of the use of the internet for the 'dissemination of information in your field of specialization'[2] and information on 'cultural, sport and entertainment events'. The system would also give access to 'dictionaries, encyclopedias, indexes, catalogues, editing programs, teaching programs, testing programs, programming systems, databases and, most important, communication'.[3] Though originally designed as a high-speed pathway to interconnect research institutions and universities, Taylor's work was not purely academic. ARPANET, the embryonic internet, was funded by the US Department of Defense.

Right from the start the US military imposed its authority, an ominous portent for the starry-eyed computer nerds who believed they could build a better world through interconnecting everyone on the planet. One of the ARPANET's partners, the Massachusetts Institute of Technology (MIT), found it necessary to warn its users:

> It is considered illegal to use the ARPANet for anything which is not in direct support of Government business . . . personal messages to other ARPANet subscribers (for example, to arrange

a get-together or check and say a friendly hello) are generally
not considered harmful . . . Sending electronic mail over the
ARPANet for commercial profit or political purposes is both
anti-social and illegal.[4]

Significantly the university feared it ran the risk of having its
funding cut if researchers breached the rules. 'By sending such
messages, you can offend many people, and it is possible to get
MIT in serious trouble with the Government agencies which
manage the ARPANet.'[5] The early warnings were probably
taken in a spirit of openness but behind them lay a darker
purpose: the internet was controlled by those who paid for its
creation. Over the next two decades the military would split
off a large section of the net to use for its own communications channels, leaving the rest for civilian purposes. But the
United States and its military would make sure it still maintained close command and control over much that travelled
across what was then being called 'the communications super-
highway'.

In the early 1990s all the world's internet traffic travelled
through a single switching system in Washington.

As the internet grew the United States maintained its
pre-eminent position as the gateway for a system which would
dominate world communications.

Universities thrived as the government poured more and
more money into internet-related activities. No one benefited more than Stanford University. During the Cold War
Stanford was one of the top recipients of Defense Department
patronage; it was also one of the first universities to forge close
relationships to private industrial concerns, many of which
were developing war-related technologies.[6]

Founded in 1885 on 650 acres of grassy slopes and rolling
hills, privately funded Stanford set itself apart from other
American universities. As it boasts today on its website, 'From
the beginning, it was clear that Stanford would be different.

It was coeducational at a time when single-sex colleges were the norm. It was non-sectarian when most private colleges were still affiliated with a church. And it offered a broad, flexible program of study while most schools insisted on a rigid curriculum of classical studies.[7] Stanford was out to make a name for itself and it would not be following the strictures of a conventional university.

Now as the military money poured in, those who sought riches and power drew close. Surrounding the campus like bees feeding off the intellectual nectar of a huge hive of knowledge, US and international electronics companies flocked to the shores of San Francisco Bay. At last count there were 32 of the world's biggest names in international communications and computer science crowding the area around Stanford University. The intensity of computer-related company activity spawned a name for the area.

It was probably too difficult to coin a name to describe its true activity – making money out of armaments – but down the road from the university at the town of Palo Alto there is a clue to the quiet revolution that had taken place. On the wall of one of the homes is a brass plaque which reads simply, 'Birthplace of Silicon Valley', named after the silicon chips that powered computerised systems. It was here, next door in the garage, that Dave Packard and his former university colleague Bill Hewlett set up their small workshop in 1939 – the forerunner of the eponymous electronics and armaments giant. Hewlett-Packard certainly started small, most notably producing an electronic sound oscillator for the music used in the Walt Disney production of *Fantasia*, but before long Hewlett-Packard's focus shifted from the silver screen to the theatre of war.

In 1940 the company's work was deemed to be of such national importance that Packard was exempted from the Second World War draft. Instead the company worked with the US Naval Research Laboratory to build counter-radar technology and advanced artillery shell fuses.[8] As the business grew and Hewlett-Packard moved out of the garage, it added other components to its manufacturing arsenal: sophisticated electronics for B-52 nuclear bombers.[9]

The growth in the weapons industry meant more money for Stanford University. In 1950, with the Korean War starting, Stanford agreed to a US Navy request to build an electronics program, specifically to produce weapons for electronic warfare. The head of the school of engineering, Fred Terman, enthusiastically endorsed the idea: 'In the event of all out war Stanford would become one of the giant electronic research centers . . .'[10]

Whether or not much of the West Coast of the United States, and Stanford University, would have survived a nuclear exchange with the Soviet Union seems to have not been considered. Even without 'all out' war, Pentagon money still flowed into Stanford's coffers. Military funds doubled the size of the university's electronics program. Hewlett-Packard – great beneficiaries of the arms race – completed the circle of money, pouring funding back into Stanford to support innovations in electronic warfare.

By 1969 Hewlett-Packard was so much part of the military–industrial Establishment that President Richard Nixon appointed David Packard deputy secretary of defense. Forced to divest himself of the US$300 million he had tied up in the company because of conflict-of-interest issues,[11] Packard set up a charitable trust and handed over the investments. Vetting him for the appointment many US congressmen believed the trust was a sham, but Nixon got his way and Packard moved into the administration. Perhaps unsurprisingly he became one of the biggest champions of the arms race, arguing that détente with the Soviet Union was tantamount to capitulation to communism, and supporting a plan to covertly build an anti-ballistic missile system without the approval of Congress.

With anti-Vietnam War demonstrations sweeping US cities in 1971, Packard had a plan for them too: bring in the military to clear the streets. Though constitutionally it seemed illegal, and could only be effected if Congress agreed, Packard rewrote the law – Employment of Military Resources in the Event of Civil Disturbances – and pushed it through the legislature, giving the President the right to impose what many saw as martial law for the first time in the history of the United States.

When Packard left public life and returned to Hewlett-Packard, he continued his support for right-wing causes like the Heritage Foundation and, more profoundly, he began funding a group known as the 'Committee on Present Danger'. With the election of Ronald Reagan in 1980, most of the super-hawks who populated the White House Cabinet Room came from the ranks of the committee. Many were neo-cons, former Democrats who, like many newly converted believers in any faith, embraced extreme positions when they moved across to the other side.

Assistant Secretary of State for East Asian and Pacific Affairs Paul Wolfowitz believed it was America's destiny to remove 'tyrants' from power; Assistant Secretary of defense Richard Perle, known in certain quarters as the 'Prince of Darkness', aggressively opposed nuclear arms reduction; and Jeane Kirkpatrick, President Ronald Reagan's foreign policy adviser, believed that right-wing dictatorships were better than those from the left because they were more likely to give up power to democracy.

Rather than seeing the increase in Soviet nuclear weapons in the 1970s as a rational response to the American build-up of the 1960s, they argued that the Soviets were preparing to use nuclear blackmail to take over the world. That this was roundly rejected as absurd by nearly every major academic and foreign policy analyst had little effect on Packard and the neo-cons. As Alex Zaitchik, who researched security policy at the Institute of International Relations in Prague, wrote, 'given the scale of recklessness in the policies and statements of the first Reagan Administration – from medium-range missiles in Europe . . . to Strategic Defence Initiative (SDI) – Star Wars – to "winnable nuclear war" – it is remarkable that disaster was avoided'.[12]

Zaitchik says that during the early 1980s, US leadership sounded less like educated and serious men with the fate of the Earth in their hands than did General Buck Turgidson in Stanley Kubrick's film *Dr. Strangelove or: How I Learned to Stop Worrying and Love the Bomb.* The movie's general, chomping on a large cigar, tells the US President of the downside of a nuclear exchange with Russia: 'I'm not saying we won't get our hair mussed. Ten to twenty million casualties tops – depending on the breaks.'

As nuclear brinkmanship terrified the world, soaring US military expenditure filled the coffers of the arms manufacturers. Like the missiles they were making, Hewlett-Packard's profits rose into a clear blue sky. By the time it celebrated 50 years in business, orders would exceed US$10 billion per annum.

Hewlett-Packard was particularly proud of its research and development division, touting its 1968 breakthrough in the production of Light Emitting Diodes (LEDs). Hewlett-Packard had solved one of the big problems: how to make an LED that would produce enough light to be useful. '[The] breakthrough, together with improvements in the optical design, has resulted in LEDs that are now bright enough to be used in such demanding outdoor applications as automotive taillights, scoreboards and bill boards,' Hewlett-Packard boasted.[13]

But there was more to these revolutionary LEDs than cars, sport and advertising. The LEDs also had a significant military application: part of a night-vision system being used by the US military in Vietnam to identify and ambush the enemy at night.

For a person who was about to join the Nixon White House the following year, it was perhaps understandable that David Packard wanted to keep his company's relationship with defence production as quiet as possible. Yet it is extraordinary that there was not one single mention of the US Army, Navy or United States Air Force (USAF) in the company's entire annual report. Hewlett-Packard had managed to create an illusion of distance from the military. Its electronics were simply being bought by other companies who manufactured the equipment.

Just as Hewlett-Packard manufactured the impression of an arm's length relationship with the US military, the distinction between military and civilian use of its electronics systems was becoming blurred. Research and development for military products produced extraordinary spin-off benefits which spilled over into the civilian consumer market. The same software for nuclear weapons systems powered pocket calculators and Hewlett-Packard surged ahead of the field in this lucrative new market. It had already made its mark in 1968, not only with LEDs but also by manufacturing the first mass-produced personal computer.[14] Now Hewlett-Packard was about to be projected to the forefront of the biggest game in town after nuclear weapons: the internet.

—

As the Cold War ended and the superpowers had managed not to fry the planet, the future lay in using new electronics systems for more benign purposes. Once again Stanford University was in the vanguard.

Not far away from where Stanford's computers had linked up to create the first internet connection, two PhD students began researching ways to take the next step: indexing and making quickly accessible the thousands of pages on websites which were now slowly beginning to be established around the world.

The story of how Larry Page and Sergey Brin created Google runs eerily parallel to how Hewlett-Packard got off the ground. They too started work in the dorms and labs of Stanford and then moved to a garage down the road, where they set up a workshop. The means by which Larry Page, at the tender age of 25, established the concept of the prototype Google search engine is now the stuff of legend. The early search engines like Yahoo or HotBot would scan through the text of websites around the world for a key phrase or word and then direct the searcher to the website. The more frequently a site contained the word or phrase – the bigger its number of 'hits' – the higher up it would automatically appear in the results list. The problem was that it might not be what the person was looking for. For example, a search for the English football club Manchester United could direct the searcher to a clothing store stacked with soccer products carrying the insignia of the club, instead of the club itself. Page solved the problem by developing a system which recorded how many 'hits' the Manchester United home page received from searches over time by other people actually looking for that particular site. It was like a popularity contest and the most popular site was ranked no. 1 on the Google search page. As *Time* magazine explained, Google's technology was the first to 'treat the internet as a democracy', adding that 'Google interprets connections between websites as votes. The most linked-to sites win on the Google usefulness ballot and rise to the top of the search results.'[15]

Page and Brin found that the democratisation of the internet went down well with the students they used as guinea pigs to test their latest refinement of the Google search engine. The youth culture of freedom and openness which dominated much of the San Francisco Bay area – famous for its 'Summer of Love' in '67 – would give birth to an idealised way of working, an attempt to mould together two seemingly competing philosophies: big business and a big heart.

By mid-1998 it seemed like it just might work. Everyone on the Stanford campus seemed happy to know Page and Brin. Google was getting thousands of hits a day.

To expand the operation the pair scrounged computers from other departments on campus and ploughed in US$15,000 of their own money, buying a terabyte of disks, spreading the costs across three credit cards. Daunted by the debt, these somewhat reluctant entrepreneurs tried to license the search engine to other companies but – as it turned out, luckily for them – no one was interested. By chance they kept control of what would become the biggest communications goldmine in the world.

What they discovered instead was someone who was prepared to invest cold hard cash and take all the financial risks. Andy Bechtolsheim, the founder of Sun Microsystems, wrote them a cheque for US$100,000 as investment seed money. But it was no use to Page and Brin; they didn't even have a company bank account. They had to set one up in the name of Google so they could cash the cheque. As the investment community cottoned on to the hottest thing on the internet, serious investors ploughed in a further US$25 million.

Google was on its way – with some help from giant Silicon Valley trailblazer Hewlett-Packard: using two HP routers to run their mainframe systems. It wouldn't be the last time that there would be an identifiable connection between the two companies which shared similar beginnings and were both swept up in the converging interests of Silicon Valley business development and the US military.

Google was on a fast escalator to the top. In 1998, its first year of operation, the search engine indexed 24 million pages and attracted 10,000 searches every day. As word spread around the world of the super speed and incredible access provided by Google, the daily search number rapidly soared to half a million.

The investments helped Google relocate from the garage to leased premises in Mountain View, overlooking San Francisco Bay. Two years later Google bought the property outright for US$319 million and, despite the price tag, the building – which they named Googleplex – maintained that cool campus feel. Inside the huge glass and steel edifice, surrounded by gardens and cycle tracks, there was free Ben and Jerry's ice-cream, an on-site masseuse, a ping-pong table, yoga classes, and even a staff physician. Employees could bring their dogs to work, and the company cafeteria was run by a professional chef who used to work for the rock band the Grateful Dead. 'Since we started the company, we've grown twenty per cent per month. Our employees can do whatever they want,' said Brin.[16]

The staff could also work whenever they wanted to, provided they completed their tasks, and even then the company was generous. The work hours were divided up – 80 per cent for the company, with the other 20 per cent put aside for staff to concentrate on pet projects. Page and Brin hadn't forgotten how the benefits of a relaxed and support- ive university life had helped them release their creativity and get a big break. A similar work environment would not only help the staff become fulfilled, they reasoned, it would also get the best out of them. But all was not what it seemed. Not everything at Google would always be open and relaxed.

By the end of 1998, Google had an index of 60 million pages that could be accessed by its search engine. Regular internet users were voting with their keyboards: Google was outpacing its search engine competitors; HotBot, Excite, Netscape, AOL – the then darlings of the internet but barely memorable now – couldn't match them for speed or access. Google would soon leave them in a cyber funk, unable to compete. To rub it in, the term 'internet search' was being replaced with a new verb by the cool net savvy younger generation. They didn't surf the net looking for information any more, they googled.

On 19 August 2004 Google cashed in on its good fortune with a public float. A total of 19,605,052 shares offered at a price of US$85 each raised US$1.67 billion, and gave Google a market capitalisation of more than US$23 billion. Many of Google's employees, who had been given shares in the company as part of a salary package, became instant paper millionaires.

As Google refined its massive search engine, championing the cause of net freedom and an interconnected world – where knowledge would be shared and with it would come opportunity for all – its corporate motto, 'Don't Be Evil', sounded like something from a previous generation. With its religious overtones, it wasn't exactly a return to the days of peace, love and hope, but it was all part of the feel-good mantra.

All that was to change though as the company which initially had been so dismissive of using advertising to fund its ventures became drawn into the commercial world. When Google started taking advertising, the systems it used to profile its users and accordingly to target its commercials were sophisticated pieces of machinery. In many ways they were similar to the systems used by intelligence agencies, producing profiles on people they were tracking. Consequently when the National Security Agency (NSA) wanted a system to catalogue and store its huge collection of clandestine material, it went straight to Google. In 2003 Google secured a US$2.07 million contract to outfit the NSA with a Google system capable of 'searching 15 million documents in twenty-four languages'.[17]

At the same time that Google was working with the NSA it was also forging links with two other US intelligence agencies – the National Geospatial-Intelligence Agency (NGA), which provides live satellite imagery to US military battlefield operations, and the Central Intelligence Agency (CIA).

Both the CIA and the NGA had what Google wanted as it began building an extraordinary venture: an interactive system that would map the world. It would be known as Google Earth but first Google needed access to the raw materials to build its visionary product: high-resolution satellite photographs and a 3-D viewer to give the user a feeling of 'being there' as Google Earth allowed its customers to see the world from the comfort of their computer screens. The NGA, best known for providing the satellite intelligence and photographs which helped capture and kill Osama bin Laden at his Pakistan headquarters, had the imagery systems Google needed. As Google negotiated for access to the NGA's satellite database it also began talking to the CIA; an organisation which had spent years hiding its activities behind front companies was now brazenly operating in the commercial world.

The CIA's 'investment arm', In-Q-Tel, had just bought a company called Keyhole, which seemed to have not much to recommend it except that it had mastered the art of 3-D satellite projections. Close to bankruptcy, Keyhole had been reduced to handing out high-resolution copies of its imagery for free to television networks or to real estate agents in exchange for online credit. In-Q-Tel began pouring millions of dollars into the Keyhole company and suddenly it was solvent again. A few months later the CIA sold the company on – to Google.

In the kind of mangled syntax that only someone who is trying not to be too explicit can manage, CIA Director George Tenet 'explained' in his book about life in the organisation, 'We [the CIA] decided to use our limited dollars to leverage technology developed elsewhere.'[18] Tenet did manage to make one point very clear, although it did seem extraordinary. He said that while the CIA 'paid the bills', In-Q-Tel was 'independent of CIA'.[19]

Google, according to surveys one of the most trusted companies in the world, was following in the footsteps of Hewlett-Packard by forming a close-knit relationship with the arms and intelligence industries. And it would get even closer. Just a few weeks after the CIA sold the Keyhole satellite system to Google, the person who had led both the negotiations for the CIA company to buy it and the ones to on-sell it to Google, joined the Google corporation: Rob Painter was appointed as chief technologist and senior manager for Google Federal. His biography says he focused on 'evangelizing [sic] and implementing Google Enterprise solutions for a host of users across the Intelligence and Defense Communities, Homeland Security, and many others'.[20] In other words he was continuing the work with Google that he had been doing for the CIA's In-Q-Tel. Google now had very close ties with US defence and intelligence organisations. Precisely how close was the question. In the internet world the mere mention of the CIA sends many bloggers and the conspiracy obsessed looking for their escape hatches.

Google might have been able to explain away the relationship but for the emergence as a commentator of Robert Steele, a former CIA clandestine case officer. Steele worked in CIA operations at the Soviet satellite section of the US Embassy in Mexico City in the 1970s. He was also the co-founder of the intelligence wing of the Marine Corps and became its second highest ranking civilian. Steele was a maverick who had championed the use of 'open source' intelligence, which relied more on publicly available information than secret surveillance to inform decision-makers. He finally walked out of the CIA when he realised no one at the top was interested in using the cheaper open source material as it was deemed a threat to the existence of the multi-billion dollar US intelligence system.

On 27 October 2006 Steele appeared on a syndicated radio show run by shock jock Alex Jones, a cross between a right-wing libertarian supporting gun ownership and a Tea Party conservative opposed to Wall Street and socialism. Jones does not try to hide his views. Take the way his website reported the Australian government's decision to give the domestic spy agency, the Australian Security Intelligence Organisation (ASIO), more power; the headline read, 'Australian Senate Kills Civil Liberties with Draconian New Anti-Terror Law in Orwellian Orgy of Baseless Fear-Mongering'.

Perhaps Steele, founder and president of Virginia-based Open Source Solutions Inc (OSS), could have chosen a more trustworthy platform, but what he had to say was even more startling than the headlines on Jones's website. Steele told Jones that 'Google is in bed'[21] with the CIA and it had been for some time. He said he believed Google 'took money from the CIA' when the company was poor during its start-up phase: 'Unfortunately our system right now floods money into spying and other illegal and largely unethical activities, and it doesn't fund what I call the open source world,' said Steele, citing 'trusted individuals'[22] as the sources for his claim. Asked at what level Google was 'in bed' with the CIA, Steele described the bond as a 'small but significant relationship'.[23]

The former CIA officer went on to identify by name the person Google liaised with at the CIA: 'Let me say very explicitly – their contact at the CIA is named Dr. Rick Steinheiser, he's in the Office of Research and Development.'[24] Steele said later that Google 'took money from' Steinheiser, 'my old colleague'.[25]

There's little public information available about Dr Rick Steinheiser but he is cited as appearing on a panel discussion at an international conference on data mining in Florida in September 2003. The program notes say that 'challenges for security applications will be discussed'; and more significantly, 'the opportunities for funding available for data mining research and applications'. He was simply named on the conference program as 'Rick Steinheiser, United States Central Intelligence Agency (CIA)'.[26]

Presumably Google hoped Steele's claims might quickly disappear in the 24-hour news cycle, but that's not what happened. They were picked up by a blogger – and not just any blogger but one of the most respected people on the internet, John Battelle, founder of the industry 'bible' *Wired* magazine, who wrote on his blog:

This might be filed in the Tin Foil Hat category, or it might be something we look back on and wonder how we ever missed it. I don't have any idea which. That alone sort of scares me.

The story says that Google is working with the Govt. in the war on terror. It depends a lot on ex CIA agent Robert Steele, who may or may not be a trustworthy source.

I've seen this story all over the place this weekend, and it strikes me as possibly accurate on at least one level: If the CIA/ Dept. of Homeland Security was NOT trying to secretly work with Google, it's even lamer than we might imagine. After all, the company has just about the best infrastructure in the world to help them do their job. Is it legal? Moral? Right? Another question entirely . . .[27]

A professor of journalism, Battelle is the author of one of the definitive books on Google, *The Search: How Google and Its Rivals Rewrote the Rules of Business and Transformed Our Culture* (Portfolio, New York, 2005). An international bestseller, it has been translated into more than 25 languages.

Battelle was no conspiracy theorist but someone Google had to deal with, a serious commentator. Matt Cutts, a senior Google executive, took up the fight for the company using online humour:

Random Google PR person:	Hey, co-founder, can I grab a minute of your time?
Random Google Co-founder:	I'm on my way to a meeting, you can walk with me if you want.
PR person:	So a site on the web claims that Google is in bed with the CIA.
Co-founder:	Huh? What are you talking about?
PR person:	There's this site claiming that Google is, like, in bed with the CIA. So, are we?
Co-founder:	Dude, why are you bothering me with crap like this? Of course we're not! I think somebody's pulling your leg.

PR person:	No, really, it was a serious inquiry. As long as we're talking about this, can I check on just a couple other things?
Co-founder:	Sure.
PR person:	Are we a, let me find it, 'proxy NSA outfit'?
Co-founder:	What the hell are you talking about?
PR person:	Someone said that 'Google's ceaseless drive to dominate Microsoft and reap untold profits has come at the expense of privacy as the company jettison's [sic] its "don't be evil" mandate and merges itself into a proxy NSA outfit, creating all the tools necessary for the state to suffocate its subjects under an inescapable high-tech panopticon control grid.'
Co-founder:	PR person, have you been smoking crack?[28]

As a response it got plenty of laughs in cyberspace, particularly among the Google fan club, which believed the company could do no wrong. What the witty dialogue could have included but didn't was any kind of personal anecdote from Cutts about the NSA. He almost certainly had a selection of them from his time there as an NSA intern, a fact which is also omitted from his Google and Wikipedia biographies.[29]

While Google buried uncomfortable truths about itself, it continued to promote the company as a staunch defender of its customers' right to privacy. In January 2006, with the US Department of Justice seeking access to millions of searches carried out by internet users – part of an investigation into child pornography – Yahoo and Microsoft caved in and handed over their data. Google alone declared it would fight on; it became a matter for the courts.

In public statements the company argued that Google users 'trust that when they enter a search query into a Google search box, not only will they receive back the most relevant results, but that Google will keep private whatever information users communicate absent a compelling reason. The Government's demand for disclosure of untold millions of search queries . . . selected from Google's proprietary index would undermine that trust.'[30]

But documents dated 13 March 2006, filed at the US District Court in its low-rise building in San Jose, at the southern end of Silicon Valley, paint a different picture. Google had been motivated not by privacy concerns but by anxiety about losing its commercial edge over its rivals by revealing information about its extraordinarily successful search engine. In the documents, stamped with the case number 5:06-mc-80006-JW, Google argued that the data the Department of Justice had wanted 'contains valuable trade secrets and confidential commercial information' and that 'disclosure of Google's trade secrets is a significant possibility'. Google also said that 'production of the requested data will result in a chilling effect on Google's business'. It's only at the end of a long list that Google – the company that claims it puts its customers first – finally mentions the effect on 'user trust'.[31]

Google then appeared to actively squander any trust the internet community may have in its ability to remain neutral and protect its secrets. Three years after the court case ended, with Google agreeing to cooperate with the Department of Justice after it reduced the scale of its demands, Google again joined up with the CIA. This time it was a joint investment in a company that monitors the web in real time. The company, Recorded Future, scours tens of thousands of websites, blogs and Twitter accounts to find the relationships between people, organisations, actions and incidents – and then tries to predict the future actions of those involved.

Both the CIA's In-Q-Tel and Google Ventures have seats on Recorded Future's board. 'The cool thing is, you can actually predict the curve, in many cases,' says Recorded Future's CEO Christopher Ahlberg, a former Swedish Army Ranger with a PhD in computer science.[32]

It was perhaps understandable that with Google and intelligence agencies competing for a similar pool of professional talent, there were crossovers in staffing. But joint company ventures were something completely different and underscored the belief that even if Google wasn't 'in bed' with the CIA, it was certainly far too close. Google's CEO Eric Schmidt was even parroting the US intelligence agencies' argument against personal privacy, telling US cable news company CNBC, 'If you have something that you don't want anyone to know, maybe you shouldn't be doing it in the first place.'[33] For the head of an organisation millions trusted with their personal details, it was dangerous territory.

Over the years many aspects of the corporate culture of Google have changed. Perhaps inevitably the Google team of Schmidt, Page and Brin started behaving less like the cool, albeit rich, nerds who were going to make the world a better place and more like big business moguls.

Not far from Google's Mountain View headquarters is Moffett Federal Airfield. Run by the National Aeronautics and Space Administration (NASA), only aircraft being used for NASA's scientific endeavours can be hangared there. 'NASA has specific criteria to determine who can partner with us and whether they may use their aircraft at Moffett,' according to an internal NASA memo published on SpaceRef, a technology website. 'All requests . . . every request must demonstrate a relationship to NASA missions.'[34]

Page, Brin and Schmidt presented a proposal to NASA which seemed like a natural fit. Google would offer one of its aircraft for aerial reconnaissance work for the good of the community, measuring the effects of global warming and pollution. The information would be shared with NASA. But some of the 'work' that was subsequently carried out by Google appeared to have less to do with scientific research benefiting the community and more to do with the luxury lives of the rich and famous. Their private jets would have been making more pollution than they'd been measuring.[35]

The flights tracked by Consumer Watchdog, a California-based public advocacy group, show that on 13 May 2010 one of the Google team's Gulfstreams departed Moffett at 11.30 pm headed for the Nice Côte d'Azur Airport in southern France. That week, Google held an event for advertisers at the nearby Cannes Film Festival. On the night of 18 May CEO Eric Schmidt attended a party for Mick Jagger in Cannes. On 26 June one of Google's Gulfstream planes flew from Mountain View to Nice–Côte d'Azur for a second time.

On 9 July 2010 the company's Boeing 762 took off for Tahiti, where a near-total solar eclipse was visible on 11 July. Among the 'sun worshipers', according to Consumer Watchdog, were Page and Brin. Both the 762 and a Gulfstream returned to Tahiti on 15 July, according to flight records, presumably to pick up large numbers of Googlers and their companions.

Similar trips – with no apparent scientific research component – to the Caribbean were noted, including to Richard Branson's privately owned Necker Island. Late in 2014 Google entered into a more transparent arrangement with NASA and took out a lease on Moffett Airfield.

There's no doubt Google has produced incredible consumer products and systems which have revolutionised communications. It's made the founders of the company and its executives exceptionally wealthy. But there's other money washing through the company that sits uneasily with an organisation that continues to pride itself on safeguarding the public's privacy. Google has benefited substantially from the billions of dollars pouring into military intelligence. It's estimated that during the Cold War, spending on intelligence peaked at US$71 billion [in 2013 dollars], surging to US$75 billion in 2013. Since the attacks on the World Trade Center and the Pentagon in September 2001 the United States has spent an estimated US$500 billion on intelligence, according to a secret report handed to *The Washington Post* by Edward Snowden.[36]

If Google had really wanted to prove it wasn't too close to the intelligence community it could have acted differently after the FBI demanded the company hand over details of emails and IP addresses used by three WikiLeaks staffers, editors Sarah Harrison and Joseph Farrell and spokesperson Kristinn Hrafnsson. Google complied with the FBI warrant in March 2012, which included a gagging order preventing them from alerting WikiLeaks about what was happening for three years. A little more than two years later however the court suddenly lifted the suppression order. Google was now legally free to inform WikiLeaks about the FBI search of their data. But that's not what happened. Google waited a full seven months, until the following December 2014, before telling Harrison, Farrell and Hrafnsson that the FBI had seized their electronic records. WikiLeaks suspected that Google waited until Christmas to release the information in the hope that any media reports would be buried among the light-hearted fare that festoons the news in the season of goodwill. It was not a good look for an organisation that repeatedly pledged itself to be open with its customers and to protect their privacy.

—

More than 50 years ago, in his farewell address as he stepped down from office, President Dwight D. Eisenhower issued a warning to the people of the United States. A five-star general in the Second World War, Eisenhower coined a chilling phrase denoting the perils of a powerful military linked to big business – and a compliant political class: 'In the councils of government, we must guard against the acquisition of unwarranted influence, whether sought or unsought, by the military industrial complex. The potential for the disastrous rise of misplaced power exists and will persist. We must never let the

weight of this combination endanger our liberties or democratic processes. We should take nothing for granted. Only
an alert and knowledgeable citizenry can compel the proper
meshing of the huge industrial and military machinery of
defense with our peaceful methods and goals, so that security
and liberty may prosper together.'[37]

Implicitly as a counterweight to the military–industrial
complex that Eisenhower warned against more than five
decades ago was a robust media. The United States has
managed to produce the kind of journalism – with all its
faults – which questioned the supremacy of the White House,
even to the extent of bringing down a president.

After failing to interest any politicians in what he had
discovered about the lies being told to the American people,
in 1971 Daniel Ellsberg went to *The New York Times* with
the Pentagon Papers. Now the ground is far more uncer-
tain. The fact that Edward Snowden handed the biggest leak
in US history to a freelance journalist because, after its delay in
publishing the George W. Bush NSA domestic eavesdropping
story, he did not trust *The New York Times* to challenge the
government, is a damning indictment.

At the very time the media was most needed as a counter-
balance to the military–industrial complex, it was ill-equipped
to deal with the threat posed. Not only is the media's own
survival under threat, but in the vacuum created by the
absence of an independent free press, so too is the foundation
of democracy.

CHAPTER 5
Race to the Bottom

The boardroom of John Fairfax Holdings, in a swanky part of Sydney down by the harbour, was not normally the place for histrionic exhortations. Admittedly the newspaper publishing company, in existence in various forms for more than 160 years, had been through its dramas – like the time a junior member of the founder's family tried to buy the place and it ended up being owned by a criminal – but those days were long past. Now in 2004, like most other newspaper publishers around the world, Fairfax was dealing with a new threat to its existence: the rise of the internet and, consequently, haemorrhaging circulation and a rapidly downward spiral in profitability.[1]

To confront the crisis it had commissioned a report by one of Australia's most respected journalists and publishers, Eric Beecher, hoping he could show the company the way forward. Beecher's credentials were impeccable. He'd started as a reporter on *The Age* before heading around the world to work on *The Sunday Times* and *The Observer* in London and *The Washington Post*. In 1984, at age 33, he became the youngest ever editor of *The Sydney Morning Herald*. And later editor-in-chief of Rupert Murdoch's Herald and Weekly Times newspaper group. Not only did he understand the intimate workings of Fairfax and the Murdoch opposition, Beecher also brought with him an unusual mixture of journalistic excellence and business nous: he had set up the hugely successful

Text Media Group, which profitably produced newspapers, magazines and books. Fairfax had been so impressed by the company they'd recently bought it for nearly AU$66 million.

The focus of Beecher's report about Fairfax's business model and future was the internet. He was in the process of telling the directors how to deal with it in order to turn their company around. He painted a grim picture of the future, a possible 'catastrophe scenario'[2] in which the company's main form of revenue, classified advertisements, might migrate to the internet – where all those web-based sites with low overheads and cut-price advertising rates were simply waiting to pounce.

Beecher understood the threat extremely well. With some of the money Fairfax had just paid him, he bought precisely such a company: Crikey, an online niche magazine for business and politics. This was an insider's view he was sharing with his old employers. His 'key argument' was that if the board rated the risk of classified advertisements deserting its newspapers at any more than 10 per cent, it should take decisive action as an insurance policy. He put it to the directors that the financial success of Fairfax 'directly subsidises the health and effectiveness of the most important quality journalism in this country'.[3] Beecher advised the board to act quickly because 'there is now a realistic possibility of the "catastrophe scenario" occurring over the next two to four years'.[4]

Beecher may have been happy with what he had to say but not everyone in the room was. After Beecher had finished speaking, one of the directors, Roger Corbett, walked to the head of the board table. Corbett, who had made his name and money as CEO of the Woolworths supermarket chain – he had grossed up to AU$100 million in payment shares and options – clearly did not like what he had just been told. As Beecher remembers, Corbett 'picked up a copy of one of Fairfax's hefty Saturday broadsheets, bulging with classified ads, from a nearby pile. He didn't want anyone coming into that boardroom again saying that people will buy houses or cars or look for jobs without "this", he told his fellow directors. He then dropped the paper onto the table with a thud.'[5]

It turned out to be a missed opportunity. Fairfax might not have taken Beecher's advice but he certainly took it himself. The following year, Beecher went on to set up three further successful online media ventures: SmartCompany.com.au, EurekaReport.com.au and BusinessSpectator.com.

At the helm of Woolworths for 16 years, Roger Corbett had steered the supermarket chain to a pre-eminent position in the Australian retail sector – the company posted soaring profits and killed off the opposition. But while Woolworths was a huge company with a formidable international reputation, its approach to selling beans and cake mixes was not necessarily right for running a publishing behemoth like Fairfax, with its string of newspapers, prominent among them *The Sydney Morning Herald* and the Melbourne *Age*.

Beecher's only comment was that Corbett 'retired as a grocer and became a newspaper director'.[6]

Five years after Beecher raised the alarm, the Fairfax board gave the job of leading the company to the person who most doubted his warnings. On the day in 2009 the directors appointed Roger Corbett chairman of the board, Corbett insisted that the Fairfax board had fixed Fairfax's problems. 'Fairfax, like most companies, has challenges ahead,' he said, 'but the decisions taken in the last few years by management and the board have, I believe, put Fairfax in a position which is envied by media companies around the world.'[7]

It was not an especially high bar. Most of the other media organisations in the world were in a shocking state and with Corbett at the helm of Fairfax, the Australian company would follow them down. Under his chairmanship Fairfax lost almost two-thirds of its value, and by the 2012 annual report his main focus was laying off 1900 staff – slashing costs to achieve what he hoped would be an annual saving of AU$235 million by June 2015.

It didn't stop the rot. All the major Fairfax newspapers – *The Sydney Morning Herald*, *The Age* and *The Australian Financial Review* – continued to lose money. Without profitability there would be less funding for serious investigative journalism – an expensive business demanding significant resources of time, labour and money, and what was worse, it didn't always produce a result.

The kind of journalism that speaks truth to power and is an essential to keep a vibrant democracy functioning has become an unintended victim of Fairfax's business woes. It's a loss that reverberates long and hard in Australia. The fact that in 2012 *The Sydney Morning Herald* won the nation's most prestigious journalism award, a Walkley, for its exposé of corruption in New South Wales, indicates just how deep the well of substantial journalism had been at Fairfax. Given the cuts the well will soon run dry.

In an attempt to compete with the internet, the company had first allowed free and unfettered access to its newspaper sites, then it introduced a partial paywall. Though customers were paying to read the papers, the classified advertisers were charged much lower rates than for the print editions. Consequently the classifieds, once described by Rupert Murdoch as 'rivers of gold', raised nowhere near the same amount of money online. Ten years ago the newspaper could bring in AU$40,000 for each classified page. Fairfax had been selling hundreds of those pages on Saturdays alone. Now they were down to a handful. The classified ads were drying up faster than the washing on a Sydney summer's day.

It would be easy to blame the problems facing Fairfax on a succession of bad board decisions, but they were not alone in failing to understand the immensity of the threat from the internet companies that had captured such a large slice of the classified advertising market. Murdoch papers were no better. News Limited, owner of *The Australian*, the Melbourne *Herald-Sun*, the Sydney *Daily Telegraph*, Adelaide *Advertiser* and Brisbane *Courier-Mail* et al. – in all, 70 per cent of the nation's daily print output – also suffered a similar form of denial that the industry was in trouble.

Like a double act, one year after the other both Fairfax and News Limited pronounced that everything was fine with their companies and the future was rosy. First, in 2011 Greg Hywood, appointed as Fairfax CEO by Corbett, told attendees of the A.N. Smith journalism lecture at Melbourne University, 'The future of journalism has never looked stronger.' He said this was because of the internet, not despite it. 'Our readers want our journalism in a variety of formats. Tracking and fussing about print circulation is an outdated and nearing irrelevant form of measurement in the world media companies now inhabit.'

One year on, at the same gathering – named after one of the founders of the Australian Journalists Association – News Limited's CEO, Kim Williams, assured the gathering that there was much to be positive about: 'Robust continuing and truly great journalism; sustainable business models for print and shiny new business models in digital media; and a heightened and voracious appetite from consumers for diverse news and information across their spectrum of passions and interests.'

One reading of their statements could suggest that Hywood and Williams were both spruiking nonsense – Hywood with his schtick that 'journalism has never looked stronger' and Williams' of 'truly great journalism'. In a more cautious world they could be accused of misleading their investors and become the subject of an investigation by corporate regulators. Not only were the 'rivers of gold' that funded good journalism drying up at Fairfax's *Sydney Morning Herald*, with nowhere near enough money being made from online subscriptions to replace it, revenue streams were near non-existent at *The Australian*, the country's other 'quality' newspaper.

News Corp likes to hide its problems, wrapping them up in global bundles, seldom giving a country-by-country breakdown

of any business metrics. But a leaked copy of a company financial statement revealed that Rupert Murdoch's operations in
Australia are swimming in a sea of red ink, and the national
daily is the worst performer by far: in 2012–13 revenues dropped
20 per cent – from AU$135 million to AU$108 million – while
operating income fell 42 per cent, creating a loss that ballooned
from AU$19 million the previous year to AU$27 million.[8]

The story of a decline of this magnitude in such an
important institution as the fourth estate should have been
the subject of major newspaper investigations. But there
were none, the result of either bad editorial judgement, a
lack of courage or a mixture of the two. There was also the
paradox that with falling revenues, investigative journalism
was among the first areas to have its funding cut. Whatever
the reason there were plenty of signals that the old model
of newspaper publishing was entering a new world. And it
hadn't happened overnight.

—

More than 30 years ago in San Francisco two newspapers uncovered the first inkling of what the internet might deliver to the
future of journalism. The morning *San Francisco Examiner* and
the afternoon *San Francisco Chronicle* jointly carried out an elaborate experiment. At that time it was estimated that 2000 people
had personal computers in the Bay Area, covering much of what
is now Silicon Valley, and the newspapers placed advertisements
offering a chance for people to hook up with a new system – and
read the day's news online. Five hundred took up the offer.

From the 17th floor of his North Beach apartment, not far
from where the internet had been invented, Richard Halloran
became one of the guinea pigs. Using what now looks like
a museum piece, Halloran carefully dialled a telephone
number in Columbus, Ohio. It connected him to a mainframe
computer. Not far away from where Halloran lived, staff at
the *San Francisco Examiner*'s offices were busily inserting all

that day's news into the same Ohio computer, giving Halloran direct access via his dial-up connection. With his computer connected to his television Halloran was now able to trawl the news and read most of it on the screen.

Though the lines of text were not the news pages we read today online they certainly impressed Halloran. 'Anything we are interested in we can go back in again and copy it on to paper and save it,' he said.

The *Examiner* said the program, which involved eight other newspapers, was an experiment. They were trying to work out 'what it means to us' as editors and reporters and 'what it means to the home user'. In what must be one of the most wrongheaded statements in the history of journalism, the newspaper said it didn't see computer access to its news pages as a way to make money.[9]

Other newspapers too were experimenting with computerised systems. *The Australian* used a cable to transmit its content between Melbourne and Sydney in the early 1980s. It saved transmitting stories individually over the telex system and was far more efficient. With newspaper circulations still depressed from the introduction of television a quarter of a century earlier, they were desperate to find new efficiencies.

The possibility of readership decline was first taken seriously in the late 1960s when cheap computer typesetting and offset printing led to the 'explosive growth of specialised print products that could target desired audiences for advertisers'.[10]

Publishers could do little about the competition for readers from the proliferation of magazines and booklets – much of it directly mailed to readers' homes. Instead they embraced the new technology themselves as a way to save money. In Australia both Fairfax and News Limited began shifting away from using typewriters, with their carbon paper and the reams of cheap memo-sized newsprint paper on which reporters wrote their stories. In this pre-digital newsroom the 'copy' would then be handed to copy girls or boys, who took the stories to the subeditor. From there, checked for grammar and fact, they were passed on to be retyped by printing staff downstairs. Next the typed word was turned into metal letters, carefully assembled in columns to form the newspaper page.

Computers had the ability to change all that, allowing reporters to send their stories directly to a computerised printing system. This process dramatically cut down the number of printers needed and, more importantly, cut costs. Both News Limited and Fairfax embraced the new technology with gusto, but by far the biggest champion of this new form of newspaper business model was Rupert Murdoch. He had plans which went far beyond Australia's borders – and would change the way newspapers were produced forever.

But first he had to tackle the printing unions. The printers put up a spirited fight to preserve their jobs, but in the end an industrial court decision went against them.

As both News Limited and Fairfax began installing computer terminals in their Australian offices, frequent crashes meant stories were lost and whole editions could be late going to press. But financially it was a boon for the media proprietors. They were now employing considerably fewer printers to produce the same results.

Emboldened by this victory, in 1986 Rupert Murdoch set about moving his entire stable of British newspapers – *The Sun*, the then recently acquired London *Times*, and the *News of the World* – from Fleet Street, the centuries-old capital of British journalism, to a new site at Wapping in London's docklands. The rather grim purpose-built newspaper offices and printing works were specially designed to give Murdoch the freedom to run his newspapers the way he did in Australia – with fewer printers. Journalists would write their copy on computers linked directly to the printing system, saving his company vast amounts of money – and making hundreds of printers redundant.

There had been resistance in Australia to the changes, but nothing like the opposition Murdoch faced in London. For 13 months newspaper delivery trucks entering and leaving what became known as 'Fortress Wapping' ran the gauntlet of trade union pickets. As the Labour Party called for a boycott of Murdoch's newspapers, the circulation of *The Sun* began to slide. But Murdoch held firm – and the picket collapsed.[11]

Murdoch had tamed the power of the print unions, with their often bloated staffing levels and restrictive practices, but just as significantly he had brought the rest of Fleet Street with him. The publishers who had stood on the sidelines and watched the battle now also embraced the new working arrangements. Many of those who to this day detest Murdoch and his maverick opportunism concede one thing: his prevailing helped put the entire UK press on a more sound financial footing.

What was missed in all the brawling over Wapping was that the very technology which took work away from the many and put it in the hands of the few, also cut the other way. The computerised systems which reduced costs – and helped make newspapers profitable – was part of a bigger system which would in the end challenge the dictate of the press barons. It would take away the Power of One – and give it to the many.

Murdoch himself was too enamoured by the benefits of computerisation to want to deal with its consequences. For him a healthier bottom line was critical: funding his ever-spiralling debts as he borrowed heavily to build his international empire was all that mattered.

Computerisation had a close family relative. It was called the internet.

—

As the internet grew in popularity many newspapers treated it like an extension of the marketing department, putting stories online in the hope that readers would then go out and buy the print edition. When even Murdoch began granting free access to the very product he had fought so hard to create, industry figures naturally followed his lead.

In the heart of New York City, one newspaper stood against the rising tide of give-away news. It was hardly surprising that this paper, which dedicated itself to reporting business in one of the toughest cities in the world, baulked at not charging for its products. For more than a century *The Wall Street Journal*, founded in a basement round the corner from the New York Stock Exchange, has made its daily duty understanding the market and sharing that knowledge, at a price. In 1995 *The Wall Street Journal* became the first daily newspaper in the United States – out of nearly 15,000 others – to erect a full paywall, forcing its customers to take out a subscription to view the news online.

It was a significant step: the decision wasn't purely commercial, it was also philosophical – everything had a monetary value, including its journalism. It would be an argument that would play out throughout the following decades: if the net was free for everybody to use, should everything on it be free as well?

Remarkably *The Wall Street Journal* was able to run a twin-track policy: it would look to the future and charge for internet access to its newspaper, while keeping a clear view of what sustained the newspaper at that time. In its annual report to shareholders in 1997 it boasted the newspaper had just completed 'one of the most successful years in its history with news coverage sharper than ever' and 'revenue at a historic high'.[12] The *Journal* was proudly growing circulation, readership and advertising in both its print and electronic editions. It dismissed the media analysts who heralded a digital age that consigned what it called 'dead tree editions' to history's dustbin.[13]

If the *Journal*'s heart was in the past, it was ready and equipped to embrace the electronic future.

Housed today in a glittering glass tower on the Avenue of the Americas – the *Wall Street Journal* propelled itself into the internet age with enormous enthusiasm, launching itself as 'your all-day-long source of business news', asking its readers to start the day with the print edition to 'understand what the news means' then to go online throughout the day for news updates – 'breaking news sent to your mobile'.[14]

In a surprise experiment, for one day in the 1996 financial year the *Journal* overturned its maxim never to give away its information – handing out for free half a million newspapers and throwing open its online portals for no charge. Existing print subscribers who wanted to try out the benefits of searching and reading online could get a whole month's trial for free to 'see the benefits of print and online together'.[15]

By February 2007 the *Journal* was boasting that it had what appears quaint in today's language: 800,000 subscriptions, 'more than any other news site on the entire Web'.[16]

It had drawn attention to a challenge of its own making: whether its paywall policy really could produce the kind of business model which would create a profitable marriage between online and print.

While newspapers around the world tracked how the *Journal* handled the tricky balance between selling a print edition and persuading people to pay for website content, an old, nearby rival paid closer attention than most. For nearly a century, the neo-gothic *New York Times* building on 43rd Street in the centre of Manhattan was viewed as the heart of American journalism. It was here that the Pentagon Papers were published in 1971, and the newspaper's coverage of Watergate further bolstered its reputation for gutsy journalism. By 2004 *The New York Times* had won more than a hundred Pulitzer Prizes, the most prestigious award in US journalism. But despite the building's grand history, three years later the paper swapped the narrow corridors and the dingy office space for a 52-storey steel and glass tower on 8th Avenue, premises far more befitting a newspaper of the modern age.

Like *The Wall Street Journal*, *The New York Times* had run up an impressive level of readers on the web. In January of

2004 it had hit 1.4 million, 300,000 more than its print circulation. But unlike the *Journal*, the *Times* didn't charge for its news coverage. As they walked the dingy corridors of their old headquarters, executives at *The New York Times* ruminated on what might be the effect if they changed their policy. After all, the paper already charged for its crossword puzzle, news alerts and archives online; why not start charging for other portions of its content? One thing they decided for sure: *The New York Times* would not follow the *Journal* model, which barred everyone from viewing anything on its website unless they were prepared to pay.

Newspaper analyst Colby Atwood articulated the situation like this: 'A big part of the motivation for newspapers to charge for their online content is not the revenue it will generate, but the revenue it will save, by slowing the erosion of their print subscriptions.' He told *The New York Times*, 'We're in the midst of a long and painful transition.'[17]

It was a masterful understatement.

—

Three and a half thousand kilometres west of New York, nestled at the foothills of the snow-capped Rocky Mountains, the tiny *Spokesman-Review* in Spokane, Washington state, had just celebrated its 110th birthday. It was typical of the provincial dailies in the USA. Every day 100,000 copies of the paper rolled out of its three loading docks on North Monroe Street and were sent out into the sprawling hinterland, townships scattered across the surrounding plains. In 2005 *The Spokesman-Review* had just decided to take a major step into the unknown, to charge for its website. About 20,000 of those who read the print edition also received the paper online for no additional fee; just 545 people opted to pay for the web-only edition.

Ken Sands, the online publisher, who until a month earlier had been the managing editor of the print edition, said the

paper decided to charge for the web in an effort to save
the print edition. What the Spokane *Spokesman* had discovered was being experienced everywhere: if you can read a
newspaper free online, why pay for the print edition? As the
Spokesman started tinkering with the business model, they
unearthed another fact of online life: as soon as the paper
started charging for the web, new daily traffic, which had been
growing by more than 40 per cent a year, stopped cold. Sands
added that the print circulation had been steadily declining
somewhat anyway and so he could not blame the web for that.

'Print is going the way it's going, which is down, which is
unfortunate because it's the revenue engine that keeps this
whole thing going,' said Sands.[18] As the former editor of the
print edition, he'd seen the business from the other side too:
'The online business model won't ever be able to support the
whole news infrastructure.'[19]

The Newspaper Association of America was closely
monitoring the trend. Spending on print advertising in the
first three months of 2006 increased only 0.3 per cent, to
US$10.5 billion, over the corresponding period of the previous
year, not even keeping pace with inflation. At the same time,
spending for online advertising surged 35 per cent.

'I think the handwriting is kind of on the wall that there
is a large migration to the Web,' said industry analyst Colby
Atwood. 'This is a transition that's taking place over several
years here. It's not happening overnight, but it's definitely
happening.'[20]

Those who tenaciously believed the future of newspapers
would forever remain in print pointed to the small numbers
involved. And it was true; most of the money was still going
into print advertising. In the first quarter of 2006 online
advertising for the United States produced US$613 million.
Although it was up from US$454 million in the previous
year – the eighth consecutive quarter of growth for online
ads – the increase showed that while newspapers might be

learning how to harness the potential of online advertising they were not making anywhere near enough money to compensate for the fall in income from print classifieds.

The price of classified ads started falling in tandem with the drop in print sales. In one six-month period, daily circulation of American newspapers had dropped 2.5 per cent, to 45.5 million.[21]

In other words in the space of half a year, more than one million Americans had suddenly decided to stop buying the print edition of their regular newspapers. Even the relatively good news that total internet advertising revenue reached a record US$3.9 billion was tainted by the fact that the vast bulk of it had ended up on sites like Craigslist that provided a free and cut-price advertising service to its customers and reached millions of readers. Newspapers couldn't compete.

They were fast understanding that the 'rivers of gold' had lost their lustre and were making frenzied attempts to stem the tide. The *Los Angeles Times*, which had opened a paywall for its online site the previous year, shut it in 2005 just as *The New York Times* opened its version only to abandon it in 2007, passing the baton to the UK's *Financial Times*. There were no clear winners in the torturous game of paywall tag. With print advertising income and newspaper circulations continuing to drop in unison, no one knew where to run.

By 2010, with the *Financial Times* still operating a paywall while allowing readers access to a limited number of stories for free, other news publications were emboldened to try again. 'There is a danger your brand can "go dark" if you are too restrictive',[22] according to John Ridding, CEO of the *Financial Times*, one of the few newspapers in the world that still makes a profit. But the *Financial Times* and *The Wall Street Journal* were both aimed at a special niche business market: people who were prepared to pay for information which might help them make money. The other mass circulation newspapers were different. They had a more fickle readership that could find its general news elsewhere, for free on the internet.

Newspapers were in a state of full-blown panic. It's difficult to say who made the first break from the pack to try once again to find a workable formula but among the leaders were long-time French rivals *Le Figaro* – a conservative newspaper established in 1826 – and *Le Monde*, founded with the support of General Charles de Gaulle in 1944 after the liberation of Paris.

As Parisians enjoyed an unusually warm spring in 2010, the country's two favourite quality newspapers finally took the plunge, erecting what are known as 'semi-paywalls' – both still allowed some of their news pages to be seen for free, but charged a hefty fee for full access.

It had been a difficult choice and a long time in the making. As their print sales dropped and more people accessed their online web pages, like many others around the world, *Le Figaro* and *Le Monde* faced difficult choices. They could give open access to everyone for free, thus increasing the number of hits so they could sell more online advertising at a higher rate, while keeping 'premium content' for those prepared to pay for full online access. Then there was another alternative: lock everyone out, unless they were prepared to pay for everything. That was *The Wall Street Journal* option, and as a niche business paper it seemed to be having some success, but the concept had never been tried by a mass circulation newspaper producing general news until Rupert Murdoch decided otherwise.

In July 2010 Murdoch slapped a padlock on the London *Times*. There would be no more free access. The price of reading anything in *The Thunderer*, as it was called in its heyday, was a full subscription. Murdoch was leading again, and the rest of the ex-Fleet Street papers, who had followed him to Wapping, were once more watching on in amazement. It's rare that newspapers make headlines themselves but within days of the London *Times* shutting the gate it did just that. *The Times* lost 90 per cent of the readers who read it online when it was free because they wouldn't pay to read it online behind a paywall. It was a cruel parody on an old joke about *The Times*: years ago, it ran a billboard advertising campaign worded, 'Top People Take The Times'. A wag had scrawled underneath, 'The others pay for it!' Now it seemed that wasn't true either, at least for the online version.

Not that you would know that if you listened to the head of News Corporation's Digital Media Group. Speaking at a business conference at New York's Time Warner Center in December 2010, Jonathan Miller said that since the introduction of the paywall the paper's 'total economics have improved'.[23] The venerable *Forbes* magazine, best known for annually publishing the list of the 400 richest people in America, asked could Miller possibly have meant that the paper is already making more money, in the form of subscription sales and higher ad rates, than it lost from all those hits from visits when the site was free?

Not quite, said Miller. *The Times*, he insisted, was 'on an immediate path' to replacing the lost revenues, and would get there in a matter of months, not years. 'It's predictive,' he said.[24]

Three years later the joke was again on *The Times*. Not enough people were prepared to pay to read it online, even with trial subscriptions at giveaway prices. In what must be a novel first, even for the mavericks in News Corp, the chief executive of News International, Mike Darcey, began attacking a whole class of the people that *The Times* once so assiduously courted. Of the casual online reader who had failed to take up *The Times*' subscription offers he asked, 'What have we really lost? A long tail of passing trade, many from overseas, many popping in for only one article, referred by Google or a social media link, not even aware they are on a *Times* . . . website?'[25] The fact that the advertisements on *The Times* Online were no longer being read by this 'passing trade' seemed not to matter to Darcey.

He dismissed the former free visitors as not generating 'any meaningful revenue' and argued that pursuing them as customers 'undermines the piece of the business that does make money' – the printed edition. Taking a stand against what most other newspaper publishers in the world were doing – allowing at least some of their content to be seen free – he argued that giving digital content away undermined the print business, which was still by far and away the engine room of revenues and profits.[26]

By the end of 2014, print-at-any-cost was a difficult argument for News Corp to sustain. Like every other national daily, from the red tops to the qualities, *The Times* had witnessed a considerable fall in its circulation, down from 633,000 in January 2008 to a paltry 396,000. Yet News was desperate to prove the critics wrong. It wasn't merely ego that was at stake; if the circulation numbers fell too far, advertisers would immediately start negotiating with News to cut its ad prices.

The official UK Audit Bureau of Circulations figures covering the six years between January 2008 and January 2014 reveal exactly how desperate News Corp had been to claim success for its *Times* paywall. At first glance it looks as though the newspaper had increased its sales between January 2014 and January 2015. But *The Times* figures include what are known as 'bulk sales' – 22,000 newspapers either given away free to every bored airline passenger, poked under every hotel bedroom door or sold at giveaway prices. Once *The Times* circulation is measured the same way as its rivals – *The Daily Telegraph* and *The Guardian*, which don't include bulk sales – the circulation is revealed as falling dramatically, like all the other UK national dailies.

The numbers make chilling reading, showing an industry in dramatic decline from 2008 to 2014:

The Sun, down from 3.2m (million) early in 2008 to 2.2m

The *Daily Mail*, down from 2.3m to 1.7m

The *Daily Mirror*, down from 1.5m to just below 1m

The Daily Telegraph, down from 890,000 to 544,000

The Times, down from 633,000 to 384,000

The Independent, down from 250,000 to 66,000 – a debilitating drop of 73%

The *Financial Times*, down from 450,000 to 217,000

The *Guardian*, down from 378,000 to 234,000.[27]

Over the same six-year period, the daily newspapers in Australia suffered a similar fate:

The *Australian*, down from 136,000 to 104,774

The *Australian Financial Review*, down from 89,329 to 57,451

The *Daily Telegraph*, down from 385,000 to 273,241

The *Sydney Morning Herald*, down from 212,500 to 113,634

The *Age*, down from 208,000 to 106,843.[28]

In Australia, all newspapers added discount sales to lift their numbers, but, as in the UK, News was the gold-star performer in ramping up its circulation figures, giving away its papers to hotels, airlines and schools and handing them out at major events such as rugby matches. *The Daily Telegraph* used this ruse to increase 'sales' by more than 20,000 copies and *The Australian* by nearly 9000 whereas *The Sydney Morning Herald* only added 6300. *The Australian Financial Review* – which had earlier decided to take a novel approach, solely reporting the number of copies people paid for – now joined the throng, adding 9202 copies.[29]

The only good news for any newspapers anywhere in the world was that digital subscriptions were increasing. But while many more readers were now paying for their news, the income they produced for newspapers was tiny compared to the overheads. Those costs were still being almost entirely met by the classified ads carried in the print editions. And as print sales dropped, advertisers began looking elsewhere to place their advertising. Inevitably they also started demanding lower rates. This combination of falling readership and declining classified ad revenue created an unsustainable level of debt. As newspapers cut staff to contain costs and pay down the debt, the remaining staff were expected to pick up the workload to fill the paper. Perhaps not surprisingly readers noticed the quality slipping.

—

It became common practice for newspapers which operated a partial paywall to try to lure more readers in with juicy stories. But there was a downside. The demands of continually updating information to attract new viewers online, so they would stop at a 'new' story and click through, started to dominate the journalistic culture. At *The Washington Post*, stories were being tailored with keywords so that they would hit the demographic target audiences that the newspapers were guaranteeing advertisers they would reach.

It was a strategy being copied around the world. Search engines like Google and social network companies like Facebook – which directed surfers to the newspaper websites – cashed in on the opportunity. If newspapers needed traffic to boost their advertising revenue, they would provide it. In the end they were directing so many readers to the newspapers it was now Google and Facebook that were determining the kind of stories that were being published. It was the web equivalent of the tail wagging the dog.

The vast amount of personal information that Google gathered when people entered newspaper websites using their search engine – if not a river of gold – was able to be transformed by Google into a solid stream of silver. Google was producing extraordinary amounts of personal information on people, from their likes and dislikes, the films they watched and their politics, to their sexual orientation. It wasn't only using that information to send targeted advertising to anyone who used their systems, it was also making money out of selling the information to others.

A novel category of business was born: dataminers, or aggregators – companies that trawled the internet gathering all the information they could from search engines – would build comprehensive profiles of newspaper readers. They on-sold those profiles to advertising placement agencies, who consequently knew where best to place their ads. For the newspapers this was another attack on their revenue stream, for the aggregators charged the advertisers a fraction of what newspapers used to ask for this valuable information.

While News Corp, which had by now bought *The Wall Street Journal*, had become a keen advocate of full-scale paywalls to protect content, it was incensed to discover it could not keep secret from search engines like Google valuable personal information about those who entered their site. What annoyed News Corp was that aggregators were selling access to the demographic details of 75 per cent of *The Wall Street Journal*'s customers at 25 per cent of the News Corp asking price. News Corp chief Robert Thomson wrote a blistering missive to the European Commission, which was investigating Google's power in Europe. He accused Google of 'undermining the business model of the content creator'.[30] Thomson argued that although the process was at a relatively early stage, it needed 'constant monitoring to ensure that abuses were halted and that there is a fair return for newspapers, publishers and other investors in original content'.[31] The Google goliath with its cute motto 'Don't Be Evil' was up against the Murdoch empire, whose *New York Post* had been famously described in the *Columbia Journalism Review* as 'a force for evil'.[32]

The European Commission gave Thomson a good reception, though wickedness wasn't the issue. It was more concerned about Google recycling information produced in Europe and then on-selling it for a profit. It was an unlikely alliance: the anti-European Murdoch and the anti-Murdoch Europeans. Google was the loser.

Not long before taking over his job in 2014, Gunther Oettinger, the EU's new Commissioner for Digital Affairs, stated his intention to reform European copyright law in 2015. Oettinger announced few details of his plans but in an interview with the German daily newspaper *Handelsblatt*, he made it clear that he wanted to tackle the profits Google made from listing European companies in search results. 'If Google takes intellectual property from the EU and works with that, then the EU can protect that property and demand Google pay for that,' he said.[33]

Copyright laws nicknamed 'Google taxes' – though any fee Google is forced to pay will be paid to content publishers, not governments – have been passed in several European countries. Spain passed a law that charges search engines that include snippets from, and links to, news websites. In 2013, France's government settled news publishers' demands for copyright reform by striking a deal with Google: for a flat rate of €60 million the company was allowed to continue listing news articles in search results.

There's no doubt these arguments resonated well with News Corp. Thomson pointed to Google routinely displaying YouTube results at the top of its search pages, even if YouTube was not the original source of that content. The reason for that 'bias', according to Thomson, was that YouTube – owned by Google – 'gets a cut of the revenue',[34] taking income away from the person who created and posted the video.

On purely economic grounds there was a reasonable argument for controlling the power of Google. But the basis for the objections to its practices became more treacherous when Thomson began arguing morality. He warned the European Commission that Google's 'Undermining the basic business model of professional content creators will lead to a less informed, more vexatious level of dialogue in our society.'[35]

The outburst left News Corp wide open. Google replied, 'People probably have enough evidence to judge that one for themselves :)',[36] accompanying the post with an image of the infamous 1990 'Up Yours Delors' *Sun* headline, an attack on the former European Commission President Jacques Delors.

Desperate for readership, no matter what the demographic, newspapers industry wide jumped on the bandwagon and began pumping out lightweight stories – known in the industry as 'click-bait' – to encourage online readership. No one was immune, not even the newspapers which had been the first to identify the web as a means of connecting with a new kind of readership. In San Francisco both the *Examiner* and the *Chronicle*, which had once championed social causes and published extraordinary exposés, rapidly moved downmarket. It had been nine years since the *San Francisco Chronicle* had won a Pulitzer Prize for reaching the pinnacle of US journalism. Since then both the *Chronicle* and the *Examiner* had been focused on another kind of reward, staying alive. Now with a partial paywall, their online front-page stories had a single aim: to draw in the maximum number of readers. 'Pack of Pit Bulls Mauls Seniors', 'SF [San Francisco] Woman Shot by Lover Dies' and 'Man Injured in Shooting at Fisherman's Wharf', the headlines howled.

Sadly the story that revealed so much about what was happening to journalism in the United States, the death of campaigning newspaper *The San Francisco Bay Guardian*, received much smaller treatment. In a bitter twist, the fate of the 48-year-old paper had partly been sealed by a lawsuit brought by Craigslist, the company that had wounded so many newspapers with its free and cut-price online advertising.

For newspapers in the digital era it seemed that nothing was working in their favour. The full paywall wasn't delivering anything like enough subscribers for *The Times*; the semi-paywall wasn't delivering enough website hits for the rest.

One feature of new technology is the open-ended promise of improvement; there had to be other options to explore. No longer constrained by national borders, many newspapers broke out into the wider online world in order to attract more readers. Among the first was the British *Daily Mail*, its free online pages (dailymail.co.uk) flooding the world with salacious and populist stories, whetting the appetite of its historically prudish and conservative readers. It recently extended its reach into Australia to become the third player in an already hotly contested struggle between the right-wing daily *The Australian* and the leftist *Guardian Australia*.

Unlike the *Mail*, which looks like a circus show more than a newspaper, what *The Australian* and the *Guardian Australia* have in common is that neither has to worry too much about how many people read what they write. In a world dominated by journalism in freefall, Australia has become perhaps the home of a surprising experiment, reinventing a model of newspaper journalism that dates back to the post-Middle Ages.

Like the first press barons in the making, Rupert Murdoch underwrites *The Australian*, using it to attack his political enemies and at other times to blatantly promote his personal so-called free-market economic views. In a front-page lead story in October 2014 under the headline 'West Faces More Inequality', *The Australian*'s editor-at-large Paul Kelly reported Murdoch believed the poor would be better off if 'governments got out of the way' of business. In his unquestioning report there was no suggestion that it was the 'free market' which nearly destroyed the world economy in the Global Financial Crisis.

On the left, the financial roots of *The Guardian* – funded by the Scott Trust – can be traced back to the time of *noblesse oblige*, when the wealthy bankrolled 'good works'.

In the digital landscape Australia is like an ark of social history, with two newspapers – heavily influenced by a bygone age – battling it out for national influence, while *The Sydney Morning Herald* and *The Age* simply try to stay afloat. Australia has become a microcosm of what might produce the model that finally saves quality journalism from oblivion, a kind of philanthropy. Everything else appears to be in danger of total collapse.

Back in England *The Sun* and the *News of the World* had allowed themselves to get carried away fighting their rivals for readers. Increasingly tawdry stories had become the staple diet of their front pages, particularly at the *News of the World*. In their zeal to produce often sensationalist click-bait reports to boost their online presence they broke the law.

They had been seeking salvation; now they were in for a big surprise.

CHAPTER 6
Trash Sells

Although it was the cream pie thrown at the most powerful media mogul the world has ever seen that got the headlines, of more symbolic importance is that it missed its mark. Rupert Murdoch has a history of dodging attacks and this was no exception. He managed to avoid the full force of the missile, thanks to his then wife Wendi Deng exhibiting all the speed and agility she had honed in a former life as a basketball player. In a way the attack played to Murdoch's narrative as a somewhat hesitant, doddery octogenarian needing help to avoid a clumsy assault. It was July 2011 and the pie incident occurred as the media mogul was winding up his testimony before a UK House of Commons committee investigating phone-hacking – the latest surreal event in a drama of Shakespearean dimensions. Anything appeared possible, even that Murdoch had been unaware of what had happened at the most tabloid of his tabloids, the UK's *News of the World*. Everyone from showbiz luminaries such as Hugh Grant to the family of murdered schoolgirl Milly Dowler had become victims of the story-at-any-price mentality of the *News of the World*.

As Murdoch wiped spatters of shaving cream from his face and security guards marched away the attacker, he may well have relished the break in proceedings of the appropriately named Committee of Culture, Media and Sport. His son James, Chairman and Chief Executive of News International, had been facing detailed questioning about hush money paid to phone-hacking victims, in the hope of fending off further investigations. Of course the cream pie only temporarily slowed the inquiry as it zeroed in on News International's cover-ups and assiduously cultivated political connections, which went all the way to the highest office in the land, 10 Downing Street, the home of Prime Minister David Cameron.

When the Murdochs had earlier presented themselves at the first-floor committee room in Portcullis House, the name on the door – The Wilson Room – might have rung a bell with Murdoch senior, the Chairman and CEO of News Corporation. It commemorates the prominent Labour Prime Minister Harold Wilson, who spent his time in power battling a faltering economy, a hostile intelligence service, the military and, crucially, the ego of the UK's then most powerful media baron, Cecil King, Chairman of IPC, publishers of the *Daily Mirror*. Murdoch, who replaced King as Britain's most feared media boss, was easier to understand. His conservative politics coupled with an eye for commercial advantage formed the basis of how he dealt with Britain's governments. The game he played was a familiar one, whereby editors – and their newspaper owners – try to influence the direction of politics, often for commercial advantage. He was master of the classic stand-off: the struggle between parliament and the fourth estate.

This time Murdoch was on the back foot. Despite his best efforts, he had been unable to brush off the inquiry's request for him and his son James to appear. Eventually they had been compelled to attend by parliamentary order. Hauled before this parliamentary committee, one of the most powerful men in the world and his heir were having to choose their words carefully and be very formally civil.

As theatre it was not only absurd; at times it verged on the ridiculous. For two men who had made their way through the cutthroat world of newspaper publishing, they seemed to have astonishingly bad memories when questioned about events. On countless occasions Rupert Murdoch's responses were that he could not remember, could not recall or, to the best of his knowledge, did not know. His son's ability to recollect was no better.

The Murdochs found themselves the uncomfortable targets of traditional journalistic pursuit: what did they know and when did they know it? If James Murdoch was clear about one thing it was that he knew nothing about how prevalent phone-hacking was at the *News of the World*. Both Murdochs repeatedly maintained it was just one rogue reporter who'd caused all the trouble. Several months later, their story would change when fresh evidence revealed the extent of the hacking. It was rife at the *News of the World* and it had been for years.

—

In 2005 Clive Goodman, a reporter who made his living writing about the royal family for the *News of the World*, discovered an innovative way to get scoops. Instead of pains-takingly piecing together fragments of information and talking to dozens of people then cross-referencing what they said to build a credible story, he had found a short cut. The stories started rolling in. Goodman became the toast of the *News of the World*.

Like most newspapers its sales had been in rapid decline since the advent of the internet. In 1988 the paper had sold 5.4 million copies supplying readers with a rich diet of sordid sex – usually involving the royals, the rich and the famous – but the 2005 figure was hovering around 3.8 million. The audience reach of the newspaper was falling even faster. In 1994 the *News of the World* was read by 28 per cent of the popu-lation. But that number had plummeted to around 15 per cent. In a desperate attempt to boost readership the paper went even further downmarket, if that were possible, to slake the nation's thirst for celebrity tittle-tattle. There was no better titillation in the UK than a royal story. And Goodman was the reporter who had the inside dope.

In November 2005 Clive Goodman – with his trademark pin-striped suits and oiled, slicked-back hair – began an extraordinary run of exclusive stories about the royal family. It seemed that Goodman, known as 'Raffles' after the notorious London conman, could not put a foot wrong. But Goodman quickly became the victim of his own success. By early January 2006, detectives from London's Metropolitan Police Service had Clive Goodman and his collaborator – private investigator, Glenn Mulcaire, who frequently freelanced for the *News of the World* – in their sights.

A world away from the grimy Wapping docks in London's East End – where the *News of the World* shared an austere brick building with other News International titles, *The Sun* and *The Times* – the Met set an elaborate trap. They thought they had the answer to how Goodman was getting his scoops. At Clarence House, a 19th-century mansion in The Mall, central London, where Prince Charles and Diana, Princess of Wales, had lived and now the home of Prince Charles and Camilla the Duchess of Cornwall, the detectives briefed the royal staff.

In journalism there are few greater rivalries than among newspapers owned by the same company. So when *The Sun*, another News International paper, splashed a front-page story about Prince Harry visiting a strip club under the headline 'Harry Buried Face in Margo's Mega-Boobs. Stripper Jiggled . . . Prince Giggled', Goodman became desperate to get a follow-up and within a few days he did precisely that.

The secret to Goodman's success wasn't shoe leather, contacts and an astute mind. His short cut was far more effective: Mulcaire had managed to obtain the PIN numbers of several of the royal household's phones. It allowed Goodman and Mulcaire to access the mobile phone message boxes and listen to the recordings. Given such incredible access, the two did not waste time; on more than 600 separate occasions they tapped into the voicemail boxes of royal staff.

For Mulcaire it was a good little earner. The *News of the World* paid him £100,000 a year for his services. But if the idea was to carry out the snooping unnoticed, Goodman and Mulcaire failed badly. For all their trickery in acquiring the PIN numbers they left behind telltale clues as they did their hacking. When the staff at Clarence House checked their messages, they saw some of them had already been listened to, and not by them! Goodman, in his eagerness, had beaten them to it.

As Goodman and Mulcaire continued their covert surveillance of the day-to-day lives of the royal household, the police in turn began spying on them, closely monitoring their mobile phones.

On 9 April 2006 Goodman produced a follow-up article in the *News of the World* about the apparent distress of Prince Harry's girlfriend over *The Sun*'s strip-club story. Headlined 'Chelsy Tears Strip Off Harry!' the piece quoted, verbatim, a voicemail Prince Harry had received from his brother, Prince William, passing on how apparently upset his girlfriend had been when she heard about the story.

Four months later the detectives felt they had gathered enough information. Goodman and Mulcaire made their own headlines. Police arrested them.

At London's well-known criminal court, the Old Bailey, Goodman and Mulcaire pleaded guilty to illegally intercepting private communications. Goodman received a four-month sentence; Mulcaire was jailed for six months.

More than anything else it was the accuracy of the reporting, which faithfully reproduced parts of the mobile phone messages, which helped trap Goodman: one of the few cases where accuracy led to a journalist's downfall. If he had made some errors the police may well have been thrown off his trail.

Sentencing Goodman, presiding judge Mr Justice Gross told him, 'This was low conduct, reprehensible in the extreme.'[1] The case was not about press freedom, he said. 'It is about grave, inexcusable and illegal invasion of privacy.'[2]

Despite the stern reprimand, the pair may have got off lightly for it wasn't only the royals that Goodman and Mulcaire had had in their sights. In the course of their investigation, the police had found that other targets may have included David Blunkett, while he was home secretary, and the then Labour minister David Miliband. Such was the competition for scoops inside the News camp that even the phone of *The Sun* editor Rebekah Brooks, who herself would be charged with involvement in the phone-hacking saga a few years later, was targeted by the *News of the World* team. Goodman was particularly worried about being scooped by other News International papers.

Immediately the repercussions began. With the jailing of Goodman and Mulcaire, *News of the World* editor Andy Coulson fell on his sword, not that he fell far. Though he denied it, he'd overseen the systematic campaign of organised hacking by his reporters. Such is the cosy relationship in Britain between journalists and political power he then became Prime Minister Cameron's media adviser. David Cameron should have known better than to take a Murdoch reject. He would later bitterly regret that decision.

As far as News International was concerned, that was the end of the matter. The police too seemed to be losing interest. Counter-terrorism now soaked up the Met's time. Goodman and Mulcaire had simply been bad apples in an otherwise pristine journalistic environment. The Press Complaints Commission, a self-regulating body run by newspaper and magazine proprietors, launched an investigation and rapidly came to a similar conclusion. As the *News of the World* might have said, 'The Guilty Men had been Shamed and Jailed'.

Yet above and beyond the murky phone-hacking episode, there was something deeply troubling about the kind of journalism being practised by the *News of the World*. Known by journalists as the *News of the Screws*, nothing was too lowbrow for the *News of the World*.

—

When Rebekah Brooks became editor in 2900, she launched a salacious campaign against convicted paedophiles, publishing a list of their names and the locality in which they lived. Police warned the newspaper that if it genuinely wanted to help children at risk, it was counterproductive, since most paedophiles were already known to the families of the children they abused. More importantly vigilante groups were liable to use the information and take the law into their own hands. The *News of the World* ignored the warnings. Within days of the first stories appearing, vandals hit the home of a paediatrician in Wales, daubing the front door with the word 'Pedo' – an ignorant attack on a doctor who helped children. And in Manchester a mob attacked the home of a man whose neck brace made him look similar to a convicted paedophile who had been 'outed' in the *News of the World*.

In 2003 when Brooks left to take up the editorship at *The Sun*, she handed over to Andy Coulson. When Coulson resigned in 2007 in the wake of the jailing of his royal reporter, it could have been reasonable to assume that Murdoch might go looking for a competent person to edit the *News of the World*. Instead he appointed Colin Myler, whose reputation did nothing to encourage the belief that things might change at the newspaper.

Like Hugh Cudlipp (see chapter 3), who had done so much to produce clever and incisive journalism for a mass market, Myler too had worked his way up from a provincial newsroom. But it was there the similarity ended. Myler's journalism was more brutality than brilliance. In 1993 as editor of the *Sunday Mirror*, Myler had created a storm by publishing covert photos of Princess Di working out in a leotard. While editor of the same newspaper, he caused the trial of two footballers accused of assault to be aborted and was found guilty of contempt of court.

Forced out of the *Sunday Mirror*, Myler was given a job by Murdoch in New York. Perhaps unsurprisingly he found it difficult working alongside the abrasive Col Allan, the Australian ex-pat who edited the *New York Post*. When Murdoch subsequently offered Myler the highly paid job of editing the *News of the World*, he jumped at it.

Myler arrived at the *News of the World* in January 2007 and found that the phone-hacking scandal was only one of the tabloid's problems. Circulation was dropping, advertisers were restless. His response was to return to his old tricks.

In the summer of 2008 Myler was offered a story which, on the face of it, was rather humdrum by *News of the World* standards. A very powerful person in the car racing business, the head of the Fédération Internationale de l'Automobile (F1), liked the occasional sex orgy. What made it appealing to Myler was that the individual concerned was Max Mosley, son of the former British fascist leader Sir Oswald Mosley.

The *News of the World* decided to set up an elaborate sting operation, hiring prostitutes and organising an orgy at a fashionable Chelsea apartment. Mosley walked into the trap and was filmed being hit on the bare buttocks by a woman wearing a German military uniform. For the hacks at the *News of the World*, a woman in uniform equalled a Nazi. The front-page story ran under the headline 'F1 Boss has Sick Nazi Orgy with Five Hookers'.

Mosley immediately sued. He challenged the publication under Article 8 of the European Convention on Human Rights, which protects an individual's privacy. More than anything else it was the word 'Nazi' that most offended Mosley. The story said that Mosley had spoken German, and that stripped naked he had been spanked by the girls, all of them wearing German military uniforms.

The *News of the World* argued that the public had a right to know Mosley was involved in Nazi role-play because he held a public position. In his ruling, Mr Justice Eady had some good news and some bad news for the *News of the World*. The bad news was that even in cases of adultery, sadomaso-chistic behaviour was generally not deemed to be a matter of public interest. The good news was that there could be a public interest if the behaviour involved the mocking of Jews or the Holocaust. Unfortunately for the *News of the World*, Justice Eady found that wasn't the case as there had been no Nazi role-playing. He awarded Mosley damages of £60,000 (approximately AU$95,000).

Furious at the findings, and without any sense of irony, the *News of the World* ran an editorial exclaiming that public figures must maintain standards. 'It is not for the powerful and the influential to run to the courts to gag newspapers from publishing stories that are TRUE,' it said. 'This is all about the public's right to know.'[3]

Colin Myler had done it again, this time handing ammunition directly to those who argue for further press restrictions. Max Mosley grabbed the opportunity with both hands. Within days of the High Court finding he lodged an application in France – which has strict privacy laws – to force Google to block its search engine from accessing the *News of the World* photographs. The French court upheld his right to privacy; though the photographs can be found with effort by using other search engines in France, it was a symbolic loss for those who support the internet's freedom of access and freedom of expression.

What Mosley said he objected to wasn't that the pictures were available, but that they were available to everybody. 'The fundamental point is that Google could stop this material appearing but they don't, or they won't as a matter of princi-ple,' he said.[4]

Mosley's argument went to the heart of the issue: elected governments should be held accountable, but at the same time members of the public, even influential and powerful ones like him, had a right to a private life. In its story the *News of the World* described Mosley as a pervert but it was the newspaper that had created the greatest perversion of all. It had twisted a valid journalistic argument about the public right to know, to produce a tawdry tale, damaging the best defence journalists have in exposing government secrecy.

The strident nature of the *News of the World* editorial following the High Court result seemed to be solely an attack on the decision. With hindsight it can also be interpreted as a clever defensive move. Few outside the newspaper knew but, at the time, the *News of the World* had plenty of secrets to hide. It was rife with phone-hacking.

—

As odd as this appears we may never have known about the corruption at the *News of the World* if it hadn't been for a staunchly independent freelance journalist. Nick Davies had developed a formidable reputation as an investigative reporter, winning many awards, including Reporter of the Year in 2000. The fact that Davies was a contributor to *The Guardian* but was not on staff meant that he lived a separate cultural life, free to explore his own ideas, uncontrolled by the influences of a more conformist journalistic world. Even though *The Guardian* cannot be described as conformist, Davies' freelance status gave him an added degree of independence.

It served Davies well. He was alone in forensically pursuing the WikiLeaks revelations, which delivered him the then biggest scoop in the history of journalism (see chapter 8). Davies had also closely followed the *News of the World* phone-hacking case from the beginning. He always disbelieved News International's assertion that only the telephones of the royal family's household had been compromised and that Goodman was a lone rogue reporter.

In 2009 Davies got a break: he discovered that News International was being sued for breach of privacy by the Chief

Executive of the Professional Footballers' Association, Gordon Taylor, and it had something to do with the 2006 police investigation of *News of the World* phone-hackers, Goodman and Mulcaire.

The British awoke on the morning of 8 July 2009 to a continuation of the muggy weather which had made sleeping so difficult over the previous few nights. What *The Guardian* newspaper carried on its front page that morning would generate plenty more sleepless nights for people in the News International camp.

Under the headline 'Murdoch Papers Paid £1M to Gag Phone-Hacking Victims', Nick Davies revealed mesmerising details of Gordon Taylor's phone-hacking case and demonstrated also that it was the tip of an iceberg. When Taylor took out a civil case against News Group Newspapers (NGN) for its undisclosed involvement in the illegal interception of messages left on his mobile phone, News responded by marshalling untold amounts of cash and an army of QCs to stop Taylor's story being made public. By negotiating an out-of-court settlement with Taylor for his legal costs plus paying more than £400,000 in damages in exchange for his silence, then persuading the High Court to seal the file – effectively locking up the evidence – NGN prevented the public from knowing anything about the hundreds of pages of evidence which had been gathered by police in the 2006 phone-hacking investigation which Taylor's lawyers had assembled to support his case. Included was evidence of potentially criminal behaviour by journalists on NGN's payroll. Davies highlighted that NGN's strategy protected some powerful and influential people.

'Rupert Murdoch's News Group Newspapers has paid out more than £1m to settle legal cases that threatened to reveal evidence of his journalists' repeated involvement in the use of criminal methods to get stories,' Davies wrote. He added that the payments 'secured secrecy over out-of-court settlements in three cases that threatened to expose evidence of Murdoch journalists using private investigators who illegally hacked into the mobile phone messages of numerous public figures'.

Another revelation was that the hackers had also gained 'unlawful access to confidential personal data, including tax records, social security files, bank statements and itemised phone bills'.

The report aired the first hard evidence to crack open News International's position that the phone-hacking had been just one rogue reporter eavesdropping on royal conversations. Not only were journalists – plural – victims of the practice, cabinet ministers, MPs, actors and sports stars were all targets.

Davies' story landed in the laps of the hitherto comfortably smug Murdoch hierarchy like an exploding grenade. They had been confident that the hacking story had been put to bed. And why wouldn't they be? London's Metropolitan Police, the Director of Public Prosecutions and the Press Complaints Commission had all conducted their own follow-up investigations into the phone-hacking saga. They had all found no case to answer for the *News of the World*. The accepted narrative was that royal reporter Clive Goodman and Glenn Mulcaire had acted alone.

The only critical voice came much later in 2012 from the House of Commons Culture, Media and Sport Committee. It rejected News's 'lone rogue' reporter defence and observed that the 'evidence we have seen makes it inconceivable that no-one else at the *News of the World*, bar Clive Goodman, knew about the phone-hacking'.[5]

The committee was particularly unimpressed by the forgetfulness of News International which, they said, reached new levels when on one day the former Executive Chairman of News International, Les Hinton, stated that he 'did not know, could not recall, did not remember or was not familiar with the events under scrutiny a total of 72 times'.[6]

So sure was News International that the matter was at an end that when the Commons committee published its

findings, it unleashed a ferocious attack on the MPs who had
dared question its supremacy. On 28 February 2010 in a full-
page editorial headlined 'YOUR Right to Know Is Mired in
MPs' Bias. But a Free Press Is Far Too Precious to Lose', the
News of the World stated, 'Sadly, the victims here are YOU,
the public.' The newspaper said that if MPs got their way
the media landscape would be changed forever. It reminded
readers that every time they read of a revelation in the *News
of the World* they should bear in mind 'the forces that are at
work trying to silence us and keep you in ignorance. They
are many and they are powerful. And right now they're doing
their damndest [sic] to wreck the most precious of basic press
freedoms – your right to know.'

Despite the righteous indignation of the editorial, thanks
to Davies' reporting questions were being asked about why
earlier inquiries had not discovered the real state of play in
the Murdoch empire. It turned out that there were hundreds
of pages of documentation of systemic criminal acts, and this
is where the story becomes quite complex. There was something rather strange about the way the investigation had been
conducted. The Met believed it was only illegal to hack into
a message, if that message had not already been accessed and
heard. All messages not already listened to could be hacked by
anyone, seemingly without breaking the law. It appeared like a
ridiculous interpretation of the law designed to hide the truth
and reduce the number of people who could legitimately lodge
a claim against News International. Whatever the reason for
the interpretation it certainly reduced the number of people
who could claim that their phones had been hacked.

Even as the veil that concealed the corruption extending
from Wapping to Whitehall was about to be torn away, the
Press Complaints Commission was unmoved. It criticised
Davies for producing stories with 'anonymous sources' against
a number of 'on the record statements' from those who have
'first-hand knowledge of events at the newspaper'.[7]

Davies had admirably discharged his duty as a reporter, raising in the public domain matters of extraordinary importance to the British people. Yet the very organisation whose job it is to represent the public interest had dismissed his courageous reporting as irrelevant. As is often the case, the truth lay buried, just waiting to be uncovered.

—

The highly regarded London law firm of Harbottle & Lewis has its offices in an elegant building on the corner of fashionable Hanover Square in the heart of Mayfair. In 2007 it was Harbottle & Lewis that News International had asked to investigate and then store emails relating to the phone-hacking investigation. Harbottle & Lewis were being sucked into an impossible situation.

Buried in those News International documents – where they would remain for another three years – were the notes of a transcript of a telephone conversation which had been intercepted from Gordon Taylor's phone. Marked 'For Neville' – believed to be Neville Thurlbeck, a reporter for the *News of the World* – they were the smoking gun: there was at least one more *News of the World* reporter involved. The notes laid out finally the lie that Clive Goodman had been a one-off rogue – the basis of the News defence. And they had been in the papers held by News International's lawyers all along.

Another explosive letter from Goodman to News International underscored the fact that others at the *News of the World* knew about the phone-hacking – and that on top of the year's salary he'd been paid when he was jailed, he wanted a substantial amount of money as compensation for what he said was his 'unfair dismissal'. It was an unusual request given that Rupert Murdoch makes repeated public assertions that he always insists on a 'commitment to ethics and integrity'[8] among his staff. How could Goodman believe he would extract a payment from News International when he'd just been jailed for a crime?

It seems that Goodman was banking on News being willing to settle with him. If Goodman decided to pursue the matter through the courts – or more likely a special tribunal which hears cases of alleged unfair dismissal – then the cache of incriminating records and other documentation would become evidence. At the very least this would be awkward for News.

Goodman's ploy worked. Although News had already paid him £40,000 compensation followed by another £90,000, it topped that up with a further amount in the vicinity of £90,000.

Somehow Goodman's letter – which proved that the practice of phone-hacking was much wider than commonly believed – was missed when the first search was made in 2007. A good deal of backtracking and explaining went on. It emerged that News International, when handing over to Harbottle & Lewis relevant documents, defined the search criteria so narrowly that it prevented any incriminating material ever being found by an investigation. Harbottle & Lewis had searched 2500 emails from the News International's archives and declared Goodman's assertions about a criminal syndicate operating in the *News of the World* newsroom unfounded.

News Limited must have believed their tactics were working. It wasn't until three years later that the phone-hacking scandal again rose to prominence.

On 2 February 2010 *The Guardian* published on its front page a report that phone companies had discovered another 120 victims who had been hacked.

In March 2010 News International reached a million-pound settlement with publicist Max Clifford which included a restriction on him ever discussing the case of his phone being hacked. Clifford was best known among the British tabloids for persuading *The Sun* to publish a front-page story about one of his clients under the headline 'Freddie Starr Ate My Hamster'.[9]

In September 2010 *The New York Times* published a long investigation into the phone-hacking affair. It didn't raise much which was new, but it did put pressure on the Metropolitan Police and the British judiciary.

On 15 January 2011 the Crown Prosecution Service announced a review of the evidence collected in the Metropolitan Police Service's original phone-hacking investigation. News International still clung to its argument of the lone reporter, publicly at least. It would be another seven months before News's defences would finally collapse.

On 5 July 2011 a piece by Davies and fellow journalist Amelia Hill in *The Guardian* reported that the mobile phone of Milly Dowler, a schoolgirl from Surrey who was murdered in 2002, had been hacked by the *News of the World*. At the time of her disappearance – it was several months before her body was discovered – the newspaper had published misleading stories which said her phone messages had been answered, giving false hope to her parents that she might be alive. It was the final blow which brought undone News International.

On 6 July 2011 Davies co-wrote a story which revealed that the phones of the families of soldiers killed in Afghanistan and the families of victims of the 7/7 London bus bombings had also been hacked to produce stories for the *News of the World*.

On 7 July 2011 News International announced that the 168-year-old *News of the World* would close.

On 10 July 2011 Harbottle & Lewis were cited in reports by *The Guardian*, the BBC and *The Independent* as being involved in what they described as smoking gun emails in the hacking scandal.

Now that the story was out, Harbottle & Lewis were instructed by News International to reinvestigate the emails. It would be true to say that the Hanover Square law firm was unimpressed by the request. Particularly when Rupert Murdoch told the Commons Culture, Media and Sport Committee he blamed Harbottles' lawyers for having misled News International in 2007. With their client now turning on them, Harbottle handballed the investigation off to someone who knew a thing or two about the case: Lord Macdonald, a former director of public prosecutions. Lord Macdonald took one look at the News International emails and immediately put the matter in the hands of the police.

The net was closing on News International. James Murdoch issued a carefully worded statement. It distanced himself and his father from the cover-up, highlighting to the committee that the *News of the World* had made statements to 'parliament without being in full possession of the facts. This was wrong.'[10]

The Commons Culture, Media and Sport Committee was, to put it mildly, disbelieving. It saw right through the tactic, pointing out that 'News Corporation's strategy has been to lay the blame on certain individuals'.[11] It found that *News of the World* editor Colin Myler, News International's senior legal counsel Tom Crone and the company's chief legal officer Jonathan Chapman 'should certainly have acted on information they had about phone-hacking and other wrongdoing, but they cannot be allowed to carry the whole of the blame as News Corporation has clearly intended'.[12]

The committee pulled up short of calling the whole News International defence a transparent lie, but it came close: 'Far from having an epiphany at the end of 2010, the truth, we believe, is that by spring 2011, because of the civil actions, the company finally realised that its containment approach had failed, and that a "one rogue reporter" – or even "two rogue journalists" – stance no longer had any shred of credibility.'[13]

Paul Farrelly, a committee member, observed that 'any 10-year-old' would have asked how the royal reporter Goodman could have been the only journalist guilty of phone-hacking when Professional Footballers' Association Executive Chairman Gordon Taylor – the person whose civil case against News and extraordinarily large settlement had alerted Davies to the extensive nature of the phone-hacking – was clearly 'not a member of the royal family'.[14]

James Murdoch purported not to remember the payout to Taylor, which did his credibility with the committee no good. A Conservative member, Philip Davies, was astounded that Murdoch could not remember the first payment to Taylor, which amounted to £250,000. He told Murdoch junior, 'I find it incredible, absolutely incredible, that you didn't say, "A quarter of a million? Let me look at that." I can't begin to believe that that is the action that any self-respecting chief operating officer would take, when so much of the company's money and reputation is at stake.'[15]

On 8 July 2011 Prime Minister Cameron announced a judicial inquiry into the conduct of the media; it was headed by Brian Leveson. The balding and bespectacled Leveson seemed well suited for the job of investigating the relationship between politicians, the police and the media. He'd recently been elevated to one of the highest judicial ranks in the country as a Lord Justice of Appeal, having made a name for himself dealing with a range of highly complex cases.

Perhaps appropriately for an inquiry into the media he opened the proceedings by issuing a clarification: 'Although flattered that various politicians and members of the press have elevated me to the rank of peerage, I am not Lord Leveson: my judicial rank is that of a Lord Justice of Appeal.'[16]

Even before his four-volume report was published, as if to compound the arrogance and disregard that abounded, a group calling itself 'Free Press Network' took out huge advertisements in newspapers carrying photographs of international leaders Vladimir Putin, Robert Mugabe and Fidel Castro and bearing the words, 'These people believe in state control of the press. Do you?'[17]

Far from advocating state control, Leveson was suggesting that the press adopt a system of public accountability similar to the one which keeps the BBC – the most trusted news organisation in the UK – accountable for its accuracy and fairness.

Apart from stirring up fear in the population the heavy-handed campaign ensured that the focus remained solely on control of the press, deflecting attention from the central culprit of so much hurtful, grubby and deceitful work: News International.

The audacity didn't stop there. Leveson had got off lightly compared to the Commons committee. It emerged that the *News of the World*, the very newspaper that had been charged with spying in some of the most sordid cases, and which barely passed the description for journalism, had employed private detectives to delve into the domestic lives of the committee members to find any possible dirt with which to discredit them. As an attempt at intimidation it was of little use. The committee's findings were damning:

> On the basis of the facts and evidence before the Committee, we conclude that, if at all relevant times Rupert Murdoch did not take steps to become fully informed about phone-hacking, he turned a blind eye and exhibited wilful blindness to what was going on in his companies and publications. This culture, we consider, permeated from the top throughout the organisation and speaks volumes about the lack of effective corporate governance at News Corporation and News International. We conclude, therefore, that Rupert Murdoch is not a fit person to exercise the stewardship of a major international company.[18]

David Cameron would have none of it. He shelved the Commons committee's report and dismissed the Leveson recommendations. He also fired his media adviser Andy Coulson, the ex-*News of the World* editor, who had helped him win the national election a few months earlier.

Worse was to come for Coulson. He was jailed for allowing the phone-hacking at the *News of the World*, while his ex-lover Rebekah Brooks continued her charmed life. Rupert Murdoch's protégée, Brooks had had a meteoric rise from the typing pool to *News of the World* editor, then Chief Executive Officer of News International; now she walked free from the court. There was not enough direct evidence to convict her. Three million News International emails had been deleted and only a handful involving Brooks' time as editor had been kept. The hard drives had been removed from her computers for so-called safekeeping – then lost.

But News International did not escape completely. The months of bad publicity – and thousands of complaints to Ofcom, the government body which overseas broadcasting in the UK – forced Murdoch to drop his plans to take full control of BSkyB, the money-making cable network he part-owns.

BSkyB, which produces some of the highest quality news in the UK, paid a high price for the seedy and illegal activities of its downmarket stablemate. The reason the public was so appalled about what had happened had less to do with the means that were used to gather information – phone-hacking – and more to do with the subject matter – missing school-children, the families of dead soldiers and royal celebrity tittle-tattle.

If the *News of the World* had used similar methods to reveal the truth about the Iraq War before the bombing started, its reporters may well have been hailed as heroes. They might also have been prosecuted but it would have been for a worthwhile cause.

Of course such a thing would never happen as Murdoch was in favour of the war: Murdoch editors toe the line on the truly important stories. Some of the world's most esteemed broadsheets do too. Despite their high-handed views about the tabloid press, they are sometimes no better than the red tops they so despise.

CHAPTER 7

Source for the Goose

The Franz Josef Strauss Airport, nearly 30 kilometres north-east of Munich, is named after one of Germany's less savoury politicians. As a member of the German federal cabinet, in the early 1960s Strauss managed to have the head of the country's investigative magazine *Der Spiegel* jailed for more than three months on false charges. And Strauss went to his grave dogged by allegations that while Minister of Defence he had received a US$10 million bribe from the US Lockheed Aircraft Corporation. It was probably fitting then that the Franz Josef Strauss Airport should be the gateway through which Rafid Ahmed al-Janabi entered his new life after he fled Iraq in 1999, leaving behind a trail of debts and suspected criminal activity.

As he moved through the imposing concrete and glass terminal building, al-Janabi may well have approached the immigration barrier with a certain degree of trepidation. Possessing just a tourist visa, he would have to argue – if questioned – that his only plans were for visiting the BMW Museum and sampling the local pretzel. But al-Janabi had much more on his mind. Not only had the Iraqi Justice Department put out an international warrant for his arrest for selling stolen camera equipment on the Baghdad black market, he had had to leave his new wife in Morocco and he wanted to bring her to Germany to join him.

Speaking Arabic and halting English, the Baghdad-born chemical engineer promptly discarded the tourist visa that had facilitated his trip and applied for political asylum. He told the German immigration officials he had embezzled Iraqi government money and faced prison or worse if sent home. Sent to a refugee centre located in Zirndorf, near Nuremberg, he joined a long line of Iraqi exiles seeking permanent German residency visas. Desperate to jump the queue, al-Janabi abruptly changed his story.

If the Germans hadn't been all that interested in his problems back home, they were certainly fixated on what he now told them he had been doing there. Al-Janabi said he once led a team of officers that equipped trucks to brew deadly bio-agents. He named six sites where Iraq might be hiding biological warfare vehicles, three of which were already operating. A farm program to boost crop yields was cover for Iraq's new biological weapons production program, he claimed.

The immigration officers called in the BND – Germany's federal intelligence service. What al-Janabi told his BND interrogators fitted perfectly the story that western intelligence agencies had been piecing together about Saddam Hussein's bio-weapons program. They had always been suspicious of Saddam's sworn promise that Iraq had destroyed all its chemical weapons in 1991 after the first Gulf War.

For al-Janabi, relieved to have attracted the attention of German authorities, the timing could not have been better. A few months before he defected, the CIA issued a national intelligence estimate on worldwide biological warfare (BW) programs. It was a regular assessment by the agency, sent to other agencies and the White House. It accused Iraq of 'probably continuing work to develop and produce BW agents'.[1] Ominously it added that Iraq could restart production in six months.

Al-Janabi painted a picture of an elaborate deception created by the Iraqi government, convincing his BND handlers that the Djerf al Nadaf warehouses, where he had worked as an engineer, were part of Iraq's secret germ weapons program.

He claimed that mobile biochemical laboratories were hidden in a two-storey building that could be driven into from both sides.

Al-Janabi had other significant information: there were plans to build mobile biochemical factories at six sites across Iraq, from An Numaniyah in the south to Tikrit in the north.

His claims might have seemed implausible but, cunningly, al-Janabi added the kind of local colour that only a person with accurate inside information could know. Al-Janabi explained how the Iraqis had deceived the teams of United Nations weapons inspectors sent in to scour the country looking for weapons of mass destruction (WMDs) after the first Gulf War. He told the BND that when the inspectors entered Iraq, the production of the biological weapons agent always began at midnight on Thursdays because it was thought the inspectors would not work on the Muslim holy day, which ran from Thursday night to Friday night. The fact that weapons inspectors did work on Fridays seemed to have escaped the Germans.[2]

While BND officials launched what would turn out to be nearly two years of interrogation of al-Janabi, their counterparts in immigration started processing his refugee claim. In the bleak surroundings of the Zirndorf refugee camp – used to house Soviet defectors during the Cold War – al-Janabi must have hoped his past wouldn't catch up with him. If his family's close relationship with the Iraqi regime were ever made known to the German authorities, he would have trouble explaining why he feared persecution.

The youngest of five children in a family of Sunni Muslims, he had grown up in a middle-class neighbourhood of Baghdad. His eldest brother became a brigadier in Saddam Hussein's Republican Guard. Al-Janabi had also worked as a technician in a film and TV company which made propaganda films for the Iraqi dictator. But there was more than that, if anyone dug deeper into his past.

Los Angeles Times reporters Bob Drogin and John Geotz managed to track down someone who knew al-Janabi well:

Hilal Freah, who said he had been picked up and tortured by the CIA during the war, then left Iraq for Jordan. Freah had been al-Janabi's supervisor at the Djerf al Nadaf warehouses, 15 kilometres south of Baghdad, where al-Janabi was employed as an engineer. Freah, who had viewed himself as al-Janabi's mentor, understood his protégé all too well. He would not have been surprised at the facility with which al-Jalabi was weaving tales for the BND.

'Rafid [al-Janabi] told five or 10 stories every day,' he said. 'I'd ask, "Where have you been?" And he'd say: "I had a problem with my car," or, "My family was sick." But I knew he was lying.' He had a gift for it and 'was not embarrassed when caught in a lie', according to Freah.[3]

Far from being a chemical weapons centre, the Djerf al Nadaf warehouses performed a genuinely useful function for the local farmers scraping a living off the land. It was there that they brought their seeds to be treated with fungicides to prevent mould and rot. There were certainly no WMDs anywhere to be seen.

Even in Germany, where al-Janabi found work at a local Burger King after gaining the right of residency, his co-workers couldn't decide whether he was dangerous or crazy. He told co-workers that he spied for Iraqi intelligence and would report any fellow Iraqi workers who criticised the Hussein regime. 'During breaks he told stories about what a big man he was in Baghdad,' recalled Hamza Hamad, one of al-Janabi's fellow restaurant employees. Calling to mind an odd scene with a pudgy al-Janabi in his too-tight Burger King uniform praising Saddam, Hamad observed, 'He always lied. We never believed anything he said.'[4]

Though the staff at the Burger King tired of al-Janabi's tales, the same couldn't be said for the BND. Between 2000 and the end of 2001, they met him on 52 separate occasions. He became such a vital source of information they gave him a secret codename – Curveball. Why the Germans chose that name is not clear, but during the Cold War western intelligence agencies used the suffix 'ball' to indicate a source was connected to WMDs. Other commentators speculated that the word's common usage as a US baseball term was meaningful. But since the BND jealously guarded Curveball as a source – and did not allow the Americans to directly interview him – a perhaps more likely explanation is that they believed what he said was potentially dubious, or not straight.

—

The name Curveball would echo through Washington's corridors of power for years to come as the White House assiduously sought intelligence to bolster its argument for a war against Iraq. Over the period of al-Janabi's debriefing, the BND sent a total of 95 reports from Germany to the US Defense Intelligence Agency headquarters in Clarendon, Virginia. From its nondescript brown high-rise building, the information passed to the Weapons, Intelligence, Nonproliferation, and Arms Control Center – known as WINPAC – at CIA headquarters in nearby Langley.

The CIA called in experts, including an independent laboratory, to help evaluate the data. Spy satellites were directed to focus on Curveball's sites. CIA artists prepared detailed drawings from Curveball's crude sketches. Al-Janabi consistently provided evidence which fitted perfectly what the CIA already believed: Iraq was running a covert operation to build WMDs.

The CIA's suspicions had a reasonable basis. In mid-1995 Iraqi officials admitted that before the first Gulf War they had secretly produced 30,000 litres of anthrax, botulinum toxin, aflatoxin and other lethal bio-agents. They had also deployed hundreds of germ-filled munitions and researched other deadly diseases for military use. Curveball's story to the Germans neatly dovetailed with that history and continuing CIA suspicions.

In December 2000, after a year of Curveball's reports, another national intelligence estimate cautiously noted that 'new intelligence' had caused US intelligence 'to adjust our assessment upward' and 'suggests Baghdad has expanded' its bio-weapons program.[5] Al-Janabi's little ruse had created a snowball effect.

In Washington the snowball gathered pace thanks to the political imperative of the neo-cons – the so-called new conservatives – who were looking for any excuse to reassert US power over a dictator who had once been a trusted ally. When two hijacked passenger planes struck the World Trade Center towers in central New York on a crisp autumn morning in 2001, the neo-cons, led by Defense Secretary Donald Rumsfeld, went into overdrive.

As the rest of the United States – and much of the rest of the world – reeled in shock at the terrorist atrocity, the White House used the attack as an opportunity. It went looking for evidence that America's adversary Saddam Hussein was involved. Five hours after the planes hit the towers, an aide to Rumsfeld made a diary note that revealed just how keen the White House was to use the al-Qaeda attack as an excuse to hit Saddam Hussein. The aide wrote, 'Best info fast. Judge whether good enough [to] hit SH [Saddam Hussein] @ same time. Not only UBL [Usama bin Laden].'[6]

The following day, 12 September, President Bush's head of counter-terrorism, Richard Clarke, had just left the Secure Video Conferencing Center – near the Situation Room in the basement of the West Wing of the White House – when he says he saw the President 'wandering alone. He grabbed a few of us and closed the door to the conference room. "Look," he told us, "I know you have a lot to do and all, but I want you, as soon as you can, to go back over everything, everything. See if Saddam did this. See if he's linked in any way."'[7]

Clarke says he was 'taken aback, incredulous, and it showed. "But, Mr. President, Al Qaeda did this."

"'I know, I know, but – see if Saddam was involved. Just look. I want to know any shred.'"[8]

Clarke gave an undertaking to look again. He was, he said, 'trying to be more respectful, more responsive. "But you know, we have looked several times for state sponsorship of Al Qaeda and not found any real linkages to Iraq."'[9] Clarke maintains that he told Bush, 'Iran plays a little, as does Pakistan, and Saudi Arabia, Yemen.' But Bush was not persuaded: "'Look into Iraq, Saddam," the president said testily and left us.'[10]

One month later, in October 2001, Curveball's information helped ramp up the argument that Iraq was building a deadly arsenal. The CIA said Iraq 'continues to produce at least . . . three BW agents' and its mobile germ factories provide 'capabilities surpassing the pre-Gulf War era'.[11]

The CIA's extraordinary assertions weren't based on any new intelligence about Iraq's biological weapons. Instead analysts had simply estimated what they believed would be the maximum output from seven mobile labs – only one of which Curveball said he had seen – operating nonstop for six months. They had developed a hypothesis using Curveball's unsubstantiated claims to produce a frightening scenario.

It later emerged that Curveball was returning a favour to those who had helped him defect from Iraq to build a new life in Germany. Known as the Iraqi National Congress (INC), a strong mix of Kurds, Shia and Sunnis who wanted Saddam ousted, they were closely connected to hawks in the US administration who were determined to reassert America's authority over oil-rich countries. The INC was headed by Ahmed Chalabi, an Iraqi-born but US and UK educated can-do guy with all the charm of a snake oil salesman. Chalabi had been anointed to lead the INC by one of the most powerful men in Washington, John Rendon, who owned the Rendon Group. Rendon, ruggedly handsome and smooth-talking, had been an advisor to Democrat President Jimmy Carter.

With its US headquarters in Washington's Dupont Circle, the Rendon Group was but a few kilometres from the US Congress and the White House. In terms of political influence, though, it was even closer.

The Rendon Group prides itself on being the leader in a strategic field known as 'perception management manipulating information and the news media. In other words spinning stories – and placing them in an often unquestioning press.'[12] The Rendon Group had been specifically hired by the CIA in 1991 to help 'create the conditions for the removal of Hussein from power' – a demand by George H.W. Bush after the first Gulf War ended with Saddam still in control.[13]

When Frank Anderson, the chief of the CIA's Near East division, was handed a copy of the President's order, which became known as 'regime change', he scrawled in the margin, 'I don't like this.'[14]

The President expected the CIA to do what the first Gulf War had failed to do – remove Saddam. 'The agency wanted to clean their hands of the whole mess,' said one ex-intelligence official, 'so they gave it to Rendon.'[15]

Rendon became the de facto leader of the Iraqi Opposition. 'The INC was clueless. They needed a lot of help and didn't know where to start. That is why Rendon was brought in,' said Thomas Twetten, the CIA's former deputy director of operations.[16]

The CIA contract paid The Rendon Group extremely well – '[US]$23 million in the first year alone'.[17] According to the author of 'Flacks Americana: John Rendon's Shallow PR War on Terrorism' (*New Republic*, 20 May 2002), The Rendon Group expanded dramatically. The open-ended contract gave John Rendon a free hand and he splashed the money around. In 1991 several of his operatives in London earned more than the director of the CIA – about US$19,000 per month. The Rendon Group was feeding the media free vision shot by freelance journalists it had commissioned itself. It had other freelance journalists producing stories for a CIA-funded radio station which had just been established in northern Iraq – an area protected by the UN no-fly zone established after the end of the war to stop the Iraqi Air Force attacking the local Kurds.

Though Rendon was a smooth operator, not everything went smoothly. CIA accountants who investigated the company's accounts found no examples of fraud, but they did produce a report which contained criticism of the way the company operated. The CIA agents who worked with Rendon on the INC conceded that Rendon's Langley bosses simply didn't monitor his work. 'They were broadcasting into Iraq,' said one, 'but there was no due diligence.'[18]

By 1995 a new team was in charge of the CIA's Iraqi Operations Group and they severed the agency's relationship with Rendon altogether.

Six years later, shortly after the 9/11 attacks, Rendon was back inside the beltway – with a new client: the Pentagon. Just a few weeks after the World Trade Center attack, the Pentagon secretly awarded The Rendon Group a US$16 million contract. The mission statement: help remove Saddam Hussein from power. Rendon simply picked up where he had left off with the CIA: working with the INC and, in particular, Ahmed Chalabi.

No one – publicly at least – questioned the fact Chalabi was on the run after being found guilty of embezzling millions of dollars which destroyed a Jordanian bank. The Rendon Group just wanted Chalabi, who had already delivered up Curveball, to repeat the performance. They would not be disappointed. He was about to give them another extraordinary 'gift'.

—

The tiny beachside town of Pattaya on the Gulf of Thailand was a popular haunt for the US military on R&R leave in the 1960s during the Vietnam War. Nowadays, with its high-rise buildings curling along the bay, the Vietnam vets who used to while away the hours in the former fishing village would hardly recognise the place. Some things have remained the same. The market the US soldiers created for bars, sex shops and prostitution is still there. And in 2001 it continued to be favoured by the CIA: a place far enough from Bangkok where business could be done discreetly and yet a town with its own international airport. It was from Pattaya that US B-52s launched their bombing raids against North Vietnam and even now the US military presence was still strong.

In December 2001 a team of Defense Intelligence Agency (DIA) and CIA officers headed into town, checking in at one of Pattaya's many hotels. Already there was someone who didn't quite fit the military mould, a man in his middle forties who probably wished he was somewhere else. It was one particular CIA officer who took charge. He told the man to sit in a padded chair while he attached metal electrodes to his ring and index fingers. He then wrapped a black rubber tube, pleated like an accordion, around the man's chest and another across his abdomen. Finally, he slipped a thick cover like a blood pressure strap over the man's arm. Wired up to the polygraph machine was Adnan Ihsan Saeed al-Haideri, who had fled his homeland in Kurdistan and was determined to do his part in bringing down Saddam Hussein. As a civil engineer he claimed to have personally visited 20 top-secret WMD sites in Iraq. The Pentagon had sent one of the CIA's best polygraph experts to confirm once and for all whether Saddam Hussein had a secret WMD stockpile.

Over the hours as the relentless questioning continued, al-Haideri didn't waver. He insisted repeatedly that he was a civil engineer who had helped Saddam's men to secretly bury tons of biological, chemical and nuclear weapons. The illegal arms, according to al-Haideri, were buried in subterranean wells, hidden in private villas and even stashed beneath the Saddam Hussein Hospital, the largest medical facility in Baghdad.

As al-Haideri spoke, all in the room were acutely aware that if what he was telling them was true, it would make war with Iraq inevitable.

After he finished the questioning, the CIA officer began the painstaking business of analysing al-Haideri's responses; his blood pressure, pulse rate, breathing rate and perspiration all produced a complex graph on the polygraph's computer screen. As the CIA officer matched up the scratchy lines tracing how al-Haideri had reacted to every question, the mood in the room darkened. The analyst had bad news for the Pentagon: the results indicated al-Haideri was a fabricator at best and probably a liar. Whatever the truth, his assertions about biological and nuclear weapons were nonsense.

The destruction of al-Haideri's credibility as a witness should have spelled trouble for the people who had vouched for him as a reliable informant – Chalabi and The Rendon Group. After the Pattaya meeting the CIA certainly believed he wasn't to be trusted. But the White House wasn't listening to the CIA any more.

Desperate for unequivocal evidence in order to justify waging war with Iraq, the neo-cons had set up their own unit, which bypassed the intelligence agencies. Vice President Dick Cheney and Richard Perle, the policy adviser to the secretary of defense and a long-time supporter of Ahmed Chalabi, established what was known as the Office of Special Plans (OSP). The OSP hired analysts and Middle East experts to re-examine the raw data gathered by the intelligence agencies, trying to get the facts to fit their beliefs about Iraq. If the intelligence agencies couldn't provide the evidence they needed, they would find it themselves with the help of Ahmed Chalabi and the INC.

When Deputy Secretary of Defense Paul Wolfowitz dined with Christopher Meyer, the British Ambassador to the United States, according to a memorandum the diplomat sent to the office of British Prime Minister Tony Blair, Wolfowitz told Meyer that Chalabi 'had a record of bringing high-grade defectors out of Iraq' like Curveball. Richard Perle believed 'the most reliable person to give us advice is Chalabi'.[19]

Chalabi was just the person to give the OSP what it wanted to hear.

It isn't the case that everyone in the Bush administration was blind to the modus operandi of the OSP. Some in the intelligence agencies believed the OSP was 'dangerous for US national security and a threat to world peace'.[20] In an interview with the Scottish *Sunday Herald*, a former CIA officer named Larry C. Johnson said the OSP lied and manipulated intelligence to further its agenda of removing Saddam. 'It's a group of ideologues with pre-determined notions of truth and reality. They take bits of intelligence to support their agenda and ignore anything contrary.'[21]

Many inside the intelligence agencies looked on in horror. W. Patrick Lang, the former chief of Middle East intelligence at the DIA, expressed outrage: 'The Pentagon has banded together to dominate the government's foreign policy, and they've pulled it off. They're running Chalabi. The DIA has been intimidated and beaten to a pulp. And there's no guts at all in the CIA.'[22]

Dismissed by the CIA and now hired by the Pentagon, The Rendon Group was only too keen to wheel out the defectors the OSP believed provided the best intelligence on Iraq. Ably assisted by Chalabi, they picked their purveyors of testimony well. A failed CIA polygraph test certainly wouldn't stand in the way. Rendon was several steps ahead of the CIA et al. and was putting together a global communications plan as things were winding up in Pattaya.

For the worldwide broadcast rights to al-Haideri's fabricated story they contacted Paul Moran. An Australian freelance journalist who had worked for the ABC, he was perfect for their purposes. An idealistic photojournalist, Moran had earlier been working with INC spokesman Zaab

Sethna on what were known as 'information operations'. In a
rare interview Sethna explained, 'We were trying to help the
Kurds and the Iraqis opposed to Saddam set up a television
station . . . The Rendon Group came to us and said, "We have
a contract to kind of do anti-Saddam propaganda on behalf of
the Iraqi opposition."'[23]

Sethna was adamant that neither he nor Moran knew – and
the Rendon Group didn't tell them – the CIA had hired them
to do this work.

Moran was certainly an unconventional journalist, according to those who worked alongside him. When it came to
being granted visas to work in Middle Eastern countries,
he acquired a reputation for achieving the near-impossible.
Cameramen who queried his methods or cast aspersions on
the connections that got him access were accused of being
jealous.

In December 2001, after the INC brought al-Haideri
to him, Paul Moran sat down with the Iraqi defector and
conducted the most important interview of his career. Within
hours of its completion the ABC had put it to air and, crucially
for the INC and The Rendon Group, this ABC TV exclusive packed with disinformation and fabrication went around
the world, picked up by dozens of TV stations. Unchecked,
uncorroborated, the ABC broadcast a pure piece of pro-war
propaganda, gratefully received by the White House.

Moran, however, would never be brought to account for
his interview. By the time questions were seriously being
asked, he had been killed by a car bomb in northern Iraq
while working as a cameraman for ABC's *Foreign Correspondent* program. One of the cameramen who worked alongside
Moran said he believed Moran had been the subject of a
'targeted killing' because of his work supporting the Kurds.[24]
What's more, he'd put others at risk. ABC journalist Eric
Campbell was also injured in the attack. Another of Moran's
former colleagues pointed to him being a 'bag man' for the

CIA, carrying cash to help fund the Kurds in their battle against Saddam Hussein.[25]

The 39-year-old Moran became the first international journalist to die in the Iraq War. He is honoured on the ABC staff memorial page set up to pay tribute to colleagues who lost their lives in the line of duty.[26]

In the wake of the broadcast the spotlight was on Moran, and details of his puzzling working life and Middle East connections were publicly pored over. The ABC's then Director of News and Current Affairs, Max Uechtritz, said the ABC knew that 'Moran had obtained the interview because of his contacts with the Iraqi National Congress.'[27] As Peter Cave, who put together the ABC story from Moran's interview, said, 'I was conned, the ABC was conned.'[28]

What has never been publicly explained is that it was common knowledge that Moran had worked for the CIA-funded Rendon Group and the ABC seemed to accept it. Moran had self-censored and failed to check the veracity of the al-Haideri story, either because he thought he was helping the Kurds or because he knew what John Rendon expected of him. It may well have been a combination of the two. For the ABC there were other reasons.

In fairness to Uechtritz and his colleagues, at the time the ABC was under extreme pressure from the Howard Government to come to heel in its reporting in the post 9/11 environment. Ministers and their media handlers called regularly complaining about the coverage – the beginning of a sustained attack on ABC journalists who questioned the government. It was in this environment that Paul Moran offered up the world exclusive.

—

The ABC was not the only media entity to be manipulated by The Rendon Group and the INC. To disseminate the international print exclusive of al-Haideri's 'revelations', Ahmed

Chalabi contacted the formidable journalist Judith Miller of *The New York Times*. A confidante of I. Lewis 'Scooter' Libby, Vice President Dick Cheney's Chief of Staff, Miller had made a name for herself writing about chemical weapons. She also had a reputation for being a ready outlet for INC propaganda.

The INC so trusted both Moran and Miller that it gave each of them access to al-Haideri in Pattaya before the CIA ran its polygraph test on him. Consequently the INC was able to get its story out before any uncomfortable truths emerged about the veracity of what he was saying. By the time al-Haideri underwent his beachside grilling Miller was already back in New York. She later made calls to the CIA and DIA but her vaunted intelligence sources must have let her down because she claimed not to know about the results of al-Haideri's lie-detector test. Instead in her piece which appeared in *The New York Times* on 20 December 2001 she reported that unnamed 'government experts' called his information 'reliable and significant'.

Miller's story scored the kind of exposure Rendon had been paid millions of dollars to provide. Headlined 'An Iraqi Defector Tells of Work on at Least 20 Hidden Weapons Sites', the article began by saying that this 'defector who described himself as a civil engineer said he personally worked on renovations of secret facilities for biological, chemical and nuclear weapons in underground wells, private villas and under the Saddam Hussein Hospital in Baghdad as recently as a year ago'. If verified, added Miller, the allegations would 'provide ammunition to officials within the Bush administration who have been arguing that Mr. Hussein should be driven from power partly because of his unwillingness to stop making weapons of mass destruction, despite his pledges to do so'.

The New York Times carried a boast in a box on the front page, 'All The News That's Fit to Print', but there should have been a caveat that not everything it printed was fit to be called news. Newspapers and television networks around the world were soon repeating the story, reinforced by Moran's on-camera interview with al-Haideri on the ABC. If it was a scoop for Miller and Moran, it was a massive victory for John Rendon, who was on his way to helping create the first ever war built entirely on disinformation planted in the media.

President George W. Bush whipped up the momentum in his State of the Union address of 29 January 2002. Wearing a sombre dark suit and grey tie, he told the applauding joint sitting of the House of Representatives and Senate that Iraq was part of an 'axis of evil'. Allied with terrorists, it posed 'a grave and growing danger' to US interests through possession of 'weapons of mass destruction'.[29]

Eight months later, with the drumbeat of war growing ever louder, *The New York Times* carried a story which showed Judith Miller had finally crossed the line from journalist to war activist. On 8 September 2002 Miller wrote in *The New York Times* about 'Mr. Hussein's dogged insistence on pursuing his nuclear ambitions'. It was a bald statement of 'fact' without any attribution.

She added, 'What defectors described in interviews as Iraq's push to improve and expand Baghdad's chemical and biological arsenals, have brought Iraq and the United States to the brink of war.'

The story, headlined 'US Says Hussein Intensified Quest for A-bomb Parts', quoted not a single person by name, and relied entirely on US government sources. 'In the last 14 months,' wrote Miller, 'Iraq has sought to buy thousands of specially designed aluminum tubes, which American officials believe were intended as components of centrifuges to enrich uranium' to a level that it could be used in making a bomb. She quoted 'American officials' as saying 'several efforts to arrange the shipment of the aluminum tubes were blocked or intercepted'.

In a dramatic flourish the story reported that the latest attempt to ship material had taken place in recent months. Specifically officials said 'the diameter, thickness and other technical specifications of the aluminum tubes had persuaded American intelligence experts that they were meant for Iraq's nuclear program'.

Another of the 8 September 2002 article's purported facts – again without any attribution or qualification – was that 'The attempted purchases are not the only signs of a renewed Iraqi interest in acquiring nuclear arms.'

Although none of this was true – not the tubes for enrichment nor the quest for atomic bomb parts; Saddam had not been 'pursuing his nuclear ambitions' – Miller and *The New York Times*, with its uncorroborated, unquestioning reporting, had provided the perfect vehicle for the White House. Over the following 24 hours they saturated the airwaves stirring fear of a nuclear Armageddon. On 8 September 2002 on NBC's *Meet the Press*, Vice President Dick Cheney cited *The New York Times* article and accused Saddam of moving aggressively to develop nuclear weapons over the past 14 months to add to his stockpile of chemical and biological arms. On CNN the same day, National Security Advisor Condoleezza Rice acknowledged that 'there will always be some uncertainty' in determining how close Iraq may be to obtaining a nuclear weapon but, in a phrase as polished as it was hollow, added, 'We don't want the smoking gun to be a mushroom cloud.' On CBS President Bush said UN weapons inspectors, before they were denied access to Iraq in 1998, concluded that Saddam was 'six months away from developing a weapon'. He cited satellite photos that showed 'unexplained construction' at Iraqi sites that weapons inspectors had previously searched for indications Saddam was trying to develop nuclear arms. 'I don't know what more evidence we need,' Bush said.

The news flashed around the world that the White House had 'confirmed a report in *The New York Times*' that Saddam Hussein has been attempting to get equipment to enrich uranium to produce nuclear weapons. Australian

Prime Minister John Howard added to the misleading game, saying the intelligence that had come out of the United States 'if accurate confirms the intelligence that we have been given'.[30] The fact is it was the same intelligence that the United States had already given to Australia. Howard made great play of the possibility that 'Iraq has not abandoned her aspiration for nuclear capacity'.[31] By suggesting *The New York Times* story added yet another layer of confirmation, Howard was taking part in the Australian version of the style of journalism that Miller and the White House specialised in: the story leaked to Judith Miller and published in *The New York Times* had been confirmed by the very people who leaked it in the first place. Iraq's nuclear ambitions were now accepted as fact.

Even the BBC's prestigious *Panorama* program 'The Case Against Saddam', broadcast on 23 September 2002, embraced the 'evidence', reporting that 'In the 14 last months, several shipments, a total of 1000 aluminum centrifuge tubes, have been intercepted by intelligence agencies before they actually reached Iraq', suggesting they could be used for nuclear weapons production.[32] Yet the International Atomic Energy Agency in Vienna and the senior expert at America's primary nuclear weapons research facility, Oak Ridge National Laboratory, had both informed the CIA the centrifuge tubes were no good for uranium enrichment.

At the State Department building in Washington, Greg Thielmann, the Acting Director of the Office of Strategic Proliferation and Military Affairs, witnessed the disinformation program firsthand. But his oath of secrecy overrode any other conditions: 'Our job was not to straighten out the press on these issues.' His frustration was that the leadership of the country was 'not being totally honest with the people on this important issue'.[33]

Like al-Janabi's 'Curveball' claims of bio-weapons and the al-Haideri stockpile of nuclear, biological and chemical weapons, the tubes for nuclear centrifuges story was complete fiction.

—

Pulling together all available intelligence information to provide an overall picture of what the US intelligence agencies believed posed the biggest threats to US interests was the job of a group of expert analysts who worked on the outskirts of Washington at Tysons Corner. Part of the Washington over-spill, it was once a sleepy township. Now Tysons Corner is home to the National Intelligence Council. Those who work there comb through the findings of all 16 US intelligence organisations to produce a crisp, tightly argued overview of the current world strategic state for senior members of the administration. It's called the National Intelligence Estimate and the one issued in October 2002 was vital. It was sent to Congress mere days before lawmakers voted to authorise the use of military force if Hussein refused to give up his 'illicit' arsenal.

For the first time, the new estimate warned with 'high confidence' that Iraq 'has now established large-scale, redundant and concealed Biological Weapons (BW) agent production capabilities'. It said 'all key aspects' of Iraq's offensive BW program 'are active and that most elements are larger and more advanced than they were before the Gulf War'. The assessment was based 'largely on information from a single source – Curveball'.[34]

Not everyone was cheering and stamping their feet at this news. Some of the biggest sceptics were inside the very intelligence agencies whose job it was to protect the United States.

In the US embassy, not far from Berlin's Brandenburg Gate, CIA European chief Tyler Drumheller was in direct contact with the German BND intelligence agency demanding to know about Curveball's credibility. The response was damning: 'Very senior officials in the BND expressed their doubts, that there may be problems with this guy.'[35]

One German official offered a startlingly candid assessment, Drumheller recalled. 'He said, "I think the guy is a fabricator. We also think he has psychological problems. We could never validate his reports."'[36]

When Drumheller relayed the warning to his superiors in October 2002, it sparked what he described as 'a series of the most contentious meetings' he'd ever seen in three decades of government work. Although no American had ever interviewed Curveball, analysts with the CIA's Weapons, Intelligence, Nonproliferation, and Arms Control Center believed the informant's technical descriptions were too detailed to be fabrications.

'People were cursing. These guys were absolutely, violently committed to it,' Drumheller said. 'They would say to us, "You're not scientists, you don't understand."'[37]

—

On the other side of the Atlantic, the British had their own version of the OSP, called 'Operation Rockingham', set up to 'cherry-pick' intelligence proving an active Iraqi WMD program and to ignore and quash intelligence which indicated that Saddam's stockpiles had been destroyed or wound down.[38] Their work provided 'evidence' for British Prime Minister Tony Blair's claims that Iraq was a major threat and could launch a WMD in 45 minutes – a now discredited claim in the so-called dodgy dossier.

The United States and Britain were in lock-step. But not everything was running to plan in the Coalition of the Willing, the countries the United Kingdom and United States had recruited to attack Iraq.

In the far distant Southern Hemisphere, in a low-rise utilitarian building housing Australia's senior analysis agency the Office of National Assessments (ONA), one of the senior officers was starting to feel uneasy about the intelligence the British and the Americans were sending to justify the war.

He was concerned about what the Australian people were being told. Andrew Wilkie, a former lieutenant colonel in the Australian Intelligence Corps, was a man of conscience. A one-time member of the Liberal Party of Australia (the country's conservative party) and trained at Canberra's elite Royal Military Academy – Duntroon, he would play a pivotal role exposing corruption at the heart of government – and the corrosive role played by sections of the media as the Iraq War plans gathered momentum.

As an intelligence officer who every day witnessed the raw intelligence data flowing into the ONA – the vast bulk of it directly from the United States – someone like Wilkie, principled and diligent, was the neo-cons' worst nightmare. He could see firsthand the disconnect between what was true and provable and what the public was being told.

While Wilkie was becoming agitated at the deception, thousands of kilometres away at Pine Gap, the joint United States–Australia spy base near Alice Springs, NSA staff were also becoming uneasy about the WMD claims being made by President Bush. David Rosenberg, who worked for the NSA at Pine Gap for 18 years as an electronics intelligence signals analyst, the author of *Inside Pine Gap: The Spy Who Came in From the Desert* (Hardie Grant, Melbourne, 2011), told me that Bush's assertions, beamed in from the United States on the nightly TV news, generated some spirited debates at Pine Gap about the need for war. Pine Gap had positioned its advanced Orion satellites to focus almost entirely on Iraq, probing for even the slightest shred of evidence that Saddam Hussein possessed WMDs or was developing them. Rosenberg said, 'We at Pine Gap had access to a significant number of the intelligence communities' tasking messages looking for proof of Iraq's WMDs, and in the 10 years that I was looking at these messages going backwards and forwards about Iraq's WMDs nothing showed [up] that [Iraq] had them.'[39]

Pine Gap had also been tasked with searching for missiles that could reach the mainland United States – one of the more alarmist claims from Washington. The former official said Pine Gap had discovered 'no missile in Iraq [was] capable of hitting the US'.[40]

This was the kind of intelligence Wilkie was reading as he worked at the ONA. In the battle to win the argument for war, the US, British and Australian governments simply ignored information that didn't fit their agenda. Instead the official message became amplified and relayed by radio shock jocks and newspapers like the *New York Post* and *The Australian*. The White House began turning up the pressure.

In October 2001 President Bush had signed a presidential order marked 'Top Secret' and 'NoFor', meaning no foreign governments were to be told. The National Security Agency, with its network of bases around the world and a secret budget in the multiple billions of dollars, already had the right under US law to spy on any person and any government overseas. But the presidential order rewrote the rule book, granting the NSA the power to spy on US citizens at home – all in the name of national security and all done without having to seek a court warrant. Bush had endowed fresh powers on the most powerful intelligence-gathering apparatus ever built.

The President pointedly had not asked Congress to include provisions for the NSA domestic surveillance program as part of the interestingly named Patriot Act, which gave authorities significantly enhanced powers of surveillance. White House lawyers had argued behind closed doors that such new laws were unnecessary; agencies already had ample power to fight terrorism. But there was another more compelling reason for secrecy about the NSA's new snooping role: seeking Congressional approval was politically risky. The White House feared that civil liberties groups would be bound to fight it – and besides, the lawyers feared they might be in breach of the Constitution.

Spying on Americans on their home soil was almost certainly in breach of the Fourth Amendment, which specifically prohibits random searches of a person's private property. Originally designed to prevent the capricious abuse of government power against its citizens, it has far greater significance today in protecting a more sophisticated form of civil liberties – private electronic communications.

Bush and his legal advisers believed that in the wake of the 9/11 attacks, what might have been seen as crossing the legal line before would be acceptable now in order to prevent another terrorist attack on the United States. A few days after 9/11, a US Justice Department lawyer wrote an internal memorandum that argued the government might use 'electronic surveillance techniques and equipment that are more powerful and sophisticated than those available to law enforcement agencies in order to intercept telephonic communications and observe the movement of persons but without obtaining warrants for such uses'.[41]

The legal advice noted that while such actions could raise constitutional issues, 'the government may be justified in taking measures which in less troubled conditions could be seen as infringements of individual liberties'.[42]

By the beginning of 2003 any chance of a realistic assessment of the intelligence on Iraq had long disappeared. On 4 February 2003, the night before Secretary of State Colin Powell made his now infamous appeal to the United Nations Security Council for backing to invade Iraq, Tyler Drumheller, the CIA's European Director – who had already passed on his concerns to the CIA Director George Tenet – called the deputy head of the CIA to remind him that Curveball was a fabricator. The following day, when he turned on the television in Germany to watch Powell address the Security Council, he realised that Curveball wasn't the only person who couldn't be trusted. Despite Drumheller's warnings, Curveball's confected stories formed the main thrust of Powell's address – from the non-existent WMD sites, to the mobile facilities.

Like many others in the intelligence community, Andrew Wilkie of Australia's ONA was only too aware what was happening. The United States was going to war no matter what. But unlike any of his intelligence colleagues, Wilkie decided not to be part of the deception. On Friday 7 March 2003 Wilkie drove to the home of well-respected Australian television journalist Laurie Oakes. He wrote a message for Oakes to call him, put it in a plain envelope and slipped it into the letterbox. The trouble was Oakes didn't see the envelope until much later. The biggest story about Iraq, and certainly one of the biggest in Oakes' long and illustrious career, sat in a Canberra letterbox waiting to be read.

Once Oakes had received the letter and made contact, Wilkie made his move. Not long after taking part in an Iraq planning meeting at 4.30 pm on 11 March 2003, he walked out of his ONA office – and resigned. That night on the Channel Nine news, on national Australian television, he told Oakes that the arguments used by Colin Powell did not measure up with what the Australian intelligence community had been told by the United States. He was particularly angry that the federal government had repeatedly linked Iraq with terrorism to justify its bellicose threats of war. 'We have not seen any hard intelligence that establishes that Iraq is actively co-operating with al-Qaeda. It is quite clear to me that the Iraq issue is totally unrelated to the war on terror,' Wilkie said.

Wilkie told Oakes that although he would be 'a pariah in the public service and around the government', he hoped that by speaking out the government would rethink its position.

> The reason I have done what I have done – and it's obviously a very dramatic action – is that I am convinced that a war against Iraq would be wrong at this point in time and not a risk worth taking.

Iraq does not pose a security threat to the US, to the UK, to Australia or any other country at this point in time. Their military is very small, their weapons of mass destruction program is fragmented and contained, because of the way it has been managed since the last Gulf War, and there is no hard evidence for any active co-operation between Iraq and al-Qaeda.

A war is the course of action that is most likely to cause Saddam to do the things that we're trying to prevent; to make him feel cornered and force him to act recklessly, including possibly using weapons of mass destruction, possibly against his own people. It could also cause him to engineer a humanitarian disaster or to play the terrorism card and push him closer to terror organizations like al-Qaeda.[43]

Other intelligence officers would join him in condemning the war after the invasion but Wilkie was the only intelligence officer in the world to break ranks and speak out about the folly of the war before it started. Many would regard Wilkie as courageous and heroic, but he would pay dearly for his public-spirited action.

Wilkie had chosen to speak to Oakes in particular because, like the good intelligence officer he was, he had correctly assessed Oakes as an honourable journalist driven by the pursuit of truth. The INC had chosen Judith Miller for completely different reasons: she appeared more concerned with the removal of Saddam than any journalistic principle.

—

The trouble for the Coalition of the Willing – and particularly for *The New York Times* and Judith Miller – started as the first US ground troops moved into Iraq after days of heavy bombing. Search as they did, they could find no WMDs. Given how vehemently the WMD argument had been put by the Bush administration, it might have been reasonable for Miller to now temper her enthusiasm. Instead she switched tack. In a story published in *The New York Times* on 21 April 2003, bearing the by-line 'Judith Miller, with the 101st Airborne Division, south of Baghdad', she wrote that a scientist who claimed to have worked for 'Iraq's chemical weapons program' had told an American military team that Iraq destroyed chemical weapons and biological warfare equipment only days before the war began. Conveying what the military officials had told her, Miller wrote that the scientist 'led Americans to a supply of material that proved to be the building blocks of illegal weapons, which he claimed to have buried as evidence of Iraq's illicit weapons programs'. Just for good measure she threw in the allegation from an unnamed military source that 'Iraq was cooperating with Al Qaeda'. There was no mention of Andrew Wilkie's comprehensive firsthand rebuttal of that spurious link six weeks earlier.

In what must be one of the greatest ironic explanations in journalism, Miller wrote that US officials had asked that details of what chemicals were uncovered be deleted from her story. 'They said they feared that such information could jeopardize the scientist's safety by identifying the part of the weapons program where he worked.' An alternative explanation hung in the air: that they were simply hiding the identity of someone who was gravely mistaken or a straight-out liar.

Miller also wrote that she was not able to interview the scientist but only 'permitted to see him from a distance at the sites where he said that material from the arms program was buried'. In what turned a black propaganda operation into black comedy, the credibility of the WMD fear campaign was reduced to Miller being shown a man in the distance pointing at various areas on the ground. 'Clad in nondescript clothes and a baseball cap,' she wrote, he indicated 'several spots in the sand where he said chemical precursors and other weapons material were buried'.

The next day Miller appeared on US national television, including the Public Broadcasting Service's prestigious

The NewsHour with Jim Lehrer, proclaiming that what had been discovered was 'more than a smoking gun' and was a 'silver bullet in the form of an Iraqi scientist'.[44] She praised the Bush administration for creating a 'political atmosphere where these scientists can come forward'.[45]

The story spread like wildfire: it was trumpeted by conservative talk-show hosts Bill O'Reilly and Rush Limbaugh; sent to regional newspapers via *The New York Times* wire service, it acquired even more dramatic impact. 'Illegal Material Spotted' the *Rocky Mountain News* blared with a subhead that distorted even more: 'Iraqi Scientist Leads U.S. Team to Illicit Weapons Location'. 'Outlawed Material Destroyed by the Iraqis Before the War' was the headline of the *Seattle Post-Intelligencer*.

Out in the Iraqi desert the reporter who more than anyone else had produced unverified and unquestioning journalism championing the war did perhaps finally stumble across the truth: the scientist, like all the other defectors and informants who'd spoken of Iraqi WMDs, simply wanted a green card or a visa – and was prepared to say anything to get it.

As Miller breathlessly reported, the scientist was offering US troops information about WMDs 'and seeking their protection'.[46]

Miller's stories became increasingly bizarre. If she had earlier crossed the line between journalism and public relations for the White House, she outdid herself now. She asserted that the reason the WMDs hadn't been found yet was possibly because 'the Pentagon-led teams, which include specialists from several Pentagon agencies, have been hampered by a lack of resources and by geography'.[47] It looked as though Miller was searching desperately for excuses for the Bush administration's warmongering. But if anyone at *The New York Times* was challenging her about the non-existence of WMDs, no sense of that appeared in the stories she continued to write.

Two days later Miller reported that the US military had moved on from whether or not Iraq had destroyed the WMDs and its 'Mobile Exploitation Team Alpha', the team dedicated to hunting for unconventional weapons in Iraq, was now focused on locating key people who worked on the programs. As she shared with her readers, Miller was told, 'The paradigm has shifted. We've had a conceptual jump in how we think about, and what we look for in Iraq's program. We must look at the infrastructure, not just for the weapons.'[48]

So what had the baseball cap-wearing Iraqi 'scientist' been pointing at on the ground? He seemed to have disappeared. The following day Miller is reporting a fresh lead: 'American-led forces have occupied a vast warehouse complex in Baghdad filled with chemicals where Iraqi scientists are suspected of having tested unconventional agents on dogs within the past year, according to military officers and weapons experts.'[49] That also, of course, turned out to be untrue.

Although Miller was one of hundreds of journalists who had been 'embedded' with military units, the veteran reporter was closer than most to the US military. She was given special clearance by the Pentagon to access information classified 'Secret'. What Miller either didn't understand or didn't attach importance to was that this access compromised her. It even prevented Miller discussing with her *New York Times* editors 'some of the more sensitive information'[50] about Iraq. To whom did Judith give her allegiance, the Pentagon or *The New York Times*? There were many inside the newspaper who raised similar questions about Miller's relationship with the Iraqi National Congress and its leader, Ahmed Chalabi.

She openly boasted of her professional relationship with Chalabi and the 'scoops' he had delivered to her. During a disagreement with *New York Times* Baghdad bureau chief John F. Burns, she wrote, 'I've been covering Chalabi for about 10 years, and have done most of the stories about him for our paper . . . He has provided most of the front page exclusives on WMD to our paper.'[51] With that disclosure, Miller might have been big-noting herself but in doing so she possibly broke another golden journalistic rule: protect your sources if they want anonymity.

A former CIA analyst who had observed Miller's stories and relationships for years explained to James C. Moore on the US website Salon how simple it was to manipulate the correspondent and her newspaper. 'The White House had a perfect deal with Miller,' the ex-CIA officer told Moore. 'Chalabi is providing the Bush people with the information they need to support their political objectives with Iraq, and he is supplying the same material to Judy Miller. Chalabi tips her on something and then she goes to the White House, which has already heard the same thing from Chalabi, and she gets it corroborated by some insider she always describes as a "senior administration official." She also got the Pentagon to confirm things for her, which made sense, since they were working so closely with Chalabi. Too bad Judy didn't spend a little more time talking to those of us in the intelligence community who had information that contradicted almost everything Chalabi said.'[52]

—

When former British Labour minister Clare Short publicly revealed that the United States had been bugging the conversations of the UN Secretary-General, Kofi Annan, the howls of condemnation from the right-wing press were resounding. 'Woman of Mass Destruction', splashed the *Daily Mail*. London's *Daily Telegraph* even proposed prosecuting Short under the Official Secrets Act. *The Sun* wanted Short sacked. 'What the Leftie loudmouth has done is bloody disgraceful,' raged the paper. 'The fact is that all major countries spend a lot of time, money and energy spying on others. It's not necessarily sinister but is more a common sense precaution, particularly when a war is imminent.'[53] The media did not constrain itself with criticising politicians. It turned on itself when it was revealed that UN Secretary-General Kofi Annan wasn't alone in having his phone bugged by US intelligence. I had just revealed in an ABC report the Americans were also listening in to UN weapons inspector Hans Blix during his fruitless search for WMDs and was asked by Rupert Murdoch's London-based Sky TV in an interview, 'Why was that a story?'[54] It was an extraordinary moment. What that brief query revealed was either that the Sky presenter did not recognise the story, in which case why carry out the interview, or alternatively how unquestioning journalists could be when expected to conform to their news organisation's prejudice. The argument that journalism should suspend its questioning of government is a recurring issue in times of national conflict. The War on Terror – a potentially never-ending war – is a propaganda gift for politicians and media proprietors who want to quash debate.

Others in the Murdoch camp lashed out at those who had dared question the rightness of the invasion of Iraq. *The Australian*'s foreign editor, Greg Sheridan, stoked the nuclear fears. 'Hussein could invade Kuwait for a second time on his way to dominating the Persian Gulf and all its strategic oil deposits . . . [H]e could prevent the US coming to Kuwait's rescue by nuclear blackmail.'[55]

When US troops reached Baghdad, *The Australian* published an editorial, 'Coalition of the Whining Got it Wrong', which ended with words that gave perfect meaning to irony: 'Never underestimate the power of ideology and myth – in this case anti-Americanism – to trump reality. But at least we know for sure it is not love, but being a left-wing intellectual, that means never having to say you're sorry.'[56]

The complete absence of WMDs did not temper the belligerent assertions.

Though all of Murdoch's newspapers and media outlets had championed the war, without exception, giving the lie to the oft-repeated assertion by Murdoch that his editors make up their own minds, it was in Australia that some of the most unquestioning support for the war came. Those who stood in the way became victims of a powerful alliance between the Murdoch papers and the federal government.

If the official leak can sometimes be a nuanced affair, there was nothing subtle about what the government did to pay back Andrew Wilkie. Spiteful revenge appeared to consume the government of John Howard and his Foreign Minister Alexander Downer. As a champion of the Iraq invasion, Downer frequently baited his political opponents with the somewhat childish assertion that if they didn't support removing Saddam then they must be supporting a dictator. Downer was particularly angry at Wilkie's unmasking of the truth. It made him look foolish.

In December 2002 Wilkie had written a secret assessment of Iraq for the ONA. Sent to a restricted list of people in the government, all copies were later returned to the ONA under its strict procedures for classified material. Six months later, on 20 June 2003, Downer's office requested a copy of Wilkie's report – the only such request during the six-month period. On 23 June journalist Andrew Bolt – the darling of the right, who would later rise to infamy when found guilty of racial discrimination – published an article quoting extensively from Wilkie's secret document. As noted by *Sydney Morning Herald* journalists Tom Allard and Deborah Snow in their 19 June 2004 article, if indeed Downer's office leaked the report, it would be 'a serious offence under the Crimes Act'. At the end of the article, a spokesman for Mr Downer was quoted as saying, 'We are not interested in Mr Wilkie's hysterical claims. Speak to the AFP [Australian Federal Police].'

In journalistic terms what Bolt wrote was a smear job. In the article, which appeared in the Melbourne *Herald-Sun* on 23 June 2003, Bolt wrote that Wilkie had asserted in the ONA report that Saddam had WMDs and Wilkie was therefore a hypocrite to speak out against the war. A detail he failed to include was that Wilkie said those weapons did not pose a threat to anyone, except possibly the Iraqi people. Bolt's report was a complete distortion of Wilkie's position, but it suited the hawkish agenda of the Murdoch media and a government increasingly embarrassed as the likelihood of discovering WMDs dwindled.

The leaking of a secret document marked AUSTEO – Australian Eyes Only – is no small matter and there was a furore in the press. If convicted the leaker could face years in prison under the Crimes Act. But nobody was ever prosecuted and the Australian Federal Police simply issued a statement saying there was 'no direct admissible evidence to identify any of the recipients of the report as the source of the disclosure to the journalist Andrew Bolt'.[57] It is unknown whether or not the Federal Police interviewed Downer or anyone in his office – such details have never been made public – but any serious investigator would have started by checking on those who benefited from the smear against Wilkie. Logic would suggest that someone in the government, probably in Downer's office, handed over Wilkie's classified report in order to settle a political score. Regardless of how it happened, whoever tried to damage Wilkie's reputation has never been called to account for their actions.

—

Lack of accountability for journalists who had helped create a horrific war based on lies is a major theme of the Iraq invasion. Exactly how many Iraqis lost their lives in the war, stoked in large part by a media which failed to challenge its governments, is difficult to accurately access. What is clear is that it is a shocking figure.

One detailed study, based on a cluster of 2000 randomly selected households in the then 18 Iraqi governorates, found that the death rate rose from 2.89 per thousand in the two years prior to the invasion to 4.55 per thousand between March 2003 and June 2011. The majority of the extra deaths were violent. Thirty-five per cent were killed by Coalition forces; 32 per cent by Iraqi militias. Death by shooting was more common than death by explosion. In total, there were some 500,000 Iraqis who died as a consequence of the invasion by the United States, Britain and Australia.[58]

In the United States, *The New York Times* apologised, albeit grudgingly, for its flawed reporting: 'We have found . . . instances of coverage that was not as rigorous as it should have been . . . In some cases, the information that was controversial then, and seems questionable now, was insufficiently qualified or allowed to stand unchallenged.'[59] *New York Times* executive editor Bill Keller disputed the paper's public position, writing that he 'did not see a prima facie case for recanting or repudi- ating the stories. The brief against the coverage was that it was insufficiently sceptical, but that is an easier claim to make in hindsight than in context.'[60] Perhaps one reason why Keller was so supportive of Miller was the fact that he was dealing with his own journalistic demons which would soon be made public.

Rather than scrutinise Judith Miller's work, Keller chose to base his assessment of her WMD articles on her past perfor- mances. Describing his high-profile correspondent as 'smart, well-sourced, industrious and fearless',[61] Keller dismissed criticisms that her work was fatally flawed.

If Miller's boss had done some investigative reporting of his own, he might have discovered evidence of Miller's political predisposition. The Middle East Forum, an organisation that openly advocated that the US overthrow Saddam, listed Miller as an expert speaker on its website and held a launch party for her book *God Has Ninety-Nine Names* (Touchstone, New York, 1996), which many critics have interpreted as anti-Muslim. She was represented by Benador Associates, a speakers' bureau that specialises in conservative thinkers with Middle East expertise. Asked if she supported Bush politically, Miller responded, 'My views are well known. I understood that these people . . . who hated us so much . . . that if they ever got their hands on WMD, they would use them. Do I have a belief that the WMD exist, and a fear? Yeah, I have real fear for my country.'[62]

Both Miller and Keller portray themselves as patriotic Americans doing the right thing for their country. But while it could be said of Miller than she was wilfully ignorant of the truth about Iraq, the same could not be said of Keller. In 2004, in the months leading up to the US presidential election, *New York Times* reporters James Risen and Eric Lichtblau unearthed the story of George W. Bush's decision to authorise the NSA to spy on the US public. When the White House argued that revealing this might aid terrorists, Keller made a decision not to publish the exposé. Keller says it wasn't just the issue of national security that made him hold back the story. He believed the facts needed closer checking. But the story that eventually appeared in *The New York Times* after Bush had been re-elected was not substantially different from the one that Risen had offered almost a year earlier, and the threat of terrorism hadn't changed. If *The New York Times* had published the NSA story before November 2004, it could have affected the outcome of the election.[63]

For the NSA to have been eavesdropping on billions of phone calls around the world and intercepting data on a massive scale, even from friendly countries, was one thing but the knock-on effects of the NSA's upgraded role would have repercussions the agency could never have imagined. When the truth came out about what the super-secret NSA in connivance with the neo-cons in the White House had been up to, it would set off a chain of events which would break open the real role of the NSA, further damage the credibility of *The New York Times*, set off a firestorm around the world, changing forever our understanding of what it is to have a private life. It would also put journalists on notice that they were now seen as potential enemies of the state – especially those who exposed the questionable activities of executive government and their intelligence agencies.

It would not be the last time that Keller was accused of being too close to the Bush White House . . . and doing its bidding. In years to come the repercussions would be harsh for a newspaper that had built its history on confronting government wrongdoing.

In essence, it was because *The New York Times* had held back Risen's NSA story that NSA whistleblower Edward Snowden did not offer the *Times* the biggest scoop in the history of journalism – thousands of pages of classified data detailing the NSA's eavesdropping program. 'Hiding that story changed history,' Snowden said.[64]

—

If *The New York Times* paid a price for the way it dealt with the NSA story, what happened next pointed to a deeper malaise in the newspaper. Under pressure from falling revenue and failing sales it lost its critical journalistic edge and with it went its high ethical standards. It was an incident that went to the heart of journalism, the protection of sources, and once again Judith Miller was the culprit, the perpetrator of a careless and callous act.

In April 2003, just three blocks away from *The New York Times* bureau in central Washington, Miller interviewed an expert from the Henry L. Stimson Center – a non-partisan think-tank which specialised in nuclear proliferation and WMD issues. The discussion was on background only and the person's name was not to be used. But Miller made up a quote and attributed it to the person, who she then named. Outing a source and quoting them might have been a sackable offence elsewhere, but on 9 April 2003 *The New York Times* simply published an editor's note: 'An article on Saturday about the search by United States forces for chemical, biological and radiation weapons in Iraq included a comment attributed to Amy Smithson, a chemical weapons expert at the [Stimson] Center . . . Ms. Smithson was depicted as suggesting that Bush administration officials might be less certain of finding such weapons now than before the war. She was quoted as saying that "they may be trying to dampen expectations because they are worried they won't find anything significant".'

The New York Times pointed out the comments were paraphrases of a remark Smithson made in an email exchange for 'The Times's background information, on the condition that she would not be quoted by name. Attempts to reach her before publication were unsuccessful. Thus the comments should not have been treated as quotations or attributed to her.' There was no apology.[62]

The fact that Miller had burned a source seemed of little consequence to *The New York Times*. But when it came to more important people in her life, it was a different and intriguing story. Many journalists who detested her reporting style grudgingly admitted they admired her for sticking by the journalistic principle of not compromising a source. When she was summoned to give evidence at a grand jury investigation into how a CIA officer, Valerie Plame, had been 'outed' in the media, Miller stood her ground. She went to prison for nearly three months rather than give evidence.

Miller had not written about Plame but a grand jury prosecutor investigating the leak believed she had been given the name – and they wanted to ask her questions. For Miller the problem was that the person who was actually under investigation was a major source for many of her stories about WMD and Iraq.

When Miller went to prison on 6 July 2005, adamantly refusing to talk to the prosecutor, *The New York Times* ran a syrupy editorial headlined, 'Judith Miller Goes to Jail'. It read, 'This is a proud but awful moment for *The New York Times* and its employees. One of our reporters, Judith Miller, has decided to accept a jail sentence rather than testify before a grand jury about one of her confidential sources. Ms. Miller has taken a path that will be lonely and painful for her and her family and friends. We wish she did not have to choose it, but we are certain she did the right thing.'

The only problem with all this hand-wringing is that it has never been clear why she decided not to give evidence. The source had already lifted the 'confidentiality' agreement, allowing her to testify. Other reporters had also been told by the source they could speak, but Miller steadfastly refused. The source had not contacted her directly, she said, and there was a suggestion that the White House had stood over him, forcing him to lift the 'confidentiality agreement'. Intriguingly all of Miller's stated public fears disappeared when, one year later, the source wrote to her and also telephoned, pleading with her to give evidence. 'This is the rare case where this "source" would be better off if you testified,' he wrote. 'If you can find a way to testify about discussions we had . . . I remain today just as interested as I was over a year ago.'[66]

There has been much speculation about why the source wanted Miller to give evidence. One thing remained unchanged: his story that it was okay to testify. Judith Miller, who had earlier outed a source who wanted to be kept secret, was now keeping secret a source that wanted the details of their relationship made public. Perhaps it was embarrassment, because what we now know is that Scooter Libby, Vice President Dick Cheney's chief of staff, was the source of so much discredited WMD material fed to the press. Perhaps Miller was concerned about what might be revealed about her journalism and that made her resist being questioned before the grand jury.

Under investigation Libby said that he had first heard that Valerie Plame was a CIA officer from a journalist. But the court determined differently: he had been told by Vice President Dick Cheney; it was simple payback for Plame's husband – Joe Wilson – who had played a major role in revealing that Iraq did not have nuclear weapons. And that meant

Scooter Libby lied to the FBI when they were investigating the leak. Libby was jailed for a year.

Judith Miller put herself forward as a journalistic martyr, but after all the deception few believed it was that simple.

In all the lying, cheating and what some have labelled war crimes involving US President George Bush, British Prime Minister Tony Blair and Australian Prime Minister John Howard, the only person convicted was Scooter Libby – a foot soldier in the sordid business of making the facts fit a war.

Judith Miller's problems run deeper than one journalist's failing: the ultimate insider had been captured by her sources. Miller might have become a megaphone for a war looking for a reason. She certainly helped create that reason by failing one of the first principles of journalism – scepticism. But the ultimate responsibility must rest with the editors at *The New York Times* for not sufficiently questioning the government's reasons for a war which led to more than 500,000 people dead and a shattered country. What is so damning for *The New York Times* is that inside the newspaper, Miller was known as a strong supporter for the overthrow of Saddam Hussein's regime and had openly accepted fees to make public speeches to that effect. She was also known as being extremely pro-Israel and participated in conferences partly funded by the Israeli government.

Elucidating how Miller operated can best be explained by the concept of revolving-door journalism. She cultivates senior officials; they give her a story; she reports it uncritically; it appears prominently in the newspaper of record. The senior officials then confirm it or choose not to comment. Everyone is happy, and if it is an exclusive, so much the better.

This systemic problem at the *Times* has also been described as journalistic materialism. Miller has delivered 'exclusives', even if in a prosecutorial, hyperventilated voice. But no one wanted to admit that most of those exclusives were wrong.

In fact even as Miller was preparing to gather up her files and leave *The New York Times* – in its huge 52-storey open-plan glass tower on the south side of 8th Avenue, a hopeful symbol of transparency and openness – she was being nothing of the sort. Miller maintained that the only reason she was leaving was because she had become too much part of the story.

It was like an echo of her time in the desert, when she repeatedly reported that mobile trucks for producing chemical weapons had been discovered. Their existence had formed a key part of Colin Powell's address to the United Nations on 5 February 2003, as he tried to persuade the assembly that Iraq posed a threat to world peace. Even after the story fell apart and the trucks were about to be revealed as nothing more than vehicles used for producing hydrogen for weather balloons or just plain farm machinery, Miller had lashed out at her critics. 'You know what,' she said. 'I was proved fucking right. That's what happened. People who disagreed with me were saying, "There she goes again." But I was proved fucking right.'[67]

As she quit the building for a new job as a commentator on Rupert Murdoch's Fox TV, her journalistic reputation in tatters, there was no contrition, merely unrelenting arrogance.

Yet the powerful vested interests which had fostered Judith Miller's kind of journalism were about to come under a sustained attack. The following year – on the other side of the world, in a Melbourne terraced house – an idea was being born which would blow open the cosy relationships between governments and insiders like Judith Miller. Julian Assange got up from his chair, walked over to a whiteboard and wrote one word on it – WikiLeaks.

CHAPTER 8

WikiLeaks

Julian Assange bounds into the boardroom of the Ecuadorian Embassy and sits down next to an open window. As he talks a deep-green-coloured truck from the local supermarket for the rich and famous, Harrods, passes by, the noise temporarily interrupting our conversation. So near and yet so far. But any thoughts of jumping from the first floor to freedom are tempered by the knowledge that London's Metropolitan police spend £4 million a year keeping Assange's place of refuge under constant surveillance. Police in uniform and plain clothes occupy the buildings and narrow side streets that criss-cross this part of London's Knightsbridge.

It was 19 August 2014. Recently, for the first time in many months, the crowd outside outnumbered the security services. They weren't what are known as 'Assangists' – Assange's fan club – who often turn up in groups to give their support, but the exact opposite: dozens of representative of the media. There had been a rumour that after more than two years inside the embassy, Assange was going to walk out and surrender to the British police. The story had been sparked by a report in *The Sunday Mail* – the weekend sister of one of Britain's popular right-wing tabloids – that Assange was ill. It coincided with a visit by the Ecuadorian Foreign Minister, who decided to hold a press conference at 9 am the following day with Assange to discuss changes in the extradition laws. In the ever-insatiable demand for 'celebrity' news – and Assange is one of the most recognisable people in the world – the journalists besieged the embassy from the early hours. TV cameras formed a line of triffid-like three-legged beasts on the far side of Hans Crescent, each Cyclopic eye trained unblinkingly on the embassy entrance. Though the story of Assange's surrender, like much of what has been written about him wasn't true, and the newsrooms of Britain had merely jumped to conclusions, some of the more credulous were still there the next day. They believed he might walk out the door at any moment.

Inside Assange smiles at the media's antics. It underscores his belief, to repeat that old journalistic shibboleth, that large sections of the media don't let the facts get in the way of a good story.

It's seemingly paradoxical that Assange, garlanded with awards for his journalism, including the prestigious Australian Walkley, the 2011 Sydney Peace Foundation Gold Medal, and *Le Monde* readers' Man of the Year in 2011, threw himself on the mercy of this tiny South American country. The Ecuador government has deservedly received withering criticism for its treatment of journalists. Reporters Without Borders, Human Rights Watch and Amnesty International have all spoken out against Ecuador. The most damning critique came from the Committee to Protect Journalists (CPJ). It said Ecuador President Rafael Correa's administration 'has led Ecuador into an era of widespread repression by systematically filing defamation lawsuits and smearing critics'.[1]

There's no doubt that Correa had been dealing with a full-scale assault by entrenched interests – those who were threatened by his reforming leftist government, but it still sits uneasily with Assange's campaign for transparency and openness. Yet like Edward Snowden's asylum in Russia, another country with a heavily restricted press, it appears there was little choice. Those who exposed the intelligence secrets of the Western Alliance are by necessity forced into the arms of the Opposition.

As Assange told me shortly after he sought sanctuary in the embassy, 'I'm not saying that Ecuador is not without its problems, but the freedom of speech problems in Ecuador are certainly no worse than the ones here in the United Kingdom. The attempts to sort of look at Ecuador through that window and therefore try and suggest that I'm hypocritical in some way, well, look – any other country wants to walk up to the bat to give me asylum, we'll consider it, but at the moment only Ecuador is courageous enough.'

It had been a long journey to the embassy from a terraced house in Melbourne's Carlton. It was here, in 2006, not far from the university where Assange studied, that he conceived the WikiLeaks idea. Assange, the child genius who had excelled at mathematics and computer science, had been brought up by his mother, Christine, an artist and a radical free thinker. There's little doubt her views helped form his; from an early age Assange took an intense interest in philosophy and politics.

Prior to setting up WikiLeaks, Assange established a group of hactivists who called themselves the International Subversives. From hacking into the Los Alamos nuclear weapons research centre in the US during the Cold War, to using Melbourne's Lonsdale Street telephone exchange as a springboard to beef up the power of their computers, the group had but one mission: to discover what was going on in the world and holding governments and powerful institutions accountable for their actions. Eventually one of the institutions, the Australia Federal Police, caught up with Assange. Arrested and charged with illegally entering a computer system, he reluctantly pleaded guilty, but argued that since he had not altered any of the data or stolen anything, he had not committed a crime. The court saw differently, but Assange did have a point. In the following years parliament would change the law. What he had done would no longer be a crime. It seemed that Assange once again was ahead of his time.

The feeling of being wrongly accused would become a further spur to take on the powerful, whom Assange believed acted in secret, not to protect the public but to shield themselves from being held accountable. At the heart of WikiLeaks' philosophy was the belief that without accurate information the public was incapable of making informed decisions.

The foray through the computers at Los Alamos had to some extent been driven by the International Subversives' desire for knowledge. In the late 1980s, with the Cold War in danger of turning hot, perhaps naively Assange had wanted to find out for himself what was going on inside these systems which had the potential to bring the world to an end. He had read a huge amount on the subject of nuclear weapons but the problem with contemporary journalism, as Assange saw it, was the power imbalance between the journalist and reader. The journalist had superior access to information and could use it to manipulate what Assange called the 'ignorant' reader; there was no easy way for the reader to check 'whether they are being lied to by the journalists'.[2] The WikiLeaks model would solve that problem, he believed, by wherever possible releasing 'full primary source material',[3] to give readers and other journalists the opportunity to check the veracity of the reported information. The bedrock of WikiLeaks' 'new journalism', he explained to me, was accountability and verification. He was convinced these ideas would garner support among the public who wanted a game-changer after the debacle of the Iraq War reporting.

As Assange raced to get WikiLeaks online though, the high ideals that had given birth to the loose-knit association of hactivists and activists who supported the organisation came up against the oldest obstacle faced by publishers and reporters alike – the looming deadline.

—

It was late in 2006 and WikiLeaks had one document they thought might make a splash. It had been handed to the

Chinese government and secretly given to WikiLeaks by an informant. If the document, supposedly written by one of the most important leaders in Somalia, Sheik Hassan Dahir Aweys, was authentic, it revealed a secret plan to assassinate the Somali government and impose sharia law on the country. It was a red-hot story about to go cold if they didn't act quickly.

How the story was eventually published offers an insight into how WikiLeaks worked in its very early days. Instead of handing the document over to an outside journalist, Assange and his small team did all the work themselves. Though scornful of much of the mainstream media and its rush to churn out material without proper scrutiny, he took a lesson from the journalists he so often despised: the need to hook the reader. Temporarily setting aside his obsession with accuracy, Assange tapped into his ability to entertain and pulled together some ringing phrases describing Aweys: 'There he is, flame on his chin, holy book in his hand and anti-aircraft cannon between his legs.'4

With the press release about the story ready to roll out, what the WikiLeaks editorial team did next was a textbook example of the power of the collective process; it also demonstrated the fledgling organisation's forensic attention to detail. Using the same technology that revealed how the Iraq War intelligence reports were changed and 'sexed up' by the British government to justify the war, WikiLeaks unpicked the software that had left traces of the pedigree and provenance of the Somalian document: when it was first written, when it was changed, even the name of the person who changed it. They were particularly careful to excise the name of one of the draft document's author in case he was the whistleblower.

WikiLeaks had established a system whereby its sources of information remained anonymous even to Assange. But the major question remained unanswered: was the document a fake? No one in WikiLeaks knew, so Assange decided to deal with both possibilities as a journalistic exercise. Positing both propositions, WikiLeaks would publish a highly readable, analytical story that examined whether the CIA was up to its old tricks, and fabricating documents to sow dissent, or whether radical Islam was about to turn Somalia into another Iran.

Assange was unsure where to publish the document. He favoured *Counterpunch*, a US magazine described by its editors as 'muckraking with a radical attitude'.[5] In the end, the Somalian report stayed with WikiLeaks. Assange decided that WikiLeaks would become a kind of online newspaper and wouldn't rely on the editorial judgement of others to decide what was published. It was a big step to take for an organisation still trying to define its role in the world of journalism. Assange believed that if he couldn't find an outlet he liked or trusted, he would publish himself.

The same kind of attitude impels others to self-publish books and magazines, an enterprise often the preserve of the deluded or the desperate. Julian Assange was neither, but he was firm in the conviction that only he would decide what would be published and what would not. It was a decision that would define Julian Assange and WikiLeaks. The question of control would be a recurring problem in the years ahead. *The New York Times* picked up the Somalia story from the WikiLeaks website and ran a brief mention in its news pages. WikiLeaks had engaged the mass media, but Assange held a very different view of the role of journalism.

WikiLeaks was born of high ideals. Assange was committed to what he called 'scientific journalism', publishing stories and including the original documents, thereby allowing readers to not only make up their own minds about whether the report and its analysis was right or wrong but also permitting them to contribute their own comments online. This concept of the reader as co-contributor in a transparent online environment has its best known expression in Wikipedia, the web-based citizen-collaboration encyclopedia; Wikipedia has no connection whatsoever with Assange. The 'Wiki' in 'WikiLeaks', like Wikipedia, merely denotes that the site is a collaborative effort that can be edited by a community of users.

It might seem normal now to involve readers directly in the editorial practice, but back then enabling readers to add their comments and make alterations to the text of the original story if they could prove that the facts or the analysis were wrong was a revolutionary act. Assange was scornful of closed-door editorial practices and told me that the Somalian document and others of its ilk would face the scrutiny of readers cutting, cutting, cutting apart their pages 'until all is dancing confetti and the truth'. That statement may have sounded like a theatrical flourish, but it underpinned the philosophy of WikiLeaks, an organisation that went beyond its journalistic mandate and aimed to become the most powerful intelligence agency on Earth, an intelligence agency of the people – open sourced, democratic and 'far more principled' than any government intelligence agency. It would have no national or commercial interests at heart; its only interests would be truth and freedom of information.

Unlike the covert activities of national intelligence agencies, Assange wanted WikiLeaks to rely on the power of what he called 'open fact' to inform citizens about the truths of their world. He maintains that there is a direct correlation between closed and unjust organisations and their inability to handle the truth. The more secretive and unjust an organisation is, Assange argues, the more any leaks within it will produce fear and paranoia. Everyone becomes a suspect and whatever trust there is breaks down, destroying the power structure inside the organisation. It's why leaking the truth is such a revolutionary act.

As Assange wrote close to the time of WikiLeaks' launch, 'Only revealed injustice can be answered; for man [sic] to do anything intelligent he has to know what's actually going on.'[6]

WikiLeaks would not 'resonate to the sound of money or guns or the flow of oil', but to the 'grievances of oppressed and exploited people around the world'. It would be 'the outlet for every government official, every bureaucrat, every corporate worker' who became 'privy to embarrassing information which the institution wants to hide but the public needs to know. What conscience cannot contain, and institutional secrecy unjustly conceals', WikiLeaks could 'broadcast to the world'.[7]

—

To protect its whistleblowers WikiLeaks developed an electronic drop box, which allowed material to be deposited anonymously. A world first, the concept has since been copied many times over by the mass media. But not even Assange could have imagined just how big a drop it would collect. Out in the barren Iraq desert at US Forward Operating Base Hammer, a then unknown military analyst named Bradley (later Chelsea) Manning might not have read the fine print of Assange's manifesto in late 2009, but he understood the WikiLeaks message. Manning began uploading gigabytes of documents. Among the first he sent were records which showed that an Icelandic bank's corrupt action had sent the country to the edge of bankruptcy.

The Icelandic capital Reykjavik with its quaint multi-coloured wood-clad homes hosted a high-profile summit between US President Ronald Reagan and Soviet leader Mikhail Gorbachev aimed at reducing nuclear weapons. It would now become the site of the first shots fired in the metaphorical and yet devastating WikiLeaks internet war. The banking cable caused a sensation in Iceland when the story broke on the local television station and was then released online in full when the station belatedly tried to censor the news. It was a perfect example of Assange's scientific journalism. It also garnered WikiLeaks widespread support among the people of Iceland – many of whom had lost their life savings because of the bank's actions. WikiLeaks had become politically untouchable in the country. Consequently it was from Iceland that WikiLeaks made its next release, and it was even more jaw-dropping.

The second batch of material uploaded by Manning consisted of raw vision from two US Apache helicopters providing air support to a ground operation in suburban Baghdad. The US gunships fired on a large group of people, a couple of whom were carrying weapons. Among victims of the air strikes were two Reuters journalists and passers-by who tried to assist the wounded; two children were seriously wounded. Missiles were also fired into an apartment building. Assange recruited local internet activists and Icelandic MP Birgitta Jonsdottir to work on producing what would become known as Collateral Murder – a chilling video created from the leaked footage.

In what must rate as either foolhardiness or an act of derring-do, Assange decided to take the fight to the enemy – Washington, and more precisely the Washington press corps. WikiLeaks hired a room at the National Press Club in the US capital and invited the media to a 5 April 2010 screening of the video. While the video immediately went viral round the world, what viewers saw at home on the evening news did not feature the gunning down of the journalists. Even CNN, known then for being the least compromising of the US networks, censored the more horrific pictures. CNN explained to its viewers that it had done this to protect the families of the two children who had been wounded. As it happened, days before the viewing those same families had already been shown the video by WikiLeaks' Kristinn Hrafnsson, though this went largely unreported. Assange had sent a team into Iraq to find the victims of the families – and to assure them that their story would be told. After the TV broadcasts of the 'censored video', the families could be forgiven for thinking that practically no one knew about what had happened. But that was far from the case.

Not far from the National Press Club at the offices of *The Washington Post* the Collateral Murder video exposed journalistically just how far the once mighty media institution had fallen. On 12 July 2007, when the Collateral Murder killings occurred, David Finkel, a Pulitzer Prize-winning journalist with the newspaper, was embedded with the US troops in Baghdad, gathering material for a book called *The Good Soldiers*. In the book, he gives a vivid description of the killings and includes verbatim much of the dialogue in the gunsight footage. Naturally when Finkel's book came out, *The Washington Post* gave it plenty of coverage; it even ran a story that addressed the events of 12 July 2007. But that's as far as it went. There was no follow-up investigation by *The Washington Post* on the killings of the journalists. Was it self-censorship? Had Finkel become too close to his sources – the military that protected him as he gathered information to tell their stories? Or was it just lazy journalism? Whatever it was, it was a stain on the once beacon of investigative journalism, *The Washington Post*.

Consider this: Collateral Murder was released in 2010 and *The Good Soldiers* was published in September 2009, well before Manning uploaded the footage to the WikiLeaks drop box. *The Washington Post* had possessed first-hand knowledge of the 12 July 2007 killings – what many lawyers believed was a possible war crime – but kept it secret.

Asked if he could say when he saw the 12 July 2007 gunsight footage Finkel responded, 'I can't' and added, 'I don't need advice from WikiLeaks how to do my journalism.'[8] Finkel, the Washington insider, did not like being held to account by outsiders. It was something he and the rest of the mainstream media were going to have to get used to.

A US military investigation found no necessity for further inquiry into the events of that day in July 2007. As for David

Finkel, he maintained he had done nothing wrong. And his book sold well, lauded by his fellow journalists. It was yet another example of why WikiLeaks would have such a huge impact on the mainstream media. As outsiders Assange and his cohorts were simply doing what many journalists had stopped doing: investigating and holding powerful organisations to account.

———

In May 2010, on assignment for ABC TV's *Foreign Correspondent* program, I conducted the first of what would be many interviews with Assange. As my colleagues and I tried to encourage him to walk down the street in Melbourne, close to where we had talked, so we could film him for the program, Assange became agitated. Asked to play the piano (he is quite a good pianist) he declined, saying that the keyboard sequence might be used by others for a story saying he was a hacker. By the time he finally agreed to allow us to film him in the street it appeared that either Assange was delusional or had delusions of grandeur. Unbeknown to us Assange had good reason to be paranoid. He had teased us during the interview that he had a big story. Not only would it turn out to be substantial, it would challenge and change journalism.

On that autumn night in Melbourne Julian Assange had tucked away in his backpack more than half a million classified US cables. And he knew the United States was now hunting for them, and almost certainly hunting for him. He'd just learnt Manning had been arrested.

A few days later and 17,000 kilometres away, British investigative journalist Nick Davies read the news of Manning's arrest. Whereas most of his peers simply wanted to interview the somewhat elusive Assange, Davies formulated bigger plans. He sought access to the documents Manning had supposedly leaked.

Even as a favourite of *The Guardian*, Davies, the consummate freelancer, was subject to few, if any, editorial dictates. From his position as an outsider he was the first to spot the significance of Manning's arrest, yet again demonstrating sharper journalistic wits than most. It was this dedication to a story he believed in – his capacity to stay focused when the natural journalistic inclination was to move on – which made him the scourge of News Corp.

It took Davies weeks to finally make contact with Assange. When he did they arranged to meet in Belgium. Assange, suspecting the net of the US government was closing on him, travelled via Hong Kong – a better transit point than Singapore, with its close links to the west and western intelligence agencies. Edward Snowden had chosen Hong Kong for similar reasons, though Davies' trip was far simpler: he caught the Eurostar from St Pancras.

In a Brussels café Davies persuaded Assange to share the files. With that commitment he triggered a domino effect, initially involving *The Guardian*, *Der Spiegel* and *The New York Times*.

Bill Keller, editor of *The New York Times*, took a phone call from *The Guardian* in the early summer of 2010 and was offered exactly the tonic he needed. From its often unquestioning coverage of the White House in the lead-up to the Iraq War, to reporters found guilty of plagiarism and fabrication, the newspaper had been suffering an identity crisis. That was the context in which two senior editors resigned in 2003. As executive editor, Keller had recently come under fire for holding back the story about how the NSA was spying domestically. Now Alan Rusbridger was offering *The New York Times* the perfect antidote: a strong revelatory story with the promise of more to come.

The next domino to move was Washington journalist Eric Schmitt. Although he had just returned from a reporting stint in Pakistan and had barely had time to settle back into his office, *The New York Times* bureau chief, Dean Banquet, told him he'd have to be on a plane quickly for a special project in London. Schmitt had covered the military for many years, and Keller saw him as a journalist with 'excellent judgment and an unflappable demeanor'.[9] Schmitt's plane touched down in London late on Saturday 26 June 2010. The next day he met with *The Guardian*'s highly experienced investigations editor, David Leigh, and they began discussing how to tackle what was emerging as one of the biggest ever stories about the Afghan War. The so-called Afghan War Diary disclosed how Coalition forces had killed hundreds of civilians. What they probably didn't prepare for was a clash of cultures. Julian Assange had little time for prevailing orthodoxies.

When Assange arrived at *The Guardian* offices to meet Leigh and Schmitt he was a day late. Eric Schmitt, a snappy dresser with an eye for detail, described his first encounter with Assange in an email to his boss Bill Keller: 'He's tall – probably 6-foot-2 or 6-3 – and lanky, with pale skin, grey eyes and a shock of white hair that seizes your attention.'[10] Schmitt observed too that although Assange was alert he was also 'dishevelled, like a bag lady walking in off the street, wearing a dingy, light-coloured sport coat and cargo pants, dirty white shirt, beat-up sneakers and filthy white socks that collapsed around his ankles. He smelled as if he hadn't bathed in days.'[11] Schmitt's immediate dislike for Assange did not augur well for the relationship.

Though Assange had worked with mainstream media before, this was his first venture into the big time. The audience reach and impact provided by collaborating simultaneously with three of the most influential publications in the world was huge for WikiLeaks, but then so too were the stakes. Assange would have to relinquish some control over the WikiLeaks information – the demand of the media stakeholders for exclusivity went with the territory.

Although journalists are traditionally competitive, not known for showing much largesse towards one another, because of the detail that needed to be understood, self-interest forced them to collaborate and share resources, research and analysis. But when Assange later spoke of working on what became known as the Afghan War Diary 'in a collaborative basement' and identified the three outlets – *The Guardian*, *The New York Times* and *Der Spiegel* – as WikiLeaks' 'media partners',[12] Eric Schmitt, in particular, was infuriated by that description of the relationship. If Keller had sent him to London because he was unflappable, he'd certainly shaken off that moniker.

'I've seen Julian Assange in the last couple of days kind of flouncing around talking about this collaboration like the four of us were working all this together,' said Schmitt. 'But we were not in any kind of partnership or collaboration with him. This was a source relationship. He's making it sound like this was some sort of journalistic enterprise between WikiLeaks, *The New York Times*, *The Guardian*, and *Der Spiegel*, and that's not what it was.'[13]

That *The New York Times* should take umbrage at Assange's description wasn't purely arrogance. The deep hostility Schmitt expressed was born of a division between the journalists, who dealt with what was, a man who dreamed of what might be, and the new environment which was forcing the mainstream media to recognise that the old order was changing. The cosy relationships with governments were under threat.

Schmitt was used to dealing with the Pentagon. *The New York Times*, as do most other US media outlets, regularly discloses details of its national security stories to the government – before they're published. Assange was definitely a different kind of journalist. Schmitt complained that Assange would arrive and 'you'd ask him questions about certain types of data, and certain questions – some of them he answered and some of them he didn't'.[14] Schmitt appeared to be almost goading him. '"Where did you get this material?" He wouldn't answer that.'[15] Schmitt admits that he even pressed Assange to divulge the name of the source of the material. 'Did it come from Bradley Manning?' he asked.[16]

Schmitt's questioning exposed a growing rift in the relationship between WikiLeaks and *The New York Times*. Sources are only discussed when journalists have complete trust in one another. There was now only a fragile relationship at best between Assange and the *Times*. Yet despite their disagreements they had successfully worked together to produce The Afghan War Diary and there were plenty more stories to come.

—

Across the Atlantic, the people at the Pentagon – Schmitt's home ground as a reporter – had been tracking WikiLeaks' work since Collateral Murder was broadcast the previous month, April 2010.

Now as the Pentagon sharpened its focus on WikiLeaks, the issue of whether or not Assange was a journalist became more than a matter of reporter pride or professional jealousy. While it's generally accepted by the US courts that journalists are covered by the freedom of speech provision enshrined in the Constitution, this does not apply to their sources. There are serious consequences for individuals when information they provide to the media is deemed to have put at risk the security of the United States.

When US Defense Secretary Robert Gates said WikiLeaks had endangered lives, it raised the alarm at *The New York Times*. WikiLeaks might well be able to argue it was protected by the First Amendment for the material it published online, but even that argument could be swept away if it could be proved that WikiLeaks had deliberately conspired to publish information damaging to the security of the United States.

'The battlefield consequences of the release of these documents are potentially severe and dangerous for our troops, our allies and Afghan partners, and may well damage our relationships and reputation in that key part of the world,' Gates said. 'Intelligence sources and methods, as well as military tactics, techniques and procedures, will become known to our adversaries.'[17]

The Chairman of the Joint Chiefs of Staff, Admiral Mike Mullen, portrayed WikiLeaks as recklessly endangering people in order to satisfy its 'need to make a point . . . Mr. Assange can say whatever he likes about the greater good he thinks he and his source are doing, but the truth is they might already have on their hands the blood of some young soldier or that of an Afghan family,' Admiral Mullen said.[18]

Ominously for Assange, Gates said he had called in the FBI to assist army investigators. This was no longer a military matter: by calling in the FBI Gates had broadened the investigation to the wider instruments of the US government.

The New York Times reported on 28 July 2010 in an article titled 'US Military Scrutinizes Leaks for Risks to Afghans' that according to unnamed sources in the Justice Department, lawyers 'are exploring whether Mr Assange and WikiLeaks could be charged with inducing or conspiring in violation of the Espionage Act, a 1917 law that prohibits the unauthorised disclosure of national security information'. The author of that report, Eric Schmitt, and his editor, Bill Keller, were anything but impartial observers.

By arguing that Assange was only a source, *The New York Times* could distance itself from Assange, stressing that it just took his information and had nothing else to do with him. If he was a journalist, the relationship was much closer and *The New York Times* ran the risk of being implicated in any connection Assange had with Manning.

The New York Times had cut Assange adrift. And to make life even more difficult for the scruffy interloper, Keller implied Assange had a political agenda – potentially stripping him of any free speech arguments he may be able to run as a journalist. Keller reported that Assange was 'openly contemptuous of the American government' and self-servingly added, 'I would hesitate to describe what WikiLeaks does as journalism'.[19]

Keller had gone out of his way to strip Assange of even his journalistic protection. Keller might not have liked Assange, and Schmitt almost certainly took a dislike to him. But as an act of self-serving bastardry it took some beating. Whatever Assange was to *The New York Times*, others considered him a journalist.

Not everyone saw things Keller's way. After interviewing Assange for six hours, the US *60 Minutes* reporter Steve Kroft said, 'I definitely consider him to be a publisher, which is the important thing. I mean, if he is not a publisher, then people at *60 Minutes* online or *The New York Times* online aren't publishers either. I mean, he operates an internet site and he publishes material.'[20]

The fact remained that Assange had dared to confront the close relationship between journalists and the US government and for that he would be made to pay. There were some people for whom the media–government nexus was not news, and Department of Justice lawyer Jack Godsmith was one of them. He hailed as 'an under-appreciated phenomenon: the patriotism of the American Press.'[21]

In this environment, when Assange joined in with the finger pointing, his focus was security. Nick Davies had been early to recognise the possibility of government eavesdropping as a problem. In 2010 he had raised concerns that his phone calls might be being intercepted by the NSA and the British equivalent, the Government Communications Headquarters (GCHQ). To Davies it stood to reason that they would be trying to figure out what WikiLeaks would leak next. Few of his fellow journalists picked up on this, and Julian Assange had been appalled by the gung-ho attitude towards security he had observed.

When I interviewed him, Assange saved a particular level of vitriol for *The Guardian* and *The New York Times*. The editors of both newspapers, he said, often spoke on open, unencrypted phones and communicated by Gmail. With its main servers in California, Gmail was instantly accessible by the United States government. He pointed out what he saw as the sickness in journalism: 'The Guardian doesn't care that the government knows, The New York Times doesn't care if the government knows. The New York Times just doesn't want The Washington Post to know and The Guardian just doesn't want the Telegraph to know, or The Times. The Times, they don't care, because they're not trying to get a maximum reform impact.'[22] He said stories were all about increasing the 'journalistic prestige' of individual journalists, to get 'awards and so on'. So much for the optimism and collegiality of the early days at The Guardian offices.

—

If the Afghan War Diary caused a furore, its follow-up, the Iraq War Logs, published in October 2010 was truly sensational journalism. This amazing cache of documents gave a near real-time view of how the United States was fighting the war. The stories, page after page of headlines, rolled around the world, revealing Washington's deception when it had denied keeping a body count of civilian deaths. The documents proved they did precisely that. And the number of Iraqis killed, with more than 100,000 in the first few months of the war. Most horrific: the story of a young boy shot in the back by the CIA as he ran away on their order to stop. He was deaf and had not heard the command.

For all the tensions and despite his criticism of the mainstream media, WikiLeaks had now clocked up two major hits with its media partners. The third and biggest was yet to come. In November 2010, working predominantly with The Guardian in London, Assange was preparing the staggered release of Cablegate, a monumental 251,287 classified communications between US embassies around the world and the

State Department. But then a hint of serious trouble crept into the equation: something was afoot at *The New York Times*.

A few weeks earlier the newspaper had published an exceedingly unflattering report about Julian Assange and his WikiLeaks organisation. Written by Pulitzer Prize-winning reporter John F. Burns, it had the look and feel of a tabloid-style hit. Burns told *The New York Times* readers it wasn't just governments that were denouncing Assange. His former supporters were also abandoning him for what they saw as 'erratic and imperious behavior and a nearly delusional grandeur'. They were also becoming more aware that 'the digital secrets he reveals can have a price in flesh and blood'.[23] *The New York Times* article was attacking someone who had just provided the newspaper with its best and biggest stories in years.

Assange described it as a smear against him. It was certainly true that many in the organisation were angry at what they saw as Assange's high-handed and autocratic behaviour. Like many editors-in-chief, Assange was not without ego. Rebuffing a critic who questioned WikiLeaks' failure to redact names from the Afghan War Diary, Assange wrote, 'I am the heart and soul of this organisation, its founder, philosopher, spokesperson, original coder, organiser, financier and all the rest. If you have a problem with me, piss off.'[24]

Assange was in high dander when he called Daniel Ellsberg at his home nestled in the hills overlooking the San Francisco Bay. Assange had asked Ellsberg to join WikiLeaks in the early days, but it came to nothing. Still Assange maintained the relationship. Assange told him he was going to cut out *The New York Times* from all future document releases. 'I said I thought he was absolutely right in being mad at John Burns and John Burns was inexcusable, but that I wouldn't make an enemy of *The New York Times*. He should try to work with them,' recalls Ellsberg. 'He just said, "Fuck them." He was mad at them and I know how he feels.'[25]

Next Assange made it plain to *The Guardian* that Wiki-Leaks would no longer be dealing with *The New York Times*. There would be no more shared stories.

The truth is *The New York Times* simply didn't need Assange anymore. And as it prepared to negotiate the difficult political terrain that came with publishing Cablegate, a major exposé of US foreign policy, it sought to distance itself from him. An article like Burns's would certainly help the newspaper deal with the avalanche of criticism that was bound to pour in after publication of the leaks.

Behind Assange's back *The New York Times* and *The Guardian* were in cahoots. They had set a publication date of 5 November 2010 for the first tranche of Cablegate material: 251,287 mainly classified State Department communications. The two newspapers were going to ambush WikiLeaks, only telling them of the plans to publish two days before they went to press. That the planned publication date was a Friday and *Der Spiegel* is published on a Monday meant that *Der Spiegel* was also on the outer. Like inner workings of the diplomatic alliance they were about to expose in Cablegate, *The Guardian* and *The New York Times* historically had a 'special relationship'. The Germans were being hung out to dry, like Assange.

Somehow Assange got wind of the plans to publish early. Immediately he threatened to put all the Cablegate material online. As far as his relationship with *The New York Times* was concerned, it was the last straw. Not only would there be no Cablegate exclusive, it was the end of the relationship. There would be no further dealings. For Assange it wasn't just the profile by Burns that turned him against *The Times*. He had been angry that while *Der Spiegel* ran a front-page story on Task Force 373 – the US assassination squad in Afghanistan – it received far less prominent treatment in the US newspaper, prompting the question of who was protecting who.

Over at the *Der Spiegel* offices near the Brandenberg Gate in central Berlin, the Germans looked on in horror. They demanded a meeting to sort out the differences. The magazine's editors were worried that the entire cooperative venture would fall apart and, as they put it, partners would turn into competitors. They scheduled a meeting at *The Guardian*'s offices for 6 pm on 1 November 2010.

Assange, wearing the attire he saves for special occasions, a blue suit and white shirt, was his customary half an hour late. But it was the team he brought with him that caused gasps – his lawyers Mark Stephens and Jennifer Robinson. *Guardian* editor Alan Rusbridger quickly called for the newspaper's legal representative. *Der Spiegel* didn't bring any lawyers but did have a full complement: Holger Stark, Marcel Rosenbach and the magazine's editor-in-chief, George Mascolo. It would have been the collaboration basement on steroids but for one group that was missing. As *Der Spiegel* reported, *The New York Times* did not attend.[26]

Assange walked in, sat down and got straight to the point. Does *The New York Times* have a copy of the Cablegate material? He repeated the question and, according to the *Der Spiegel* team, 'it sliced through the room', which by now was very still. 'And if so, where did it get a copy?' he asked.[27] According to Assange, his next question to the group was, 'Did you give it to them in violation of our agreement?' Assange maintains that Rusbridger scanned the room and refused to answer the question. Assange said, 'What's the point in making an agreement if people will dishonour it?'[28]

The story seemed to be that *The Guardian* had acquired another copy of the WikiLeaks cables and shared some of the information on it with *The New York Times*; if it was another copy, it wasn't governed by the same agreement as the one Assange had given to the newspaper.

The Guardian says that it got the copy of the cables from freelance journalist Heather Brooke, who was apparently given it by one of the Icelandic WikiLeaks supporters, Smari McCarthy, in early October. But according to WikiLeaks,

McCarthy said he wiped that copy from Brooke's computer. So when did *The Guardian* get its own copy? Possibly it came much later – according to one source familiar with the case, as late as 1 November, just four days before the planned publication date. The clear implication is that *The Guardian* produced the Cablegate stories using the WikiLeaks files they were supposedly holding in trust.

When Assange described it as theft, someone in the room pointed out it was all stolen material. Rusbridger put the obvious into words: the leaker had been leaked.

Whatever it was, it was a dishonourable way to deal with an individual who had delivered such history-making information to a newspaper. If Assange had ever had stars in his eyes about how so-called quality journalism worked, they should have disappeared by now.

What *The Guardian* did by bringing Brooke onto the Cablegate team on the quiet was underhand, but it was also what you might expect when the stakes are so high, even from a seemingly highly principled organisation like *The Guardian*. Rusbridger, who had written a foreword for one of her books, bound Brooke exclusively to the newspaper for the duration of Cablegate, preventing her from selling her copy to any of the newspaper's competitors. WikiLeaks was playing in the cut-throat world of journalism and it was losing control.

More than three hours later, as everyone decamped downstairs for some food at the Rotunda Restaurant, Assange was by all accounts still fuming about *The New York Times*. What Assange wanted was no more negative stories about him and even a front-page correction. His lawyer Mark Stephens, who was playing the role of mediator, came up with what seemed like the best solution to end the stand-off: *The New York Times* should publish an opinion piece by WikiLeaks.

Rusbridger got up from the table and phoned Bill Keller in New York. When he came back the news wasn't encouraging. Assange would be treated like any other complainant – he could write a letter to the newspaper. The only guarantee Keller could give was that *The New York Times* wasn't planning any sleazy hit pieces. Assange was not happy. He even gave an indication that he was going to pull out of the deal with both newspapers.

At this delicate moment Rusbridger deftly summed the situation up from Assange's point of view: Assange could cut out *The New York Times* and go with *The Washington Post* – the *Times'* historical rival – instead, but since he had already lost control of the material, that would result in chaos. The best decision was to go with the existing arrangements. Persuasively he argued, in what must have been one of the most syrupy diplomatic pitches on record, 'We're good at working together; we like each other. We've communicated well with your lot. It's gone well. Why on earth throw it away?'[29] As they parted that night, a somewhat placated Assange shook David Leigh's hand.

Though Assange felt he'd been duped by Leigh, *The Guardian*'s most senior investigative reporter, he retained a grudging respect for him. 'He is genuinely interested in the journalism that he does – that is a big tick from me, that he actually does care about his story. But that's all he fucking cares about. So it doesn't matter who he fucks to do it – it's immoral, duplicitous behaviour to get as much exclusivity, as possible.'[30]

From the outset Assange had been trying to control who had the right to use the material and how it was released. Wishing to extend WikiLeaks' reach far into the Spanish- and French-speaking areas of the world, which until then had been largely neglected, he had added to his media collaborators Spain's *El Pais*. With France's *Le Monde* he had also negotiated a side deal for access to the Iraq material. The inclusion of *Le Monde* was designed to cause problems for the dictatorships in former French colonies in Northern Africa. The cataclysmic events that would eventually unfold there, the Arab Spring, would surprise Assange as much as the rest of

the world. This took to five the number of big media organisations with exclusive access to the cables; every other media
outlet in the world would be forced to play catch-up. It was
hypocritical for Assange to argue about exclusivity.

The next day Rusbridger sent an offer for a settlement.
The Guardian, *The New York Times* and *Der Spiegel* were still
involved and now Assange also wanted to formally include
Le Monde and *El Pais*.

As Assange mulled over the offer he examined the alterna-
tives. In our interview he explained, 'We still had some levers
in this meeting; we could have gone, "Right, we can give
the whole lot to Al Jazeera; we can give it all to AP [the wire
service Associated Press] and News Corp, fuck 'em."' But with
'too many cables coming out too quickly' this would 'saturate
the market', reducing the number of investigative stories,
which in turn would limit the level of what Assange called
'political reform'.[31]

He must have been growing tired of his treatment by
The Guardian, a newspaper he admired and believed was socially
progressive. One witness to a discussion between Assange
and senior *Guardian* staff, including among them its editor and
deputy editor, said they were conceited and dismissive towards
the WikiLeaks founder. This witness was surprised by their
treatment of Assange, describing it as 'shitting on the goose
that had laid the golden egg' for their newspaper.[32]

But there was something else Assange had to consider as
he ruminated over how to respond to Rusbridger's offer: what
would be the implications of rejecting it? 'We would have
The Guardian and *The New York Times* campaigning against
us and those are two big cannons . . . at the very moment the
Pentagon and the White House were campaigning against us.'[33]

After a little horse-trading – Assange secured a caveat that
if there was a critical attack on WikiLeaks, he would be free to
release everything immediately – he finally accepted the offer.
He didn't need any more enemies than he already had. He was

increasingly worried about being picked up off the street in
London by US intelligence and whisked away to the United
States.

—

For Assange the fear of ending up in the United States would
become an understandable obsession. While in Sweden in
August 2010 searching for a safe haven for WikiLeaks servers,
what happened after he had two brief affairs – with Anna
Ardin and then with Sofia Wilen – entangled him in a legal
process which reeked of an intelligence operation.

Daniel Ellsberg, who has an intimate understanding of the
US intelligence community, told me it was likely that while
he was in Sweden Assange had every reason to fear that US
intelligence 'would pick up his credit card or his iPhone'.[34]
He believed that US intelligence 'would know about the two
women and he might actually have been physically followed;
they were on to him all this time'.[35]

Whatever the arguments about the allegations against
Assange, and they are thin at best, what is intriguing is the
role of the Swedish prosecuting authority, which is trying
to extradite him to Sweden. The first investigation by
the Sweden Chief Prosecutor, Eva Finne, decided there was
no case of rape for Assange to answer and at most only a
minor misdemeanour. Only when Ardin's lawyer, Claes
Borgström, went shopping for a second opinion, was the case
re-opened.

The timing is intriguing. In August 2010 the US administration urged several allies to file criminal charges against
Assange for the publication of the Afghan War Diary. A discussion around pressuring other nations to prosecute Assange
appears in an NSA file that the agency calls its 'Manhunting
Timeline'. It details on a country-by-country basis the efforts
of the United States and its allies to locate, prosecute, capture
and/or kill various individuals, among them alleged terrorists,

drug traffickers and Palestinian leaders.[36] As far as the United States was concerned Assange was swimming with the sharks. He was officially fair game.

On the day he left Sweden, 27 September 2010, with the permission of Marianne Ny, a senior prosecutor in Gothenburg, Ny issued a warrant for his arrest. The timing suggests something more than coincidence. Though Assange was allowed to board a plane for a long-standing appointment in Germany, mysteriously, three of his laptops, which for some reason Assange had booked as hold luggage, disappeared between the check-in desk and the conveyor belt which would have carried them to the aircraft handling area. It was almost as if Assange had been allowed to leave Sweden so the intelligence agencies could follow their quarry.

It was known that the US administration had begun actively seeking the cooperation of its allies to consider bringing charges against Assange after the July 2010 publication of the Afghan War Diary. Then the Iraq War Logs were published in October 2010, further damaging the reputation of the United States. Washington's most pressing question was: what's next? And if possible, how to prevent it.

As Assange returned to London rumours were spreading that the next WikiLeaks exposé would be even bigger than the Afghan and Iraq War logs, which had received saturation coverage around the world.

Ten days before publication of Cablegate, Marianne Ny told the international police organisation Interpol to issue a Red Alert for the arrest of Assange. For the days leading up to publication Assange lay low, finally agreeing to hand himself in at Kentish Town police station after the last stories had been printed.

If he'd been worried about his security before, now the threat ramped up. Cablegate, published on 28 November 2010, unleashed a torrent of rancid comment from the United States: Fox TV called for his execution. The Vice President,

Joe Biden, called Assange a high-tech terrorist. At the same time the Swedish government repeatedly refused to promise that Assange would not be onwardly extradited to the United States, where he faced a strong chance of prosecution. Eric Holder, US attorney general, told a press conference in Washington that Assange may not necessarily be charged with espionage. There were any number of different areas of US law that WikiLeaks may have broken, and not just the Espionage Act. He said the Espionage Act 'is certainly something that might play a role, but there are other statutes, other tools at our disposal'.[37] And former Republican presidential hopeful Mike Huckabee said bluntly, 'They've just put American lives at risk.'[38]

Even Assange's own government abandoned him. Appearing on ABC TV's *Insiders*, Foreign Minister Bob Carr skirted an all-important question about whether or not he considered Assange to be a journalist. In his obsfucating answer Carr undercut Assange's primary defence, should he be extradited to the United States. Carr went further: 'There's an amorality about what's been at work here,' he said of WikiLeaks' revelations.[39] Instead of seeking assurances that Assange would be treated fairly if he were ever to be extradited to the United States, Freedom of Information (FOI) documents show the Australian Embassy in Washington was more heavily focused on the possible political fallout back home in Canberra. According to the heavily censored FOI cables, what the Australian Embassy sought was not a promise that Assange will not be prosecuted by the US but a 'heads up' when any possible action against Assange or WikiLeaks may be about to take place. Carr maintained the Australian government was giving Assange full consular support, though its true focus appeared to be elsewhere.

For Assange, the final proof that he had been abandoned by his own government came when Attorney-General Nicola Roxon wrote to his lawyers shortly before he sought asylum

saying, 'Australia would not expect to be a party to any extradition discussions that may take place between the United
States and the United Kingdom or the United States and
Sweden, as extradition is a matter of bilateral law enforcement
co-operation.'[40] The letter added that 'should Mr Assange be
convicted of any offence in the United States and a sentence
of imprisonment imposed, he may apply for an international
prisoner transfer to Australia'.[41]

It was a letter that appeared to have been written by
someone who was bearing in mind not so much the security
of an Australian citizen as the interests of the United States.
If Assange felt he was being singled out for special treatment,
there was plenty of evidence to suggest he was right. A few
hours after the UK Supreme Court rejected his final appeal
against extradition to Sweden, in June 2012, there was a late-
night knock at the door: Assange was living under house arrest
and had been complying with strict terms. Assange answered
and was confronted by an officer from the security company
that monitors the anklet he wears: a condition of bail, it tracks
his every movement. Since it was 10.30 at night, Assange asked
them to return in the morning. 'I had been detained for 561
days by that stage so [it] seems a very unusual coincidence that
they would turn up at 10.30 pm the same night that our appeal
to the Supreme Court case was rejected,' Assange told me.[42]

The next day the security company filed a breach order
against Assange citing the interaction that had occurred
at 10.30 pm, meaning he ran the risk that his bail would be
revoked. When Assange contacted the security contractor,
they promised to send information to his lawyers proving the
visit had been for routine maintenance, but 'that information
never appeared,' he told me in our interview in 2012. The
'routine maintenance' at 10.30 at night, appeared to be either
a strange last-minute decision to visit Assange, or a deliberate
provocation. Assange became concerned about the unfolding
sequence of events.

The evening of the following day – within 48 hours of the 10.30 pm 'maintenance visit' – the contractors reappeared and fitted a new electronic manacle to his leg. Earlier in the day the Crown Prosecution Service, acting on behalf of the Swedish Prosecuting Authority, had made a formal request to the British government that the 14 days that Assange had to apply to the European Court of Human Rights be reduced to zero. Assange had been considering taking his case there to argue that his treatment was unfair.

With his legal options fast disappearing, three days later, on 19 June 2012, Assange formally sought asylum in the Ecuadorian Embassy. The manoeuvre bought him time to further challenge the validity of the European arrest warrant: Assange was convinced that since no charges had been laid against him, the warrant was not legal. The fact that the Supreme Court had ruled the warrant valid altered nothing in his mind.

Assange wasn't alone in thinking something was amiss with the European Arrest Warrant system, hurriedly cobbled together after 9/11 to allow suspected terrorists to be extradited swiftly between European countries. Two years after he took up residence at the Ecuadorian Embassy in London, the British parliament changed the law, ruling that, in future, anyone who hadn't already been charged with an extraditable offence could not be extradited from the United Kingdom. Since Assange had not been charged, only accused, the law fitted his circumstances perfectly. The problem for Assange was the law was not retrospective. Assange remained confined inside the embassy.

—

There is a relatively simple solution – a way to end the saga of Knightsbridge – and that it has not been not pursued by the Swedish government adds fuel to the belief that the pursuit of Assange is for political not legal reasons. The Swedish law clearly states that prosecutors can interview suspects either over the phone or visit them directly. The Swedish government will not give Assange a promise that he won't be extradited to the United States – and by mid-2015 it hadn't visited him either.

The British Foreign Office went so far as to reiterate that Marianne Ny was welcome to come to London to interview Assange. The Ecuadorians expressed support, stating that the Ecuadorian government 'reaffirms its offer of judicial cooperation to the Kingdom of Sweden, to reach a prompt solution to the case'.[43] Ecuador made it clear that it kept open 'its invitation to judicial officers to visit the London Embassy so that Julian Assange can be interviewed or via videoconference'.[44]

The embassy pointedly added that 'Both possibilities are explicitly referred to in the current procedural legislation in Sweden and the European Union.[45]

Even the British Foreign Minister, Hugo Swire, told the House of Commons, 'If she [Marianne Ny] wished to travel here to question Mr Assange in the embassy in London, we would do absolutely everything to facilitate that. Indeed, we would actively welcome it.'[46]

In Sweden legal opinion at a senior level swung against the prosecutor's decision not to travel to London to interview Assange, with Anne Ramberg, head of the Bar Association, labeling the current impasse a 'circus'.[47] She said that 'many voices' in Sweden took a similar view to the British Foreign Office. 'It is time for this longstanding matter to be brought to a fair and proportionate end.'[48]

As the third anniversary of being holed up at the Ecuador embassy approached Assange could draw strength from the fact that his WikiLeaks organisation was still scoring revelatory goals. The publication by WikiLeaks of thousands of internal emails from Sony Pictures in April 2015, showed how the company dealt with the hacking attack on one of its films, *The Interview*. It also shone a new light on the way large corporations circumvent the laws on political donations. Even from the embassy Assange constantly reminded the world how he shook up journalism and continued to challenge the most powerful country on earth.

It was a marker of how significant an ongoing threat the intelligence communities believed Assange to be that *Washington Post* columnist Walter Pincus, who spied on students for the CIA in the 1950s, suggested Assange had masterminded the actions of NSA whistleblower Edward Snowden. Assange's response is a big smile as he leans back in his chair. Yes, he did get a request for help from Snowden for assistance when he was in Hong Kong, but that's all. Even then, says Assange, he was hardly a willing participant. And certainly had nothing to do with Snowden's earlier plans.

At the time in September 2013 with the newly formed WikiLeaks Party contesting the Australian federal election, Assange was otherwise engaged. The election campaign was fast turning into a shambles, as the WikiLeaks Party presented as a disorganised and divided group. The fall-out lasted for months afterwards. Assange says his thoughts about helping Snowden were, 'Why do we have to do this?'[49] He finally decided to help only because, 'If Snowden had been captured and put in prison, it would have been two big ones in a row.' Chelsea Manning was already facing 35 years and Assange believed Snowden would probably get a similar sentence. Assange feared if Snowden was captured it would send a 'very negative signal' that would discourage other sources from coming forward: 'We wanted to set a counter example that you don't have to go to prison.' It was possible to 'keep your freedom and keep your voice'.[50]

In the end Assange sent one of his most trusted lieutenants, Sarah Harrison, to help Snowden. Harrison, in her mid-30s, had been with WikiLeaks since she was given what must be one of the most illuminating internships in journalism – to help Assange work with *The Guardian* on the release of the Afghan War Diary.

As she travelled to London's Heathrow airport to catch a plane to meet up with Snowden, Harrison knew she was heading into difficult territory, but could have had no idea that she was about to become involved in revelations which would dwarf even WikiLeaks' most sensational exposés.

CHAPTER 9
iSpy

When the plane turned to land at Chek Lap Kok airport on 20 May 2014, the view of Hong Kong from the air offered a glimpse of the contradictions of what lay below: the towering skyscrapers – a symbol of extraordinary private wealth – masking widespread grinding poverty. The tiny nation-state of seven million, independent from the United Kingdom since 1997, is now tied to one of the world's biggest nation-states, China. Under an agreement known as 'One Country, Two Systems', Bejing's centrally controlled economy exists in marked contrast to Hong Kong's raging capitalism. Understandably Hong Kong has a strangely schizophrenic air, operating under laws bequeathed to it by a long-gone regime, now enveloped by the latest rising empire.

As she made her way from the airport, Sarah Harrison understood why Edward Snowden had asked WikiLeaks for help, though she may have cursed the never-ending Hong Kong traffic. By comparison the London she'd left behind 12 hours earlier seemed calm and ordered. Harrison had travelled extensively and knew Hong Kong well, having been there several times. Her detailed knowledge would come in useful in the next few hours as, along with Edward Snowden's lawyers, she tried to figure out the best course of action for her new fugitive friend.

Assange too was familiar with Hong Kong. He had used it as a transit point a few years earlier while carrying his massive cache of documents from Australia to share them with Nick Davies in Brussels. For anyone on the run from western intelligence Hong Kong was a natural safe haven, outside the reach and influence of the United States and its western allies and independent enough from China for that country's security apparatus to be kept at arm's length, at least for a time. Probably most important of all for any spy on the run from US authorities, Hong Kong's laws prohibit extradition to the United States for any 'political offences' – a category that would almost certainly cover Snowden's activities.

When Snowden boarded his flight from Hawaii on 20 May 2013, he was mindful that he had to act quickly. The story he had told his employers, Booz Allen Hamilton, had a limited shelf life. It was true he had been diagnosed as suffering from epilepsy and needed extended sick leave but as soon as the first stories based on the information he was about to leak appeared, the US security net would start to close in on him. Snowden was aware that his employers would be taking a keen interest in his whereabouts, not so much because they cared about his health, but they did care about what he knew and what he might say. What they did not suspect was that Snowden had carefully assessed how to deceive the NSA in the same way it had deceived the American public.

The high-speed free internet at his accommodation wasn't its only attraction. The sprawling Kowloon Park on the other side of busy Nathan Road from The Mira provided a perfect alternative for meetings if he ran into problems in the hotel. As a former CIA officer Snowden understood that maintaining an aura of normality was key to reaching his objective. Accordingly he paid with his own credit card and used his own name. And Snowden had scheduled some meetings that were beyond critical: he was about to begin his critical collaboration with filmmaker Laura Poitras and journalist Glenn Greenwald. As leaps of faith go, it didn't get much bigger than that. The next few days would be crucial. One false step and the carefully laid out plans to reveal the biggest leak of classified documents in history would implode, wrecking everything Snowden hoped to achieve.

Yet for all his planning, Snowden was in a bind. He wanted to go public and reveal his identity, but there was danger if he moved too fast and the certainty of an horrific end if he moved too slowly. It would be a tricky balancing act. Snowden saw himself as a whistleblower, warning of the perils of mass surveillance, a patriot upholding the Constitution of the United States. He was worried he might be denigrated as a traitor and a spy before he could get his story out.

—

If Snowden had ever assumed that working with Greenwald and Poitras would be the easy part of his endeavour, he had already discovered that was not the case. For all the assertions that freelancers – in the main, media outsiders – are free agents unencumbered with the problems of mass media journalism, there are many issues which remain the same, particularly as a reporter gains notoriety. Greenwald had carved out a reputation as a fearless human rights campaigner with his online reporting, repeatedly challenging the US government over what we now know was an organised CIA torture program. If troublesome phone calls from members of the public who have discovered life on other planets go with the job for most reporters, then pity the online reporter: the internet nurtures those who give the impression they live on those planets. Self-protective measures are necessary. In a decision akin to that of the Decca Records executive who turned down The Beatles because 'guitar groups were "on the way out"',[1] Glenn Greenwald ignored Edward Snowden when he first contacted him. Though Snowden contacted Greenwald several more times, asking him to install encryption on his computer so they could communicate securely, still Greenwald took no action.

Snowden thought, 'Here I am ready to risk my liberty, perhaps even my life, to hand this guy thousands of Top Secret documents from the nation's most secretive agency – a leak that will produce dozens if not hundreds of huge journalistic scoops. And he can't even be bothered to install an encryption program.'[2]

For Greenwald it was a salutary experience: 'That's how close I came to blowing off one of the largest and most consequential national security leaks in US history.'[3]

Not the type to give up easily, Snowden turned to someone who knew Greenwald, Laura Poitras. She was adept at encryption because her work filming in war zones often entailed keeping her communications secret. Before she contacted Greenwald, with Snowden's agreement she shared some of the NSA documents with *Washington Post* reporter Barton Gellman, who had done highly acclaimed work exposing the duplicitous role of Vice President Dick Cheney in the lead-up to the Iraq War. When Greenwald eventually committed to the project – to Snowden's enormous relief – and found out about the overture made to the *Post*, he took Poitras to task – somewhat harsh of him, given that she had been the one who saved him from losing the story. Greenwald was aghast to see any involvement whatsoever for the *Post*. He regarded the newspaper as the worst example of conservative, Establishment journalism, keen to keep onside with the US government rather than expose its wrongdoings and inclined to pump out a few stories based on a leak, pick up the journalistic awards and then move on.

But Poitras remained convinced that engaging the conservative press in Washington would serve a useful purpose – blunting the inevitable attacks that would come with Snowden's disclosures.

Despite their individual reservations about dealing with the mass media, both Greenwald and Poitras could see that for Snowden's stories to have maximum impact, and to meet even

some of the enormous production costs involved for them
personally, they would have to engage with at least one newspaper from the mass media. They chose Britain's *Guardian*.
It was by far the most adventurous mainstream media outlet
in the English-speaking world, Greenwald's work had been
regularly published there and the paper had a track record of
fearless exposure.

Unavoidably there was a price to pay for dealing with *The
Guardian*: the newspaper insisted on sending one of its best
and most experienced journalists, Ewen MacAskill, to Hong
Kong as a minder. Greenwald viewed MacAskill, who had
been *The Guardian*'s defence and intelligence correspondent
and was now the newspaper's Washington bureau chief, as a
'company man'.4 MacAskill's presence would be a constant
reminder that Greenwald and Poitras were no longer totally
free agents.

Arrangements were made; flights booked. Four strong-
minded individuals were about to meet in Hong Kong under
tense circumstances.

—

First of all Poitras and Greenwald had to persuade MacAskill
that Snowden was an authentic whistleblower, not merely
a fantasist with a story to tell and nothing to back it up but
fabricated files. They arranged a meeting in Snowden's hotel
room where MacAskill would be able to challenge Snowden to
produce evidence he wasn't a fake. MacAskill wasted no time,
pressing Snowden on details of his past, probing for any sign
that his story didn't add up. The robust questioning went on
for over an hour. Snowden's answers were consistent and crisp.
As final proof Snowden showed MacAskill his old CIA identi-
fication pass and a now disused diplomatic passport. MacAskill
was convinced.

With MacAskill onside – a major achievement – Greenwald and Poitras now had to persuade the formidable Alan

Rusbridger. A tricky conversation ensued, using encrypted communications. He was the quintessential newspaperman, having come up through the ranks as a reporter, and had edited *The Guardian* since 1995. Most newspapers regularly changed editors but *The Guardian* allowed an almost academic tenure for its editorial leader. It encouraged a culture of independence and allowed the editor to make big and often controversial decisions without worrying that his job was on the line.

Rusbridger had long championed investigation and disclosure and thoroughly understood the cost, both emotional and financial, of taking on high-risk enterprises. Over the years fighting court cases had cost the newspaper millions of pounds. He was at the helm in 2009 through an absolute monster of a saga involving the oil trading company Trafigura and strong allegations about toxic waste it had dumped in Africa. When *The Guardian* reported it had received a demand to delete the online historical records of its reporting of the toxic oil disaster, Carter-Ruck, the defamation law firm engaged by Trafigura, said the reports were gravely defamatory and untrue. They maintained it was wrong to report that Trafigura's waste may have caused deaths and severe injury, even though, as *The Guardian* reported, Trafigura had agreed to pay compensation to its 30,000 West African victims. Within days Carter-Ruck obtained a super-injunction. It prevented *The Guardian* from revealing any information covered by the injunction, including the fact that there was an injunction at all. Even a question in the House of Commons about Carter-Ruck and Trafigura ran into problems: Carter-Ruck's injunction made the reporting of the parliamentary question a breach of the injunction.

The Trafigura case was a symptom of the culture of secrecy that pervades the British legal system. In relation to Snowden's story, *The Guardian* might be protected under the First Amendment for publishing in the United States but it could well fall foul of the Official Secrets Act, particularly if

British interests were exposed by Snowden – as would be the case in any disclosure involving the NSA.

Rusbridger would have been haunted too by the case of a whistleblower from GCHQ who leaked a devastating memo from the NSA before the 2003 invasion of Iraq. The memo showed that the United States was trying to manipulate the UN Security Council vote. After the story was published in *The Observer*, sister paper to *The Guardian*, Katharine Gun, working as a Chinese-language linguist at GCHQ, was arrested and charged under the Official Secrets Act. Rusbridger had observed the lengths the government was prepared to go to prosecute her; finally it decided not to proceed. It's believed what saved Gun from prosecution was the fear that any court hearing would have to produce evidence which may expose the fact the government knew the argument for going to war was based on a fraud.

Rusbridger was being encouraged by Greenwald and Poitras, and even *The Guardian*'s own reporter, to publish as soon as possible. With the history of battle weighing heavily on Rusbridger, he was not inclined to rush his decision.

If *The Guardian* was showing a sense of nervousness, *The Washington Post*'s Barton Gellman was agitating for a bigger role. Gellman was in possession of at least one major scoop handed to him by Poitras and was agitating to join Greenwald and Poitras in Hong Kong; he wanted direct access to Snowden so he could produce more stories for the *Post*.

Meanwhile senior management at the *Post* seemed to be searching for reasons not to publish. In a scene more reminiscent of Inspector Clouseau than James Bond, its lawyers argued that there was a chance Chinese intelligence might overhear Gellman discussing the Snowden documents, an act which could be seen as 'recklessly passing secrets to the Chinese'.[5] The lawyers warned such an action could 'result in criminal liability'[6] for both the *Post* and Gellman under the Espionage Act. It is a measure of the level of fear in the United

States that this advice was taken seriously by the editors of *The Washington Post*. Clearly intimidated, they prevented Barton Gellman from boarding the plane to Hong Kong. The kind of overly cautious journalism that had lost Snowden for *The New York Times* was now being repeated at the once iconic bastion of investigative reporting, *The Washington Post*. The Obama administration was piling on the pressure, and the *Post* had caved in.[7]

—

While Rusbridger continued to cogitate, over at *The Guardian*'s New York office, situated at the cheaper end of Broadway, the newspaper's US editor, Janine Gibson, was already fielding the possibility of threats from the FBI. Greenwald and Gibson were in constant contact; Gibson told him, 'They're saying the FBI could come in and shut down our office and take our files.'[8]

Things were mightily complex at this point. *The Guardian*'s lawyers thought there might be the risk of criminal exposure, not only for Snowden but – given the Obama administration's pursuit of journalists – for both Greenwald and Poitras as well. The Obama White House had brought charges against more journalists under the Espionage Act than all the other US governments in history. On top of that, news had just broken, on 24 May, that the US Justice Department might charge James Rosen, head of the Fox News Washington bureau, accusing him of being a co-conspirator in a leak from the State Department. The wording of the court filings was that Rosen may have 'aided and abetted'[9] the source's decision to leak by working closely with him to disclose classified information. If ever there was a time to stand and fight, it was now.

The Justice Department (DOJ) was pushing back hard against the First Amendment's freedom of speech provisions. There's a legal argument that journalists aren't protected by it if they take part in the process of leaking themselves – and

if the DOJ could prove that Rosen had aided and abetted the
source, his First Amendment protection could be in shreds.

With the possible Rosen charge fresh in his mind, as the
hours ticked by Greenwald became increasingly agitated. He
reminded Gibson that *The Washington Post* might publish its
story first. Neither of them had any inkling of just how likely
that would be, but the possibility did put added pressure on
The Guardian to move ahead. Even so Gibson said she could
not guarantee when the story would run. She told Greenwald
The Guardian would be meeting its lawyers the next day,
5 June.

Greenwald was itching to release one particular story –
about a secret court order allowing the NSA to collect
information on all telephone calls handled by the US communications giant Verizon. He asked when *The Guardian* planned
to run the exposé but couldn't get a straight answer.

The 12-hour time difference between New York and Hong
Kong could not have made life more difficult for *The Guardian*
and Greenwald. At 3 pm on 5 June, Janine Gibson sat down for
a meeting with lawyers in New York while Greenwald sat up
at 3 am wide awake in Hong Kong, waiting for the outcome.
It was already 6 June in Hong Kong. Two hours later Greenwald received the answer he didn't want to hear: Gibson told
him there were considerable legal questions to be addressed.
And even after that, the US government would have to be
informed so that it could make its case for non-publication.
According to the lawyers consulted by *The Guardian* editors,
publishing classified information could be deemed a crime by
the US government if it could be proved that the publication,
either recklessly or with intent, damaged US national security.
By alerting the intelligence agencies to sensitive information
it was going to publish, a newspaper felt it could protect itself
from the threat of prosecution.

Fearing *The Guardian* would give in to the US government's sustained legal threats, Greenwald began making plans

to walk away and find another publisher. He made calls to both Salon, his old publishing home for years, and *The Nation* to see if they would be happy to run the NSA stories right away. As Greenwald tells it, they offered all the support he needed, with lawyers ready to vet the articles immediately.

As concerning for Greenwald as having to switch publishers was that *The Washington Post* was working on the Snowden material they'd been given by Poitras. The possibility that they would publish first was a nightmare scenario for him, that he'd be scooped on his story by one of the mainstream institutions he loathed most.

After phoning his partner, David Miranda, at their home in Brazil and talking things over, Greenwald hit upon a fresh strategy. It involved both of them and Poitras opted in. If *The Guardian* dithered much longer they would set up their own website to upload the Snowden stories. With that fallback plan in place, Greenwald's spirits lifted tremendously. From the start he believed that 'the documents presented an opportunity to shine a light not only on secret NSA spying but on the corrupting dynamics of Establishment journalism'.[10]

To Greenwald, 'breaking one of the most important stories in years through a new and independent model was very important'.[11]

An energised Greenwald rang friends, lawyers and other journalists, asking for advice. They all told him it was too risky without the backing of an existing media structure. David Miranda was adamant however that 'only releasing the stories at a newly created website could capture the intrepid spirit driving the reporting we wanted to do'.[12]

He was also convinced it would inspire people everywhere. As for Snowden, his exact words were, 'Risky, but bold. I like it.'[13]

Resolution was imminent: either *The Guardian* was going to publish or Greenwald was on the verge of making one of the greatest mistakes of his career. Self-publishing is scorned

by journalists for good reason – either no one else is interested, which is a major obstacle for sales, or the risks outweigh
the benefits.

On Wednesday 6 June Greenwald woke early. It was still
evening the previous day in New York. He would have to wait
a full 12 hours before Janine Gibson arrived at work for what
he hoped would be the final day of negotiations. As soon as
Greenwald saw Gibson come online he asked her what the
plan was. 'Are we going to publish today?'

'I hope so,' she replied.

The Guardian intended to contact the NSA to ask for its
response. Gibson told Greenwald she would 'know our
publishing schedule only once we heard back from them'.[14]

Greenwald could not understand why *The Guardian* was
holding off publishing. 'For a story this clean and straightforward who cares what they think we should and shouldn't
publish?'[15]

Aside from his contempt for the process – the government
should not be a collaborative editorial partner with newspapers in deciding what gets published – he says he 'knew
there was no plausible national security argument against
our specific Verizon report, which involved a simple court
order showing the systemic collection of Americans' telephone records'.[16]

The idea that terrorists would benefit from exposing the
order was laughable: any terrorists capable of tying their own
shoelaces already knew that the government was trying to
monitor their telephone communications. Greenwald believed
the people who would learn something from the article weren't
the terrorists but the American people.

At around noon New York time Janine Gibson phoned the
NSA and the White House to tell them the newspaper was
planning to publish some top-secret material. The request
was met with complete silence. 'Right now, they don't think
they need to call us back,' Gibson wrote. 'They're going to

learn quickly that they need to return my calls.'[17] Gibson had asked to hear from the NSA 'by the end of the day'.[18]

A little over three hours later the phone rang. It wasn't just the NSA on the other end; there were officials from numerous agencies, including the NSA, the DOJ and the White House. What started off as an attempt to patronise Gibson by telling her she didn't understand the meaning or context of the Verizon court order ended with threats. They wanted to meet her 'some time next week'[19] to explain the sensitivity of the issues involved. Greenwald's understanding was that these callers became 'belligerent even bullying when she said she wanted to publish that day and would do so unless she heard very specific and concrete reasons not to do so'.[20]

Gibson had deftly turned the tables. The White House and the intelligence services of the United States had been mercilessly trying to undermine the use of the First Amendment, which gave journalists protection, by appealing to patriotism as a reason not to publish. They had drawn journalists into the Establishment, using the argument that the country was at war in order to silence its critics. Finally a lone whistleblower, an individual who recognised the corruption in the system, had played a different game with the powerful US media institutions, initially bypassing them, and was about to get his story told. The cosy relationships that successive administrations in Washington had so carefully tended were worthless.

The internet – a system which US intelligence agencies had exploited to gather unimaginable amounts of data on billions of people – was now being used against them. It must have been wounding that *The Guardian*, a newspaper from another country, would reinvigorate the meaning of the First Amendment, freedom of speech – using the internet to publish its stories across the United States and across the world.

The US administration was stunned. 'No normal journalistic outlet would publish this quickly without first meeting with us,' they said.[21]

Greenwald remembered thinking, 'They're probably right, that's the point. The rules in place allow the government to control and neuter the news gathering process and eliminate the adversarial relationship between press and government . . . These stories were going to be released by a different set of rules, ones that would define an independent rather than subservient press corps.'[22]

Gibson now found herself being squeezed by the US administration on one side, accusing her of acting recklessly, and Greenwald on the other, suggesting she might be too weak to face up to the challenge.

Extraordinarily, in the middle of one of the most difficult decisions *The Guardian* would make in its over 150-year history, the editor-in-chief, Alan Rusbridger, got on a plane for New York. This action puzzled some onlookers. It's possible he thought it was better for him to handle the issues firsthand, except that he had a more than capable US editor in Janine Gibson. What was stranger still, the flight to New York would put Rusbridger out of contact for seven and a half hours, during the crucial time when a decision would have to be made about whether or not to publish that day. By being unavailable Rusbridger had inadvertently – or not – placed some distance between himself and the publication of the Snowden material.

It turns out that though Rusbridger had a demonstrable zeal for investigative journalism, he also had a barely concealed contempt for Greenwald. Explaining the perils and potential of the internet age to a Sydney audience in December 2014, Rusbridger commented that Greenwald was an activist and said he would find it hard to get a job as a journalist in the United States. It was meant as a criticism but it could well have been taken as a compliment. It was an echo of the dismissive way Assange had been treated by *The Guardian* when he came to them with the WikiLeaks exposé, which until Snowden emerged, had been the world's biggest scoop. Whatever was going on, flying across the Atlantic at that moment placed firmly in Gibson's hands the final decision on whether to publish.

Greenwald decided to put on the pressure. He was weighing up whether or not to bail from *The Guardian* and go it alone, publishing the material online. David Miranda told him, 'You have no choice. If they're scared to publish, this isn't the place for you. You can't operate by fear or you won't achieve anything. That's the lesson Snowden just showed you.'[23]

After several drafts Greenwald sent Gibson a message: 'I understand that you have your concerns and have to do what you feel is right. I'm going to go ahead now and do what needs to be done too. I'm sorry it didn't work out.'[24]

Greenwald hit 'Send'.

Fifteen seconds later the phone rang in Greenwald's hotel room. It was Janine Gibson. She accused him of being unfair.

For Gibson the tension levels were reaching new peaks. She was totally out on her own, making decisions which her immediate boss, Rusbridger – who was still out of touch – might not like. Undoubtedly the entire Washington establishment, including possibly a large section of the media, might hate Gibson's decisions, firstly because they didn't get the story but also because they might take the White House argument that the story aided terrorists.

Gibson told Greenwald *The Guardian* was 'going to publish today. It will be no later than 5.30 pm.'[25]

At 5.40 pm Gibson sent Greenwald an instant message: 'It's live.'[26]

—

The story was page one on *The Guardian* website. Headlined 'NSA Collecting Phone Records of Millions of Verizon Customers Daily,' it carried that much overused but in this case deserved tag, 'Exclusive'.

> The National Security Agency is currently collecting the tele-
> phone records of millions of US customers of Verizon, one of
> America's largest telecom providers, under a top secret court
> order issued in April.
>
> The order, a copy of which has been obtained by *The
> Guardian*, requires Verizon on an 'ongoing daily basis' to give
> the NSA information on all telephone calls in its systems, both
> within the US and between the US and other countries.
>
> The document shows for the first time that under the Obama
> administration the communication records of millions of US
> citizens are being collected indiscriminately and in bulk –
> regardless of whether they are suspected of any wrongdoing.[27]

The impact was immediate and profound. The piece led the
evening news bulletins right across the United States. Greenwald appeared on CNN, MSNBC, NBC, the *Today* show
and *Good Morning America*. He found the experience of being
interviewed by what he called 'sympathetic reporters' unusually pleasant. When he criticised the administration in his
other stories he'd been pilloried, but not this time. Even *The
New York Times* supported the story with an editorial which
said, 'Mr Obama is proving the truism that the executive
branch will use any power it is given and very likely abuse it.'[28]

Snowden, sitting in his room at The Mira Hong Kong, had
watched it all. He might have sacrificed his future, even his
life, but his fear that no one would care had proved unfounded,
in a spectacular way. 'Everyone seemed to get it,' he told
Greenwald.[29]

Snowden had every reason to feel vindicated: the course of
action he had so carefully laid out had worked.

Twenty-four hours later – having allowed *The Guardian*
to take the first of the criticism from the White House –
Gellman's *Washington Post* story appeared online. It revealed
the existence of a top-secret program codenamed PRISM,
which internal NSA documents showed gave the agency direct

access to data held by Google, Facebook, Apple and other US internet giants.

There were howls from tech companies denying that they had set up backdoor access to their systems for the US government but there was no doubt that most had been compliant in giving the NSA what it wanted. According to *The New York Times*, 'Twitter declined to make it easier for the government',[30] but others developed 'technical methods to more efficiently and securely share the personal data of foreign users in response to lawful government requests'.[31]

One of the biggest corporations, Microsoft, had allegedly been only too willing to help the NSA. Though it portrayed itself as defending its customers' right to privacy – telling its 250 million worldwide users of SkyDrive, 'We believe it's important that you have control over who can and cannot access your personal data in the cloud'[32] – an NSA document detailed that Microsoft spent many months working to provide the government with easier access to that data.[33] Snowden's documents also revealed Microsoft's double-dealing on Skype. It promised its customers that 'Skype is committed to respecting your privacy and the confidentiality of your personal data, traffic and communications content',[34] while at the same time the NSA was 'celebrating the agency's steadily improving access to communications of Skype users'.[35]

The internet companies claimed that they only hand over information that they are legally required to do by special warrant, but there is no such requirement when intercepting foreign phone calls and even US citizens can have their calls bugged in the United States when the call originates from overseas. Along with the rest of the world their calls are scooped up by satellites encircling the Earth – intercepting digital transmissions and telephone calls from everywhere on the planet. The satellites, coupled with telephone cable intercepts, are controlled by a series of bases run by the NSA and the Five-Eyes countries. Australia is home to one of the largest and most important NSA bases in the world outside the United States – Pine Gap, near Alice Springs.

In recent years Australia's role has expanded dramatically. Pine Gap is not only used as a front-line weapons facility directing drones to carry out extrajudicial killings on behalf of the United States, it's taken over some of the communication intercept duties of the giant NSA base on the other side of the world at Menwith Hill near Harrogate in Yorkshire. Menwith Hill and Pine Gap now have interchangeable roles – putting the large industrial nations of Italy, Germany and France in Pine Gap's arc of coverage, which stretches from Western Europe to eastern China and Russia. Under a classified agreement, Pine Gap is not supposed to be used to intercept any phone calls originating in the United States or Australia. But as George W. Bush showed, the NSA surveillance system can just as easily be secretly turned against the host population. Under the terms of a classified agreement with the USA, the Australian attorney-general has the power to order Pine Gap to intercept Australian phone calls. It's a relatively easy operation. In the past phone calls made from Australia – which are supposedly protected – have been 'accidentally'[36] intercepted by Pine Gap as it scanned the spectrum looking for targeted numbers.

From space-based interception to tapping into fibre-optic cables and even planting bugs in internet switching equipment produced by US manufacturers, much of the NSA's capabilities were already known. What Snowden exposed was the sophistication and size of the NSA's data collection. As one of NSA's documents states baldly, its mission was to collect it all.

The amount of data now being stored has sent the NSA and its allies into a building frenzy to house it all. At Bluffdale, Utah, the NSA has been building a massive new facility: four 25,000-square-foot halls filled with servers and more than 900,000 square feet for technical support and administration. Since, according to author James Bamford, the acclaimed expert on the NSA, 'a terabyte of data can now be stored on a flash drive the size of a man's pinky'[37] the amount of information the NSA expects to hold there is inestimable.

And Bluffdale is not the sole facility. On the outskirts of Canberra, the Australian Signals Directorate has already built huge barn-like structures at HMAS Harman, a central hub for intelligence operations. Costing AU\$163.5 million, the project went 80 per cent over its original budget and five years behind schedule. Now it's in operation and, like the other NSA storage facilities around the world, it's accessible by a search system known as XKeyscore. Not only does XKeyscore allow the huge databases to be searched in milliseconds from a laptop anywhere in the world, it permits the user to monitor anyone's email and online searches in real time.

Snowden's motivation for speaking out is centred on the NSA's questionable gathering of information on US citizens, which he cites as a breach of the Fourth Amendment, which prohibits random searches. But there is another reason Snowden felt compelled to leak and it has less to do with what is happening in the United States and more to do with the extensive storage dumps of data being gathered by not only the United States but by the other members of the Five-Eyes intelligence-sharing countries: Canada, the United Kingdom, New Zealand and Australia.

The issue of mass storage became a central question of the New Zealand election in 2013. Prime Minister John Key insisted that New Zealanders had nothing to worry about and even said he would resign if the country's Government Communications Security Bureau was found to be including New Zealand citizens in its a mass surveillance program. After Snowden's documents revealed precisely such a plan Key shifted ground, arguing that mass surveillance did not rule out the mass collection of New Zealand data. Like the rest of the Five-Eyes countries New Zealand was apparently gathering it all and storing data for possible later use.

'It's getting to the point,' said Snowden, 'you don't have to have done anything wrong. You simply have to eventually fall under suspicion from somebody, even by a wrong call, and then they could use this system to go back in time and scrutinize every decision you've ever made, every friend you've ever discussed something with, and attack you on that basis, to sort of derive suspicion from an innocent life and paint anyone in the context of a wrongdoer.'[38]

—

As the stories emerged in *The Guardian* and *The Washington Post* and were picked up by other media organisations around the world, Snowden felt under increasing pressure. When an online security device at his home in Hawaii was triggered by an NSA official who had visited, Snowden decided the time had come for him to reveal his identity before the NSA did. Laura Poitras set up a camera in Snowden's hotel room and, after a quick question and answer session, cut together a film for *The Guardian* website. 'My name is Ed Snowden. I am 29 years old. I worked for Booz Allen Hamilton as an infrastructure analyst for NSA in Hawaii,' Snowden told the world.[39]

Five days after the first story appeared Snowden was finally out in the open. For someone who had just angered the most secret intelligence agency in the most powerful country in the world Snowden demonstrated the calm demeanour of a person resigned to his fate. Framed showing a reflection of the back of Snowden's head, the camera created a feeling of transparency, but also paid homage to the wilderness of mirrors in which he was now living his life.

On 14 June, three days after the video the US Department of Justice secretly indicted Snowden under the Espionage Act, charging him with theft of government property and two counts of unauthorised communication of national defence information and 'willful communication of classified communications intelligence information to an unauthorized person'.[40] Each of the three charges carries a maximum prison term of ten years.

Seven days passed before the news became public. Ironically it was *The Washington Post*, Glenn Greenwald's bête noire that broke the story of the secret indictment and alerted Snowden that he was officially a wanted man. Forty-eight hours later Snowden and Sarah Harrison were making their way through Hong Kong airport bound for Moscow.

In London Julian Assange had been working behind the scenes to facilitate Snowden's safe passage out of Hong Kong. 'The current status of Mr. Snowden and Harrison is that both are healthy and safe and they are in contact with their legal teams,' Assange told reporters from inside the Ecuadorian embassy. 'Edward Snowden left Hong Kong on June 23 bound for Ecuador via a safe pass through Russia and other states.'[41]

If the United States had stumbled as it tried to stop Snowden leaving Hong Kong by making an error in the extradition request, Assange had stumbled too. He had correctly anticipated that the US State Department would cancel Snowden's passport once it discovered he was on the flight to Moscow. But Assange didn't anticipate Ecuador reneging on a special travel document issued by the London consul at his urging to deal with that eventuality. It seems that the Ecuadorians were upset that it appeared Assange was running the country's asylum policy. Ecuador's President, Rafael Correa, cancelled Snowden's safe conduct pass – marooning him in Moscow.

Assange realised he'd overreached – and apologised. It was a smart move, for Ecuador held the key to Assange's asylum status too.

Unable to enter Russia because his US passport had been cancelled, Snowden remained in legal limbo at Moscow's Sheremetyevo airport international transit area. The plane that had been booked to take Snowden to Cuba, en route to Ecuador, took off without him.

Across Europe governments were falling into line as Washington exerted diplomatic pressure; France, Spain and Italy closed their airspace to any aircraft carrying Snowden. Such was the level of panic, any aircraft flying out of Moscow was suspect, particularly those heading for South America.

Given that flagging Snowden's intention to seek asylum in Ecuador had provided prior warning to the United States, Bolivian President Evo Morales might have chosen his words more carefully when he told Russian television he was prepared to consider the idea of giving Snowden asylum. When Morales' plane made a refuelling stop in Austria, an overexcited US diplomat demanded the plane be searched in case Snowden had sneaked aboard. Bad intelligence seemed to be a fitting fullstop to the first stage of Snowden's remarkable odyssey.

It had been just three months since Snowden had decided he had had enough of the NSA's deception. It turns out that a couple of events had triggered the start of his journey. Snowden said he left the CIA because he felt morally compromised CIA operatives were attempting to recruit a Swiss banker to obtain secret banking information. Snowden said they purposely got the banker drunk and encouraged him to drive home in his car. When the banker was arrested for drunk driving, the undercover CIA agent befriended him and offered to help. Snowden said the ruse worked and a bond was formed that led to successful recruitment.

'Much of what I saw in Geneva really disillusioned me about how my government functions and what its impact is in the world,' he said. 'I realised that I was part of something that was doing far more harm than good.'[42] Then in March 2013 he watched on TV the US Director of National Intelligence General Clapper being questioned by Democrat Senator Ron Wyden, a member of the US Select Committee on Intelligence.

Wyden quoted the Director of the NSA, Keith B. Alexander, who had earlier told a computer conference, 'Our job is foreign intelligence . . . Those who would want to weave the story that we have millions or hundreds of millions of dossiers on people, is absolutely false . . . From my perspective, this is absolute nonsense.'[43]

Senator Wyden asked Clapper, 'Does the NSA collect any type of data at all on millions or hundreds of millions of Americans?'

Clapper responded – committing the felony of lying to Congress under oath – 'No, sir.'

Wyden pressed him, asking, 'It does not?' and Clapper said, 'Not wittingly. There are cases where they could inadvertently, perhaps, collect, but not wittingly.[44]

For Edward Snowden, Clapper's denial was a flashbulb moment: he knew at that precise instant that he had to reveal the truth about the NSA's activities. 'I would say sort of the breaking point was seeing the Director of National Intelligence, James Clapper, directly lie under oath to Congress. There's no saving an intelligence community that believes it can lie to the public and the legislators who need to be able to trust it and regulate its actions. Seeing that really meant for me there was no going back.'[45]

As he prepared to spend another night in the austere surroundings of Sheremetyevo airport Snowden may well have reflected on what he had achieved. People now knew that if they wanted to regain their privacy, it would be a long hard struggle. They also knew that anyone who tried to hold intelligence organisations and government to account, like investigative journalists, would have to outmanoeuvre the very systems the surveillance state had put in place to defend itself from exposure. It was going to be a deadly game of hide-and-seek, where journalists would be hunted like criminals.

CHAPTER 10

Hide-and-Seek

Like any Washington-based representative of a major news outlet in the United States, James Rosen of Rupert Murdoch's Fox News has a small cubicle office in the Department of State building – the Harry S. Truman Building. This kind of arrangement is mutually beneficial: the government has the journalists on hand to feed them information, and the journalists have the chance to question the government. Being within walking distance of the main press briefing area, in room 2209, makes it easy to hear what the government has to say. The statements from the senior media officer, or even the secretary of state, are grist for the mill of the TV evening news.

But the journalists there, James Rosen included, know that the real game in town isn't the press briefings, which are public and available to all, but the extra information they can garner from others – especially the public officials who speak on behalf of the State Department before the cameras and then afterwards brief off-the-record to their favoured reporters. The stories generated by these briefings appear on the evening news or in newspapers citing a government official or government sources – or can at times be stated as plain fact if corroborated by sufficiently reliable information. For the Washington-based reporter, developing sources is what it's all about; gaining that extra piece of information that lifts your story above the rest. It's a symbiotic relationship and the

State Department's press office is often keen to help, putting reporters in touch with the right people.

The press office is paid to portray the government – and particularly the department – in a good light. To borrow a metaphor used by President Lyndon Johnson when discussing J. Edgar Hoover, head of the FBI, they believe it is better to have the media inside the tent, pissing out, than outside, pissing in. Unfortunately for the government, journalists tend not to be overly bothered where they piss, provided they get a good story. Allowing the press inside the State Department and then expecting them to play by the rules of government is a little like sending an alcoholic to work in a bottle shop.

Not far from James Rosen's office is one of the most critically important – and highly secure – areas in the State Department. It's home to the Bureau of Verification, Compliance, and Implementation (VCI), which monitors the development of all WMDs, including nuclear. Here the best and the brightest scientists that the State Department can assemble are gathered together to provide highly classified analysis and advice to the secretary of state and assistant secretaries whose job it is to deal with policy detail. Banks of terminals access documents from the NSA, the CIA and a myriad of other intelligence agencies, classified beyond Top Secret to Sensitive Compartmented Information (SCI) – information restricted on a need-to-know basis. Material so sensitive even those with a Top Secret clearance may be refused access.

Working in the office was one of the best nuclear arms experts in the world, Stephen Jin-Woo Kim. Kim's family migrated to the USA from South Korea when he was eight years old. The archetypal American success story, Kim earned degrees from Georgetown and Harvard and a doctorate from Yale. He worked for the Lawrence Livermore National Laboratory and the Defense and State departments. In early 2009 he briefed Vice President Dick Cheney on an area he was not only an expert in but had a cultural connection to: North Korea's nuclear ambitions. His boss, Assistant Secretary of State Paula A. DeSutter, says she had 'the highest regard for him'.[1] His fluency in the Korean language and his brilliant analytical skills made him much sought after to explain exactly what was happening in the nuclear-armed North. As a way of explaining government policy on containing North Korea, according to *The New York Times*, the State Department press office decided to put Kim in direct contact with a reporter from the press pool. The person they chose: Fox News' James Rosen. It was a one-off briefing to background Rosen.

By the middle of 2009 events on the Korean peninsula were increasingly demanding the attention of the State Department. Two journalists working for Current TV – former Democrat presidential contender Al Gore's media company – were on trial for crossing into North Korean territory without a visa; stiff penalties were in the offing for the pair. The North had just conducted a nuclear test. And the UN Security Council was deciding whether or not to introduce sanctions against the harsh regime of Kim Jong-il.

Sensing an opportunity for some good stories, James Rosen decided to reignite his contact with Kim but this time he would bypass the State Department press office. Instead he would go it alone, setting up a covert system of communication.

It's hard to understand how someone like Rosen, who had written a book on Watergate, could have made so many basic errors in handling a source but, as became apparent, he did. Perhaps a key to understanding Rosen is that his book *The Strong Man: John Mitchell and the Secrets of Watergate* (Doubleday, 2008) – about the Nixon attorney general who famously told Watergate reporter Carl Bernstein that the owner of *The Washington Post*, Katharine Graham, was 'gonna get her tit caught in a big fat wringer if that's published'[2] – was largely laudatory of Mitchell. It would be kind to say Rosen

was confused about the role of journalism in holding government accountable. But he would not have been alone in the
Fox Network, which has the barest of journalistic cover for its
role as a mouthpiece for the Republican Party. Whatever the
reasoning behind the way Rosen dealt with Kim as a source, it
did not bode well.

—

On 11 May 2009 Kim sends an email explaining that he has
returned from a trip. He attaches information about his professional life. He asks Rosen, 'Please send me your personal cell
number. I believe you have mine. It was great meeting you.'

When Rosen replies he tells Kim that his credentials had
never been in doubt and that he was nonetheless 'grateful' to
have the benefit of a chronological listing of 'your postings
and accomplishments'.[3] He adds that he only has one cell
phone number, which Kim already has.

Up until this point, the email exchange may be seen as
quite normal but now what Rosen writes on an open unencrypted public email system beggars belief. He describes a
system of codes to be used so the two can communicate. An
email containing one asterisk would indicate a need to contact
the other person 'or that previously agreed plans for communication are to proceed as agreed'; two astericks meant 'the
opposite': no contact should be made and any other arrangements which had been made are now cancelled.[4]

Exhibiting all the false optimism and naivety of Voltaire's
Candide, Rosen continues, 'With all this established, and
presuming you have read/seen enough about me to know that
I am trustworthy . . . let's get about our work! What do you
want to accomplish together? As I told you when we met, I can
always go on television and say: "Sources tell Fox News." But
I am in a much better position to advance the interests of all
concerned if I can say "Fox News has obtained . . ." Warmest
regards, James.'[5]

When he later created a secret email account to contact Kim, Rosen looked to the players in the Watergate saga for a false name. What's intriguing is that where most journalists might appropriate the mantle of Bernstein or his fellow Watergate reporter, Bob Woodward, as an alias, Rosen chose the name of Nixon's deputy assistant, Alexander Butterfield, and signed his emails 'Alex'. Forty years ago Butterfield recorded all of Nixon's Oval Office discussions, using technology that now seems incredibly outmoded. These days people with surveillance tools document far more than just conversations. But all this seemed to be beyond Rosen as he wrote to 'Leo', the alias Kim used.

Rosen bluntly states his case: 'What I am interested in, as you might expect, is breaking news ahead of my competitors.'[6] He says he wants to report authoritatively on new initiatives or shifts in US policy and events on the ground in North Korea, 'what intelligence is picking up, etc'.[7] He also would like to know 'maybe on the basis of internal memos'[8] what action the United States is planning for North Korea. Playing to Kim's genuine concern to alert the American public to the perils of a nuclear-armed North Korea, which so clearly threatened the country of his birth, Rosen wrote urging action.

'In short, let's break some news and expose muddle-headed policy when we see it – or force the administration's hand to go in the right direction, if possible. The only way to do this is to EXPOSE the policy, or what the North Korea is up to, and the only way to do that authoritatively is with EVIDENCE.'[9]

On 9 June 2009 at about 10.15 am Rosen called Kim's phone in the high-security area of the VCI and left a message. At 10.17 am Kim called Rosen and the two spoke for approximately 11 minutes. Within minutes of the release of an intelligence report on North Korea to members of the intelligence community, classified in the special compartmentalised category beyond Top Secret, Kim called Rosen. At 11.18 am. They spoke for four minutes. At 11.24 am

Kim called Rosen again. The call lasted 18 seconds. Two and a half minutes later Kim logged on to his secure computer and accessed the intelligence report at 11.27 am. At 11.37 am – with Kim again logged in to the intelligence report, he called Rosen on his desk phone, where he apparently left a message before calling Rosen's cell phone.

Rosen and Kim could not have left a clearer set of electronic fingerprints. At a little after midday they compounded the problem. When Kim walked through the security door of the entrance to the State Department on 2201 C Street in the north-west of Washington, his identity card automatically registered him leaving. The time 12.02. One minute later James Rosen left the building through the same door. Like Kim, his exact time of departure recorded. At 12.26 pm Kim walked back into the building. Four minutes later he was joined by Rosen. It probably would have been unreasonable to go to the lengths of a 2 am clandestine meeting in a car park where Deep Throat revealed the Watergate secrets, but as source protection Rosen was a terrible failure.[10]

Later that afternoon James Rosen gave Fox News what it wanted: an exclusive story on North Korea.

> U.S. intelligence officials have warned President Obama and other senior American officials that North Korea intends to respond to the passage of a U.N. Security Council resolution this week – condemning the communist country for its recent nuclear and ballistic missile tests – with another nuclear test.[11]

It was hardly an earth-shattering revelation and few, if any other news organsations followed the Fox story. North Korea had in the past responded to action against it by detonating nuclear weapons. It would have been more of a story – news in the real sense – if the North had decided to do nothing in response to planned UN sanctions. It was Rosen's attempt to boost this mediocre story with details about the source which caused so much damage.

In the second paragraph Rosen revealed 'the Central Intelligence Agency has learned, through sources inside North Korea'[12] about the planned nuclear response.

The problem with the story wasn't that it should not have been published but by specifically identifying the CIA as a source of the information on North Korea, it pointed the finger at the people who had access to the above Top Secret intelligence report, which had just been released. By a process of elimination the FBI established that of the 95 people who had accessed the intelligence report on the day that Rosen's story appeared, only Kim had had contact with Rosen. Matched together with the electronic fingerprints that Rosen and Kim had left behind with their frequent contact, it was only a matter of time before the FBI came knocking on the door.

—

By piecing together Kim's phone records as well as his access to the computer and his contact with Rosen, the FBI was sure that it had its suspected leaker. But instead of stopping there, the Department of Justice (DOJ) – which was directing the investigation – wanted to send a powerful warning to journalists: when it came to security leaks, they were not necessarily protected by the First Amendment. The Obama administration was ramping up its assault on leakers by attacking those who benefited from the leaks – journalists.

With this new focus on leaking, the hunt took the FBI to previously uncharted territory for a security investigation – a journalist's personal email account. The search warrant, served on Google's high-tech showpiece headquarters overlooking San Francisco Bay, demanded access to information the FBI knew lay hidden in far less prosaic surroundings, the large shed-like structures that are home to Google's servers, dotted across the United States. The affidavit lodged with the US District Court in Washington wanted 'subscriber information records and the contents of limited wire and electronic communications pertaining to the account'.[13]

The FBI – working under the instruction of the DOJ – wanted to leave no doubt it believed that Rosen had acted like a spy. It argued that Rosen had behaved 'much like an intelligence officer would run a clandestine intelligence source'.[14]

It said that 'From the beginning of their relationship, the Reporter asked, solicited and encouraged Mr. Kim to disclose sensitive United States internal documents and intelligence information . . .'[15]

By framing the request in this way, the FBI was arguing that Rosen was no longer protected by the First Amendment. Now Rosen could be prosecuted under the Espionage Act. He had committed a crime, and evidence that he was a 'conspirator and/or aider and abettor'[16] was likely to be contained within his Gmail correspondence. The FBI argued that the Gmail account fell squarely within the exemption permitting searches of media-related work product materials, even when possessed by a national news reporter, because there is 'probable cause to believe that the person possessing such materials has committed or is committing the criminal offense to which the materials relate'.[17]

Once the FBI had Rosen in its sights, public sympathy was with the reporter. Glossed over – at least for the time being – was the question of the responsibility that reporters have not only to protect their sources but to protect their sources from themselves.

What happened shifted the ground in the long-established procedures governing reporter–source relationships, built up over decades in the United States. It's a side effect of the protection under the First Amendment afforded to reporters that – at least until the Kim case – only the source could be in danger of being prosecuted under the Espionage Act. It could make journalists lazy about source protection, since their lives or careers were never in danger. Rosen either didn't care or had no idea how to protect his source.

The howls of protest from the journalistic community – particularly at the State Department – could be heard all the way to the White House. James Rosen, who had used flattery and charm and the potential promise of a glamorous role in a think tank to entice an émigré who had worked tirelessly for the United States, had written a story which warned the despotic regime of North Korea that it had possibly been penetrated by the CIA. As is often the case, the highest principles are frequently fought for using the worst example. Rosen would become the poster boy of press freedom.

For the first time it appeared that a journalist might be charged under the Espionage Act. So what had made the Obama White House – and the Department of Justice – so angry and fearful about leaking?

—

Just 24 hours earlier, on 27 May, at Forward Operating Base Hammer, east of Baghdad, the US Military Police had arrested Chelsea (Bradley) Manning and it had dawned on the administration that the leaking of the source material of *Collateral Murder* – the shocking video of the gunship killing unarmed civilians, including two journalists, in a Baghdad street broadcast around the world one month earlier – was not a one-off event. As they combed through Manning's computer, the US military discovered evidence that a cache of information had also been copied – it would soon be published as the Afghan War Diary and Iraq War Logs, along with hundreds of thousands of State Department communications known as Cablegate. As the WikiLeaks bomb went off in Washington, the White House ignited its campaign to stop leaks.

While Kim paid the price – swiftly tried and jailed for 13 months, his career in ruins – it was only the state of outrage across the political spectrum, from *The New York Times* to News Corporation, that stopped the case against Rosen. He managed to escape prosecution because the offence was relatively minor, but while the government retreated on one front, it continued pursuing a much bigger quarry: James Risen.

Although he might have a similar name to the Fox News presenter, that's where the similarity ends. Whereas James Rosen worked for Fox, James Risen worked for *The New York Times*. James Risen is best remembered as the reporter who had two of his exposés blocked from publication at the behest of the George W. Bush White House – on national security grounds. The first story – of how the NSA spied on Americans – was eventually published by the paper, but Risen's second story, which was equally as sensitive – about how the CIA became involved in sending blueprints for a nuclear bomb to Iran – never graced the pages of *The New York Times*. The story was killed after then National Security Advisor Condoleezza Rice told the newspaper's editors disclosure of the mission threatened US national security.

It wasn't until 2006 that Risen managed to get the story out; it was included in his book about the Bush administration titled *State of War: The Secret History of the CIA and the Bush Administration* (Simon & Schuster, New York).

State of War takes the reader through a plot by the CIA to plant fake blueprints for a nuclear bomb with the Iranian government. If it came off it would dramatically set back any plans by Tehran to put together a nuclear weapon. As though playing out a modern-day version of the Cold War classic *The Third Man*, the CIA decided to run their operation in the world's most notorious spy capital, Vienna. To add a further dash of drama, they used a Russian scientist who had recently defected to the west to be the courier for the bomb plans. The problem was the scientist was smarter than the CIA thought. When he saw the blueprints he noticed that they contained a major and obvious flaw which would stop the bomb working properly. What the CIA didn't know at the time was that the scientist, in an effort to protect himself from any Iranian revenge, opened the envelope containing the blueprints and slipped a handwritten note inside pointing out that they were faulty. So it seems the Iranians – and their intelligence agencies – knew they had been given a dud; the Russian knew it; the CIA knew it. The only people who were kept in the dark about the CIA's incompetence were the American public.

The source of Risen's information was almost certainly a former CIA officer Jeffrey Sterling, an African American. He was found guilty in January 2015 of espionage. Sterling worked as a CIA officer in the Far East and South Asia section of the agency and later took up a position recruiting Iranian nationals to work for the CIA to gain information on Iran's weapons capabilities.

Sterling had left the CIA complaining bitterly he had been passed over for promotion because of his colour. Risen then wrote a story for *The New York Times* about Sterling's claim and later, as he gathered information about the Iranian bomb hoax, the two of them left a string of electronic markers across the Washington telephone and email networks which revealed dozens of conversations over the years.

It was yet another example of lax reporter–source security. Here was a former CIA officer talking to a Pulitzer Prize-winning investigative journalist breaking all the basic rules of covert communication. Sterling might have been careless because of his anger, but Risen should have known better and been more careful.

Many legal commentators believe there was more than enough electronic evidence to bring Sterling to court and convict him of being the source. Unlike Rosen, who was not prosecuted and was not called to give evidence at Kim's trial, the DOJ subpoenaed Risen. They ordered him to appear before the court to be questioned on whether Sterling was his source. If Risen would not reveal who gave him the information he ran the risk of being jailed for contempt of court.

The DOJ had found another way to attack journalists who disclosed sensitive information about the government. They did not need to be directly charged under the Espionage Act, but could be caught by other means.

By the beginning of 2015, with the case dragging on, Obama administration Attorney General Eric Holder seemed to shift ground, suggesting that he didn't want to see any journalists jailed. There was also the suggestion that Risen would not be asked directly to name Sterling as his source.

So what was all this about? While Rosen and Risen both demonstrated extraordinarily sloppy trade craft in dealing with their sources, what the US government was doing sent an unequivocal message to whistleblowers and journalists that there was no place to hide from electronic surveillance: every phone call, every mobile phone tower, every electronic tag and every email could be used to track their movements. It was a stark threat to reporters that electronic surveillance had made any form of investigative journalism a harrowing and dangerous pursuit. The very system that allowed gigabytes of information to be downloaded could be turned against the leaker – and those who published that information.

Yet there was a solution, at least in part, to keep journalists' communications secret. It was the system that reporter Glenn Greenwald had failed to use – which nearly lost him the greatest story of his life.

—

The software system known as Pretty Good Privacy (PGP) had first come to public prominence in June 1996. The work of Phil Zimmermann, a genial, bearded computer programmer, it would allow all text sent by email to be heavily encrypted. It was doubtful even the biggest code-breakers in the world at the NSA could read this kind of encrypted material.

It came as no surprise that the NSA was in favour of a level of encryption that was woefully weak. One estimate said it would be possible to crack the 56-bit Data Encryption Standard (DES) being proposed for all US computers in just two minutes. Zimmermann thought that with its budget the NSA would be able to do it in seconds. Even so PGP, with its 1024-bit key, was going to be difficult and time-consuming for any intelligence agency to decipher.

Back in 1991 the US government had called on manufacturers of secure communications equipment to insert special trapdoors in their products, so that the government could read anyone's encrypted messages. The US National Security Council had been told three years earlier that the FBI, the NSA and the DOJ were demanding tough laws that would mandate the public to use only government-approved encryption products or adhere to government encryption criteria. Fearing that he had little time, Zimmermann acted first, releasing his new system because he wanted cryptography to be made available to the American public before it became illegal to use it. Zimmermann was so worried he gave it away for free to increase the uptake.

The result was beyond his wildest dreams. His encryption program 'spread like a prairie fire',[18] and within human rights groups, it was used to encode evidence and protect the identities of witnesses.

Called before the Subcommittee on Science, Technology and Space of the US Senate Committee on Commerce, Science and Transportation, investigating encryption, Zimmermann said under oath the government did not have a track record that inspired confidence that they 'will never abuse our civil liberties'.[19] The FBI had a bad record with civil rights, and also with targeting groups merely because they opposed government policies, spying on the anti-war movement – even wire-tapping Martin Luther King Jr's telephone.

Zimmermann already knew what it was like to be pursued by the FBI. Five years earlier when he'd put his PGP encryption online for others to use, special agents had raided his

home. It took until January 1996, just a few months before
he fronted the senators, for the Justice Department to finally
drop the possibility of prosecution. But even then, the export
of encryption systems remained classified as dangerous to the
security of the USA – on a par with fighter-bomber aircraft,
tanks and guns.

Exactly why the Justice Department didn't proceed with
a case against Zimmermann isn't clear. It's possible the US
First Amendment – enshrining freedom of speech – put the
prosecutors on shaky ground. Whatever the reason, PGP
encryption was now well and truly out of the bag.

As he left the hearing, Zimmermann made one final obser-
vation: PGP was a force for democracy. 'I want to read you a
quote from some email I got in October 1993, from someone
in Latvia, on the day that Boris Yeltsin was shelling his own
parliament building: "Phil, I wish you to know: let it never be,
but if dictatorship takes over Russia your PGP is widespread
from Baltic to Far East now and will help democratic people if
necessary. Thanks."'[20]

Nearly two decades have passed since Zimmermann
appeared before the Senate committee, but the need for journalists to cover their tracks and protect their sources has never
been greater. And once again, just as independent journalists like Greenwald and Assange injected vim into a sclerotic
industry, now it's the supporters of the independent internet
who are coming to the rescue. It's an often unusual coalition:
those who believe in free information coming to the aid of the
industry that vilifies them most. But they do have a common
purpose: freedom of the press and freedom of the net are
closely bound together.

—

It would be normal for people fighting for freedom of thought
and expression to be most comfortable in a country which
enshrines that right in its Constitution. But as the United

States hounds its whistleblowers and journalists, they have sought refuge elsewhere, along with others who have taken on the might of the international intelligence state created by the Five-Eyes agreement.

The S-Bahn train from Schönefeld airport to the centre of Berlin provides a clear view of the former East Germany's tele-communications tower which made sure all the citizens below were kept in their place. Now Berlin, and particularly the East, rebelling against decades of Nazism and communism, has once again become Europe's centre of openness and free thinking. Unable to return to the United Kingdom, fearing that she will be detained for her role in helping Snowden flee prosecution, Sarah Harrison has made Berlin her home. Jacob Appelbaum, who has worked with Assange, fled to Berlin after being repeatedly harassed by the FBI. Appelbaum, a genius computer programmer, supports the Tor Project, a system which allows internet users to hide their computers' unique identifier while they surf the net. Laura Poitras, who made contact with Snowden before Greenwald because she could operate PGP and he couldn't, cut her acclaimed film *Citizenfour* – about Edward Snowden – in an area of East Berlin where artists and filmmakers gather in cooperative efforts.

It's not that Germany has strong laws to protect journal-ists, although they are better than the United Kingdom's and certainly very much better than Australia's, it is, as Sarah Harrison points out, that, 'The surveillance revelations have struck a chord in Germany more than other countries.'[21] A critical mass of politicians, the media and the public were generally onside.

As Berlin has become the centre of opposition to state surveillance, it's formed strong links with other internet freedom groups, and few stronger than with Jérémie Zimmer-mann's La Quadrature du Net – 'Squaring the Net' – based in Paris. Zimmermann, a friend of both Appelbaum and Harrison, runs his organisation from a ground-floor office crammed with computers and with a handful of staff. Independently funded, La Quadrature du Net is a not-for-profit organisation which 'defends the rights and freedom of citizens on the internet'.[22]

A computer science engineer and an expert in encryption, Zimmermann is amazed at the lack of security employed by most journalists to protect sources. In a café near his office in the 11th arrondissement – an area of Paris akin to Sydney's Newtown, its narrow streets crammed with writers, film-makers, journalists and internet activists – Zimmermann ran through some techniques for maintaining privacy and protecting sources. There are obvious ones, like using the phone to make an arrangement to get together and then at the meeting setting up a coded system which allows you to meet the source at a different place next time. Writing down the name of the new location will prevent you being overheard.

MOBILE PHONE

Switch off 'Location Services', especially if you are going to meet a contact. If the phone is ever seized it will reveal exactly where you have been and at what time and for how long. Better still, leave the mobile phone at home or in the office.

If you need to have the mobile with you when you meet a contact, if feasible, seal it in a zip-lock bag and place it in the freezer. No phone signal can exit or enter the fridge. (Don't forget it when you leave; place your car keys in the bag as well, as a reminder.)

Note that there is the distinct possibility that your mobile phone can be tracked, even if it is turned off and the battery is removed. Zimmermann explains that if you take the battery out of your phone and then reinsert it, the clock still works – telling the correct time. That means the phone still holds a charge after the battery is removed. According to Zimmermann, if there is a bit of power there is a way to selectively turn on the phone, whether it is for recording or just sending one signal to the network saying here is my geographical location. If you have an iPhone forget about this, because the battery cannot be removed. Even if the phone is turned off it is possible for intelligence agencies like the NSA to turn it on again and listen to nearby conversations.

EMAIL

Send email messages using PGP; use instant messaging with the record of conversation turned off. It was Chelsea Manning's failure to tick the box which led to her record of conversation being accessible to the FBI and the US military.

Understand that if you use an email address based in the United States anything you write will be accessible by the US military and/or government. If you use a local email address, then your country's military, intelligence agencies or government will be able to get access.

If you use Skype, Viber or any of the other voice- and video-based systems, your entire communication will all be accessible by US authorities.

CONCEALING ELECTRONIC COMMUNICATIONS

If you want to hide from the NSA – or any other intelligence agency – for a short time, say one week because you want to publish something in two weeks, a public wi-fi in a cyber café and a fresh second-hand computer bought for $100 should be sufficient. If you need longer a good option is a system called Tails – an anonymous encrypted system that runs through the Tor Project – which routes information around the world and is almost impossible to trace. Zimmermann says it would take longer than two weeks to track your location if you use this system. But he warns that you must maintain perfect control of both the computer and the USB. No going to the swimming pool and leaving it in the locker, and it must even come to bed with you. Taking such measures, known as operational security, should give a journalist long enough to get their material broadcast or published.

Even then, warns Zimmermann, the communication will not be safe for all time. If something is protected by clever technology today, the NSA can store it until such time as they acquire the capability to break into it and open it.

—

It was only two streets from where Zimmermann had sat with me and explained the best way to protect journalists and their work from the perils of state surveillance that terrorists attacked the weekly satirical magazine *Charlie Hebdo*. Famous for its irreligious cartoons, some depicting the Prophet Muhammad, it had raised the ire of Islamic extremists, two of whom stormed the offices, killing 12 people in January 2015. As millions took to the streets in France carrying signs inscribed 'Je Suis Charlie' and millions more around the world added their support for those who had died for freedom of expression, governments moved to shut down internet websites, increase their powers of surveillance – and began clamping down on the press.

That the attack on *Charlie Hebdo* was used by those calling for increased surveillance and a restriction on freedom of information was a strange epitaph for the editor, Stéphane 'Charb' Charbonnier, who proclaimed after the *Charlie Hebdo* offices were firebombed four years previously, 'I would rather die standing, than live on my knees.'[23] As the French came together in their millions to honour the basis of the Republic – liberty, equality, fraternity – the biggest demands for more restrictions came from the members of the UK–USA intelligence-sharing cartel, particularly Britain and Australia. They used the *Charlie Hebdo* attack to fan the flames of another war: not a war on terror but a war on journalism – an intensification of police power, coupled with the loss of individual freedoms.

At least one French demonstrator seemed to recognise the contradiction. The sign he carried read: *Je marche, mais je suis conscient de la confusion et de l'hypocrisie de la situation.* I march, but I am aware of the confusion and hypocrisy of the situation.[24]

The fact that politicians might use the *Charlie Hebdo* murders as an excuse to increase state surveillance and clamp down on dissent might be expected, particularly when they presided over the very intelligence agencies that failed to adequately monitor the known jihadists who carried out the killings. What is difficult to understand is that journalists themselves would use the attacks to turn on whistleblowers who, like *Charlie Hebdo*, had relentlessly campaigned for greater freedom.

CHAPTER 11

Press One for Jingoism

The *Daily Mail* is what middle England consumes with its breakfast. But on 9 January 2015, a mere two days after the *Charlie Hebdo* killings, it would have taken more than a cast-iron stomach to hold down what they were offering up. A photo of the Kouachi brothers brandishing AK-47s was tucked under a headline, 'Why the Liberals Who Defended Traitors Like Snowden and Assange Should Look at This Photo and Admit: We Were Deluded Fools'. The article, written by columnist Sir Max Hastings, came close to blaming Assange and Snowden for the deaths. He wrote that Assange and Snowden had damaged the security of everyone by alerting the jihadists and al-Qaeda, Britain's mortal enemies, to the scale and reach of the United Kingdom's electronic eavesdropping. Hastings went on to describe Snowden as treacherous, accusing both him and Assange of broadcasting American and British secrets wholesale. What really upset Sir Max was that Snowden and Assange 'are celebrated as heroes by some people who should know better, many of them writing for *The Guardian* or broadcasting for the BBC'.[1]

Hastings unquestioningly took the side of Andrew Parker, Director-General of MI5, who warned that it was almost inevitable that an attack on the United Kingdom would get through sooner or later.

Quoting a senior intelligence officer who said he was dismayed by the risk that listening operations could be curtailed by civil liberties campaigners, Hastings wrote, 'I am convinced he is right that GCHQ, MI5 and MI6 must maintain their licence – within a legal framework – to trawl the ether, in the strongest public interest.'[2] In an attempt to give his argument credibility he conceded that 'there may be a few mavericks within intelligence services who abuse such power', but then suggests 'unless we view the very existence of government as inherently wicked and threatening, I cannot for the life of me imagine what harm can result from MI5 accessing the phone calls, bank accounts, emails of you, me or any other law-abiding citizen'.[3]

For a military historian of some note – he is the author of more than 20, mainly war, books – he could not have failed to notice that unchecked power has been a problem over the years. Yet he ploughs on – insisting that he is more fearful of large companies using his information commercially than the possibility that the intelligence agencies might do some-thing wrong.

If Hastings were just another conservative hack railing against libertarian journalists he might have been easy to dismiss. He is certainly fashioned in the tradition of conserv-ative journalism: closely trusted by the military, he was with British troops when they landed on the Falklands in 1982 – one of the world's first embedded journalists. But with Hastings the issues are more profound. He labels Snowden – who revealed the awesome information-gathering machine – as a traitor, but then says he could not vote Labour in 2010 because Gordon Brown was wholly psychologically unfit to be Prime Minister.[4]

The problem of executive government oversight on intel-ligence matters, if Hastings was right, passed him by. What if the person in No. 10 is crazy? Who would Max Hastings turn to – the military? He suffers from the delusion of most insiders: bolstered by the power and prestige they gain by their special knowledge, they are comfortable with the status quo, no matter how contradictory their positions may be. As a classic reactionary, Hastings' political perspective is seemingly as frozen in time as the Cold War, where he made his name. Hastings' views are closely mirrored by the paper he used to edit, the London *Daily Telegraph*.

In an unexpurgated piece about GCHQ, the *Telegraph* reported that 'Britain's spies now take three times as long to crack terrorist communications thanks to the Edward Snowden leaks of GCHQ techniques.'[5] It added that experts at the intelligence agency 'need up to six weeks to "deliver the magic" when tasked with tracking and monitoring targets, the *Telegraph* can disclose'.[6] Without question or attribution the *Telegraph* reported 'the scale of the damage caused by the leaks'.[7] Never once were the assertions of the security agencies, as self-interested as they were in beating up the story, ever questioned.

Investigation of the role of any of the agencies by a competent journalist would quickly uncover that a primary role of an intelligence agency is not only to gather information, but to deceive. And that includes, in particular, deceiving journalists. It is not without reason, for example, that Australia's domestic spy agency, ASIO, specifically asks its potential recruits if they know or have contact with investigative journalists. ASIO is right to worry about keeping some information secret, but what concerns it too is that the deception it practises may become public. Since the role of an intelligence agency incorporates deceiving to protect the country and its citizens, there is no reason to believe it stops deceiving when it needs to protect itself. It's a fact of life that appears completely lost to *The Australian*, even as the United States and some of its senior political figures had doubts that the NSA had been completely honest and the head of US national intelligence had been caught out lying (see end of chapter 10). The newspaper also failed to recognise that the US Congress – on both sides of the political divide –

united to launch investigations into acknowledged abuses by the NSA.

In an editorial littered with smears and inaccuracies, on 7 January 2014 Australia's national daily ignored the fact that Snowden had revealed many wrongdoings at the NSA and also alerted the world to the power and the problems of a surveillance system which stripped people of their privacy while protecting its own.

'Granting clemency to Edward Snowden after all he has done is a thoroughly bad idea,' read the editorial. 'Yet that is what US President Barack Obama is being asked to consider by *The New York Times* and left-wing London newspaper *The Guardian*.' *The Australian* asserted that the editorials of those papers had used 'misleading arguments' to support Snowden's case that he is a 'heroic whistleblower' who has 'done his country a great service'. On the contrary, asserted *The Australian*, Snowden may be responsible for one of modern history's most 'damaging intelligence leaks'. The editorial talked of Snowden's 'Russian handlers' waiting to release more from his 'trove of secrets' – seemingly oblivious to the fact that the US government has never suggested he was being controlled by Moscow and that Snowden left all his secret files in Hong Kong with Greenwald and Poitras.

The editorial smacked of long-held bitterness about *The Guardian*'s exposure in July 2009 of the phone-hacking saga and the corrupt practices at News International. What emerged about the murky inner workings of the company in subsequent parliamentary inquiries so damaged the brand name that it was difficult to take the organisation seriously on any question of ethics or lawful behaviour. Being advised by the Murdoch press on any proper course of action was akin to being lectured on the benefits of abstinence by a prostitute. Yet there was more to this spray than simply hitting back at an adversary.

In the wake of the Murdoch revelations and as the public called for greater control of the press, the British media fell into two camps. Murdoch's newspapers *The Sun* and *The Times*, perhaps self-servingly, launched strong campaigns against any restrictions. With less fanfare the Murdoch press was joined by the *Daily Mail* and *The Daily Telegraph*. Others, like *The Guardian* and *The Independent*, were more nuanced in their opposition to new laws to protect the rights of the individual from phone-hacking or other forms of invasion of privacy.

The Snowden revelations changed all that. The press was once again divided but this time the divisions were stark: those who had stood against any control of the print media – the Murdoch press, *The Daily Telegraph* and the *Daily Mail* – now wanted the media controlled. In fact the *Mail* and *The Sun* appeared to want *The Guardian* prosecuted. This was more than a petty spat. It revealed a crisis at the very centre of newspaper journalism in Britain. The editors of some of Britain's most influential newspapers had become champions of state power. The rights of the individual – and more importantly their journalistic colleagues – were swept aside. Newspapers were unquestioningly backing the most intrusive surveillance regime ever constructed in the history of the world. Privacy of the individual was dead and newspapers now supported the supremacy of the state.

The Sun ran a virulent campaign against *The Guardian*, headlining it '*Guardian* Treason Helping Terrorists'. It wrote of 'illiterate bearded jihadi maniacs piling up the ingredients in their bedsits to make bombs'.[8]

Louise Mensch, an ex-Tory MP who sat on the committee investigating the *News of the World* hacking allegations and opposed the finding that Rupert Murdoch was not a fit and proper person to run a TV station, wrote in *The Sun*, 'You know what's funny about *The Guardian* newspaper? They were all for state regulation of the press. The big cheerleaders for Leveson loved it when the *News of the World* was closed over illegal hacking. But when they break the law, they screech about press freedom.'[9]

The hysteria and inaccuracies were extraordinary. It was little wonder that *The Sun* and the *Daily Mail* were so opposed to any tightening of controls recommended by Leveson which might force newspapers to publish corrections when there are clear errors of fact.

—

The fact is *The Guardian* had not broken the law. After publishing the first story – about the Verizon phone intercepts – under heavy pressure from Glenn Greenwald to act quickly, it had strictly followed a voluntary process, where newspapers proposing to publish sensitive security and military information inform an independent committee which gives direction on what it believes should or should not be published. Housed in the Department of Defence, off London's Whitehall, the Defence, Press and Broadcasting Advisory Committee overseas a 'voluntary code' which 'operates between the UK Government departments which have responsibilities for national security and the media'.[10] *The Guardian* consistently dealt with the D-notice committee, comprised of senior representatives of government departments like Defence and the Foreign Office, and executives from newspapers, TV stations and other media bodies. Its job is to 'prevent inadvertent public disclosure of information that would compromise UK military and intelligence operations and methods, or put at risk the safety of those involved . . .' During the period that it was revealing the Snowden stories, Rusbridger estimated he had 100 meetings with Whitehall officials to discuss what *The Guardian* would report.

As *The Guardian* weighed up how to handle the first Snowden story, it was concerned that members of the committee might tell the government, which might then seek a court injunction to stop the story getting out. With Glenn Greenwald threatening to take the Snowden leaks elsewhere, the first story and by far the most important but, by comparison with what followed, also the most mundane, was the only one *The*

Guardian did not give the D-notice committee prior warning about before publishing.

Just why *The Guardian* continued dealing with the committee at all may well have exercised Rusbridger. The minutes of a meeting of the D-notice committee, the avenue prescribed by the government as the preferred method to deal with such sensitive issues, reveal that, in the middle of the Snowden exposés the government abandoned the process. Jon Thompson, the Chairman of the D-notice committee, was missing from the vital meeting on 7 November 2013 where *The Guardian*'s Snowden revelations were discussed. As Under-Secretary of State at the UK Ministry of Defence, Thompson is one of the most powerful people in the country.

The rest of the government also seemed disinterested. No representatives from the Cabinet Office turned up and the Foreign Office and Home Office sent along token representation as the D-notice committee, with its mix of government representatives and media editors, pondered the seemingly never-ending flow of Snowden revelations.[11]

Ironically it was left to Sky News associate editor Simon Bucks – whose Murdoch TV station takeover plans had fallen by the wayside following *The Guardian* phone-hacking inquiry – to bring a reasoned voice to the discussions. According to the minutes of the 7 November meeting, Bucks, the committee Vice-Chairman, told the D-notice committee it was 'important to distinguish between embarrassment and genuine concerns for national security'.[12] Bucks 'felt that much of the material published by *The Guardian* fell into the former category'.[13] In other words while what *The Guardian* had published was embarrassing to the government, it was not damaging to national security.

To show just how far the government was out of touch in dealing with the Snowden affair, Prime Minister Cameron threatened to use 'D-notices or the other tougher measures' to pull the press into line.[14]

Cameron did not understand that the D-notice system was voluntary. The committee voted to send the chairman, the missing-in-action under-secretary of State, off to educate the Prime Minister. Or as they put it more politely, 'Approach to No 10 offering a briefing on the DA Notice System'.[15] Bucks described it all as a 'greater malaise on the official side where there was worrying evidence of disengagement'.[16] On the contrary; the government would turn out to be anything but disengaged.

—

If the mass media needed a perfectly clear example to understand why it was suffering massive circulation declines, this was it: they were so close to the government, Bucks' sensibleness notwithstanding, it was difficult to tell them apart. In a time of unprecedented world peace the government was stoking fears of war and vulnerability and sections of the media were slavishly passing on the message. But the media had gone even further: instead of the classical fourth-estate questioning of the premises of the argument of the War on Terror, those sections of the media were now demanding more controls on what the public should know. Murdoch and to a lesser extent the *Daily Mail* had become the antithesis of journalism: they were demanding the government get tough on whoever refused to play the game to their liking. There were two clear targets, *The Guardian* and public broadcasters. As is often the case, Murdoch's right-wing politics and financial benefit coalesce. Woe betide anyone who stands in his way, particularly when they are commercial and political enemies working together.

—

It was bad enough when ABC TV's *The 7.30 Report* picked up a story from *The New York Times* revealing that Australian intelligence had spied on an American legal firm which was representing Indonesia in disputed trade talks and offered to share the information with Washington. The Australian agency was, apparently, '... able to continue to cover the talks, providing highly useful intelligence for interested US customers'.[17]

But the ABC really ran into trouble on 18 November 2013 when it reported that 'Australian intelligence tried to listen in to Indonesian president Susilo Bambang Yudhoyono's mobile phone, material leaked by NSA whistleblower Edward Snowden reveals.'[18]

Reporter Michael Brissenden said that documents obtained by the ABC and *Guardian Australia* from material leaked by the former contractor at the US National Security Agency, showed Australian intelligence attempted to listen in to Yudhoyono's telephone conversations 'on at least one occasion and tracked activity on his mobile phone for 15 days in August 2009'.[19] Following the revelation that German Chancellor Angela Merkel's phone had been intercepted, the story bolstered the perception that if the NSA was intercepting the phone calls of the leaders of friendly countries, then no one was safe.

Asked about the spying, Prime Minister Tony Abbott declined to change the 'long tradition of governments of both political persuasions' and comment on 'specific intelligence matters'.[20] But the long tradition didn't last long. And Abbott soon criticised the ABC for harming 'Australia's national security and long-term best interests'.[21] It was the slow beginning to what would turn into a concerted campaign against the public broadcaster and *The Guardian*.

One week after the program the Communications Minister, Malcolm Turnbull, telephoned the ABC Managing Director, who is also its editor-in-chief, and told him he had made an 'error of judgement' in broadcasting the Indonesian intercept story. He did not agree with the ABC teaming with *The Guardian* and 'amplifying'[22] the newspaper's story. As every politician knows, a rap across the knuckles has more impact with public exposure, but there are problems for ministers interfering in such delicate areas as editorial independence for a public broadcaster. A few days later Turnbull found the perfect vehicle as he strode into the Tattersalls Club in central Sydney. The Liberal Party was holding a fund-raiser, with Turnbull the star attraction. Under the ornate ceiling lights of a club founded by disgruntled bookmakers more than a century earlier, Turnbull revealed to the faithful his call to Mark Scott. In a breathtakingly disingenuous comment Turnbull said he had not 'said this publicly because you know what it's like as Communications Minister you don't want to be lecturing the public broadcasters that you're responsible for'.[23] Yet that is exactly what had happened.

Within 48 hours the full attack on the ABC was leaked to the Liberal Party's favourite newspaper, the Sydney *Daily Telegraph*, full of quotes which – perhaps predictably – Turnbull's office agreed were accurate. Sensing that the Liberal Party's old adversaries, those questioning journalists from the ABC, were feeling some discomfort, Abbott chimed in with a far more rational assessment of what troubled him. Now the argument wasn't about giving *The Guardian* free advertising on the ABC, Abbott was angry at the ABC working with a 'left-wing British newspaper'.[24] Abbott had fully adopted the language of the Murdoch press. The repeated attacks by News Corp, from the extreme right, had morphed into government policy.

The response from the ABC was barely audible. Scott did not attack the government, which had so unmercifully besmirched his organisation and interfered in its editorial independence. He simply criticised News Corp instead. In a masterful understatement Scott said that there were 'some people in News Corp who have a deep ideological opposition to public broadcasting and the ABC'.[25] But it was more than an ideological position; it was an ideology which demanded complete compliance.

Scornful of Scott's decision to run the Snowden story, Janet Albrechtsen, a former member of the ABC board which appointed Scott, called for his resignation in her column in *The Australian* of 26 November 2013. Scott, a former Liberal Party staffer, had been appointed apparently in the hope he would produce the kind of journalism Albrechtsen supported. It's hard to think that there would be many journalists who can provide what she wants. It's a strange kind of journalism. Albrechtsen pointed to the reckless publication of 'criminally obtained' material, as if journalists don't deal with leaked material on a regular basis. And neither Poitras nor Greenwald have been accused of criminal activity in receiving the Snowden information. But by far the most extraordinary claim by Albrechtsen is that although *The Guardian* had possessed the Indonesian spy story since May 2013, it made a decision 'not to publish the information before the election when it would have harmed Kevin Rudd' the then Prime Minister, but chose to 'sit on it until after the election when it was designed to damage Tony Abbott'. In an odd leap of logic she says that this 'is something the ABC must have considered. Its decision to go ahead showed a blatant political preference'.

In the not too distant future Albrechtsen may again have influence at the ABC. In 2008 the government of Kevin Rudd set up a system to stop the ABC board being stuffed with political cronies. A panel of eminent Australians, including the likes of Allan Fels, former Chairman of the consumer watchdog the Australian Competition and Consumer Commission (ACCC), and David Gonski, famous for his education reforms, would draw up a shortlist of credentialled applicants and make their decision. The person who appointed the panel would also be non-political: the Secretary of the Australian Public Service. No one saw it coming when Dr Ian Watt, who became head of the Department of the Prime Minister and Cabinet under Labor Prime Minister Julia Gillard, gave the positions to two of the most extreme right-wing culture warriors to oversee the ABC board appointments process: Neil Brown, a former Liberal Party deputy leader who wants the ABC privatised, and Albrechtsen got the nod. Dr Watt has never explained how he came to this implausible decision. He has since retired.

Two months after the Indonesian spy story, in an act of either strategic brilliance or an odd twist of fate, the ABC linked up with News Corp to produce a story advertised as a joint investigation by *Four Corners* and *The Australian*. Given the rabid attacks on the ABC's last joint venture, bystanders were interested to see how this one would play out. The program told the story of the policy of the Israeli military of targeting children in its attacks on dissent in the occupied West Bank. Reported by *The Australian*'s Middle East correspondent John Lyons, the editorial arrangement mirrored the relationship between the ABC and *The Guardian* which had produced the Indonesian spy story.

Although it was a hard-hitting report, this time there was no complaint from the Minister for Communications or the Prime Minister about 'amplifying' a commercial newspaper's product or working as an 'advertising agent' for a right-wing newspaper. And there was no comment either from Mark Scott to point out both Turnbull's and Abbott's hypocrisy.

Four months later the government, which had promised there would be 'no cuts' to the ABC, slashed the budget, forcing programs to be shut down, and hundreds to lose their jobs.[26] If Scott's strategy had been one of not publicly criticising the government in the hope he could head off the assault, it hadn't worked. The government and *The Australian* were in lock-step.

Kath Viner, *Guardian Australia*'s editor, probably had a better measure of the politics, commenting, 'I think the way *The Australian* goes after people they don't like is a misuse of power, and the extent to which News Corp has been able to skew the political discourse in this country is startling.' She added that she believed 'that influence appears to be 'waning', which it probably is, but its public outpourings are still influential.[27]

—

In the United Kingdom, the Murdoch mode of operation was back in full throttle. The attacks on *The Guardian* by News Corp press added fuel to the hysterical calls by Conservative members of parliament for an investigation into Snowden's disclosures and the role of *The Guardian*, which one of them called 'treasonous behaviour'.[28]

The focus had fallen on the truth tellers and the journalists who had been properly doing their jobs. Snowden had leaked thousands of files and only a fraction had been published. *The Guardian* and *The New York Times* were being extremely cautious about what they published. Snowden too could have put everything on the internet if he had simply wanted to cause mischief, but instead he had placed his faith in journalism to investigate and reveal what was in the public interest and at the same time protect the names of those who worked in the agencies.

Naturally nothing about this measured approach was good enough for those who ruled the secret world. Downing Street and the intelligence agencies decided to take action. Even as *The Guardian* negotiated the finer points of the D-notice committee's observations while it continued publishing the Snowden material, the government was applying the heavy hand. For all the openness that *The Guardian* championed it did not share with its readers just how much pressure it was coming under from the government.

Shortly after *The Guardian* published the first two stories – about demands by the NSA for phone data from Verizon, the US communications giant, and the revelation about PRISM, the system that eavesdrops and stores huge amounts of intercepted data from around the world – Rusbridger was contacted by two senior government officials supposedly representing the views of Prime Minister Cameron. There followed two meetings in which they demanded the return or destruction of all the material *The Guardian* was working on. According to Rusbridger 'the tone was steely, if cordial, but there was an implicit threat that others within government and Whitehall favoured a far more draconian approach'.[29]

In July the mood toughened when Rusbridger received a phone call from what he called 'the centre of government' telling him, 'You've had your fun. Now we want the stuff back.'[30]

The Guardian had just published a report on how the NSA and GCHQ spied on foreign politicians and officials attending two G20 summit meetings in London in 2009 – and had their computers monitored and their phone calls intercepted on the instructions of their British government hosts. Some delegates were tricked into using internet cafés which had been set up by British intelligence agencies to read their email traffic. The revelation came as Britain prepared to host another summit a few days later – for the G8 nations, all of whom attended the 2009 meetings which were the subject of the systematic spying.

The disclosure raised new questions about the boundaries of surveillance by GCHQ and the NSA, whose access to phone records and internet data had been defended as necessary in the fight against terrorism and serious crime. *The Guardian* had reported, 'The G20 spying appears to have been organised for the more mundane purpose of securing an advantage in meetings. Named targets include long-standing allies such as South Africa and Turkey.'[31]

What was different about this story wasn't simply that it touched a raw nerve about spying on delegates from friendly countries but that the report had been written by London-based reporters; it had no connection with Greenwald and Poitras. Whereas that duo might have had an argument that they were not based in the United Kingdom, and the story, published in the US edition of *The Guardian* was thus covered by the First Amendment, the latest offering was written by, among others, Nick Davies, the investigative star of the *News of the World* phone-hacking saga. While the government was still dealing with the officially agreed process of controlling security and intelligence through the D-notice committee, the Prime Minister sent in the heavy mob.

A shadowy figure whom Rusbridger described as a 'man from Whitehall'[32] spelled out the consequences: if *The Guardian* didn't stop publishing the Snowden stories, they would be shut down. The government would take *The Guardian* to court. Rusbridger says he explained to the man from Whitehall about the nature of international collaborations and the way in which, these days, media organisations could take advantage of the most permissive legal environments – *The Guardian* did not have to do its reporting from London. But the threat from the man from Whitehall was unambiguous: if *The Guardian* did not promise to stop publication it would have to destroy the files it had or be taken to court.

Rusbridger made what appeared to be a rational decision at the time: he agreed to the destruction of the files, but it would not be a decision without consequences. And it would be used against the newspaper in the future.

On a hot Saturday morning, 20 July 2013, two staff members from Britain's GCHQ were escorted to the basement of *The Guardian* offices not far from St Pancras railway station. Normally for jobs like this, intelligence agencies bring with them what they call 'cake mixers'. They are gadgets specifically used for destroying computers and reducing them to powder, so their drives are irretrievably damaged and all the information in them is obliterated. But this time they seemed satisfied with less conventional systems of destruction, among them electric angle grinders and a drill. Several Apple computers contained thousands of documents which formed the Snowden cache. The GCHQ staff watched as two *Guardian* staff drilled into the computer hard drives and ripped the machines to pieces. When they had finished one of the government men joked as he swept up the remains of a MacBook Pro: 'We can call off the black helicopters.'[33]

Had it not been for the heavy-handed interrogation at London's Heathrow airport of Glenn Greenwald's partner, David Miranda, on his way home to Brazil, we may never have known about what happened in *The Guardian* basement on that July morning.

Two days before Rusbridger's story appeared, Miranda was detained in the transit lounge – an international no-man's-land where the laws of the UK are murky to say the least. In a front-page comment piece, Rusbridger told how Miranda was kept there for nine hours under Schedule 7 of the UK's terror laws, which give enormous discretion to stop, search and question people who have no connection with 'terror', as anyone would normally understand it. Those held have no right to legal representation and may have their property confiscated for up to seven days. Under this measure – which applies specifically to places 'beyond the customs barrier' in international space – there are none of the checks and balances that apply once someone has crossed the 'frontier' into Britain. It's a complex and difficult area of operations for the police and intelligence agencies who are careful not to accuse anyone they detain of being a 'suspect'. For a 'suspect' has the right to a lawyer.

Police seized Miranda's laptop, phones, hard drives and camera to search for Snowden's documents. But try as they did, the best encryption experts at GCHQ could not open the files.

For Rusbridger it was a defining moment. Only now did he tell the story of the decision to allow GCHQ to destroy *The Guardian*'s copy of the Snowden files. By detaining Miranda in the Heathrow transit lounge, the security forces – in fact MI5 – had gone too far.

Rusbridger wrote, 'The state that is building such a formidable apparatus of surveillance will do its best to prevent journalists from reporting on it. Most journalists can see that. But I wonder how many have truly understood the absolute threat to journalism implicit in the idea of total surveillance, when or if it comes – and, increasingly, it looks like "when".

'We are not there yet, but it may not be long before it will be impossible for journalists to have confidential sources. Most reporting – indeed, most human life in 2013 – leaves too much of a digital fingerprint.'[34]

For journalists like Rusbridger who stood in the way, there was a price to pay. Hauled before the UK Parliamentary Home Affairs Committee to answer questions about the Snowden leaks, Rusbridger was subjected to a form of Blitz-style nationalism. Whose side are you on in the War on Terror?

In an unusual start to the hearing, Keith Vaz, chair of the committee, demanded to know if Rusbridger loved the United Kingdom. 'You and I were both born outside this country,' the Yemen-born MP told the editor, who was born in Zambia when it was a British colony. 'I love this country, do you love this country?'

Having said he was 'slightly surprised to be asked the question', Rusbridger responded, 'Yes, we are patriots and one of the things we are patriotic about is the nature of a democracy and the nature of a free press.' He said that the 'freedom to write and report' was 'one of the things I love about this country'.[35]

The most aggressive questioning came from Michael Ellis, the Conservative MP for Northampton North, who went for the editor with all the gravitas of a prosecuting counsel, accusing Rusbridger of being a criminal. 'Mr Rusbridger, you authorised files stolen by Snowden which contained the names of intelligence staff to be communicated elsewhere, didn't you – yes or no?' he demanded. 'Do you accept that from me that it is an offence, a criminal offence under section 58A of the Terrorism Act 2000?'[36]

To the question, as pompous as the questioner,
Rusbridger replied that no one had presented any evidence
that any security agents had been put at risk owing to *The
Guardian*'s Snowden stories. *The Guardian* had published no
names.

The Assistant Met Commissioner, Cressida Dick, told the
committee a Metropolitan Police investigation into material
taken from Miranda might result in 'some people' being found
to have committed an offence.[37] All this would have come as
a surprise to the British Cabinet secretary who, according
to Rusbridger, seemed unconcerned when told copies of the
Snowden material – containing all the names – had been sent
to *The New York Times* a full five months earlier.

The *Daily Mail* could hardly contain itself, salivating over
the prospect that journalists could be jailed. The *Daily Mail*
headline screamed long and very loud:

> *The Guardian* may face terror charges over stolen secrets: Met
> Deputy Commissioner confirms she is investigating whether
> newspaper broke the law
>
> Debate rages about dangers of Edward Snowden leaking US
> secrets
>
> MI6 said terror groups in Afghanistan and 'closer to home' are
> using leaks
>
> But *Guardian* editor Alan Rusbridger tells MPs only 1% of files
> published, insists the left-wing newspaper's staff are 'patriots'
> who 'loved this country'[38]

As Rusbridger succinctly put it, 'Those colleagues who deni-
grate Snowden or say reporters should trust the state to know
best (many of them in the UK, oddly, on the right) may one
day have a cruel awakening. One day it will be their reporting,
their cause, under attack.'[39]

In a curious story the following day, the *Daily Mail* bizarrely cited a so-called leaked NSA document on how to talk up the organisation's role. The headline read, '"NSA's mission is of great value to the Nation": Under fire spy agency's guide to Thanksgiving small talk revealed'.

If there was one question *The Guardian* had trouble answering it was this: if the newspaper had done nothing wrong, why did it destroy the files? For Rusbridger it was a pragmatic decision: knowing that the material was still held by *The New York Times*, he saved *The Guardian* possibly millions of pounds in court costs alone in not having to defend any legal action. Yet even if it might have been financially smart, it did hand *The Guardian*'s critics one tiny piece of ammunition, a possible reason why Rusbridger had not originally revealed the destruction of *Guardian* computers in its cellar back in July.

Not that *The Guardian*'s critics needed evidence as they whipped up their salivating response to the disclosures of unprecedented surveillance. The intelligence agencies simply wanted more power. On 17 January 2015 the London *Daily Telegraph* gave a big spread to a story which reported that intelligence agencies wanted 'updated powers' to access terror suspects' mobile phone records, emails and internet messages, when authorised by a senior Cabinet minister. It's what's known as the 'Snoopers' Charter', already rejected by parliament as being too intrusive, but resurrected by Cameron after the *Charlie Hebdo* killings. Closer examination of what happened in France, though, reveals gathering more information is not necessarily fruitful; working better with what intelligence agencies had already gathered may have been the answer: French security began closely monitoring brothers Cherif and Said Kouachi, the two gunmen, via internet, telephone and in person in 2009.[40]

The operation was beefed up in 2011, when Said returned from his trip to Yemen, which is reportedly when he met with al-Qaeda extremists to complete his jihadist training.

It was stopped in July 2014 when French security decided the brothers were no longer a threat.

Yet that didn't prevent the Australian Attorney-General, George Brandis, from making the 'atrocities in France' a pretext for proposed new surveillance laws which force telecommunications organisations to store metadata, the details of millions of phone calls and internet visits – similar to the Snoopers' Charter. Brandis not only linked the *Charlie Hebdo* attack to the need for greater surveillance powers, he connected it to the siege of Martin Place in central Sydney which left a gunman and two hostages dead shortly before Christmas 2014. Like the French agencies that had surveilled the Kouachi brothers, the Australian Security Intelligence Organisation (ASIO) had gunman Man Haron Monis on a watch list in 2008 and 2009 – but then, like the French, decided to drop him off it. Monis had come to ASIO's attention by sending a series of offensive letters to the families of dead Australian soldiers who had been serving in Afghanistan. The intelligence organisations of both France and Australia had adequate information that they were dealing with unstable and possibly dangerous people, information that they gathered using the existing laws. Both France and Australia ended the surveillance of those people – not because the laws weren't tough enough to allow that work to be carried out by its intelligence officers but because the individuals concerned had not been prioritised as sufficiently dangerous.

Now as the Australian government ramped up the fear of another attack, the Attorney-General forced through legislation – with the backing of the Opposition Labor Party – which will protect intelligence agencies from scrutiny and expose journalists to the risk of imprisonment for reporting on any one of their many bungles if it is deemed to be a Special Intelligence Operation (SIO). Journalists could be jailed for between five and ten years for revealing an SIO, even if they inadvertently do so. The person who decides whether an operation is an SIO is ASIO's director-general.

It doesn't take too much imagination to see that the director-general, or the government itself, might not want to have its errors revealed in public. Claiming an SIO provides them with the perfect cover. An investigation into how the blueprints for ASIO's new headquarters ended up on a server in China, which I revealed on a *Four Corners* program in 2013, or the case of how the Australian Secret Intelligence Service (ASIS) bugged the Cabinet office of East Timor's government to give an Australian oil company, Woodside, the edge in upcoming negotiations, might qualify for an SIO to find the leaker.

Not knowing that information in a story is part of an SIO is also not a defence. While in Opposition, Senator George Brandis broke all the rules about discussing intelligence matters to confirm the ASIO HQ debacle and embarrass the then government of Julia Gillard. Now in office as Attorney-General, he is using all the powers at his command to silence the media. If editors were apprehensive before, the threat of jail will make them even more jumpy and compliant.

CHAPTER 12

Chickenshit Editors

Just after the second passenger plane hit the World Trade Center in downtown New York on 11 September 2001, the NBC news anchor Tom Brokaw told his audience, 'There has been a declaration of war by terrorists on the United States.'[1]

If Brokaw, as is generally accepted, was the first person who gave life to the idea that terrorists were waging a war against the United States, the next day President George W. Bush neatly turned the phrase around. On 12 September he walked into the Oval Office of the White House for a TV address to the nation. Paraphrasing Brokaw, the US President for the first time used the phrase that would both define his presidency and redefine the meaning of war. He declared that the United States was now fighting a War on Terror. The birth of the catchphrase captured the symbiotic nature of what the media had become: so close to power it was barely possible to separate journalism and politics. It was NBC that had declared war. Bush had defined what kind of war it would be.

The catchphrase dominated the evening news: from the United Kingdom to Australia leaders became wartime prime ministers and Bush himself a wartime president. With the whole Western Alliance now 'at war', the fruits of an insider culture which had grown in many mass media outlets could now be harvested by governments.

Newspaper and TV proprietors have always mixed with politicians and the powerful to press their personal arguments. Until recently that had not been the case for their employees, the journalists, but then the status of journalists altered. Popular culture in the 20th and 21st centuries has been dominated by the rise of fascination with fame and one feature of that has been the emergence of the reporter as celebrity. No longer are reporters the outsiders – some might have said the outcasts – of society. The people at the top of the profession are themselves among the famous and highly paid new elites mixing with politicians and high society. The phenomenon first appeared in 1968, with the birth of US programs like *60 Minutes*, where the reporter became as important, and sometimes more important, than the story itself. By 1976 Woodward and Bernstein – the journalists who broke the Watergate story and brought down a US President – were being played by two of Hollywood's hottest actors, Robert Redford and Dustin Hoffman in *All the President's Men*. According to Edward Kosner, former editor of *Newsweek* and New York's *Daily News*, nobody really thought of journalists as celebrities until they were 'transformed into American icons'[2] by the film.

Celebrity journalism gave journalists huge power and with it came the arrival of the journalist as a political player: the ultimate insider – well connected, influential and, above all, famous. Certain vulnerabilities came with that territory, though: the notion of insider journalism has been identified as a major problem for decades. Being too close to a source means the journalist loses objectivity. Reporters talk of being 'captured by your source'. Guarding against this is easier said than done.

While *The Washington Post* was revealing Watergate, its editor, Ben Bradlee, warned the journalistic staff not to be seduced by off-the-record background briefings. Realising that the White House was leaking dubious stories to throw the paper off the track, Bradlee had had enough. He announced the 'no more unnamed sources' policy to the newsroom. From now on when an official said, 'This briefing is for background only', meaning the information couldn't be attributed to a named source, *Post* reporters were to walk out. Or if a Cabinet officer said, 'This will have to be off the record' – meaning it couldn't be used at all – *Post* reporters were to say politely that they were not allowed to listen. The experiment lasted for just two days. It was found to be unworkable and unnamed sources were once again allowed to be used in *Post* reports, but the experience indicated the degree of danger that Bradlee had identified in their use.[3]

As the place where it was born, it is probably the United States that understood more than most nations how vulnerable journalists could be to the allure of being an insider. In 2010 Professor Jay Rosen, one of the world's leading thinkers in journalistic practice, flew into Sydney from New York as a guest of the Walkley Foundation, whose awards honour the best of Australian journalism every year. Rosen, a long-time critic of journalists who see themselves as chroniclers of the insider game and members of the political class, was keen to discuss the problems of the insider culture. On his first day in the country, and still jet-lagged, he was aghast at what he had discovered: a television program which encapsulated the very essence of what was wrong with journalism.

Twenty-four hours after arriving in Australia, Rosen was interviewed on ABC's *Lateline* program:

Jay Rosen: By the way, I'm told that you actually have a program here on Sunday morning called the *Insiders.*

Leigh Sales: We do.

Jay Rosen: Is that true?

Leigh Sales: We do.

Jay Rosen: And the 'insiders' are the journalists.

Leigh Sales: That is right.
Jay Rosen: That's remarkable.[4]

Rosen didn't go any further, probably because he was too polite. And Sales immediately changed the subject, either because she failed to see its relevance or perhaps because she was wary of entering dangerous territory and being critical of another ABC program. Robust debate about journalism is rarely welcomed by journalists.

As Rosen pointed out, speaking at the Melbourne Writers Festival in August 2011, 'Promoting journalists as insiders in front of the outsiders, the viewers, the electorate . . . this is a clue to what's broken about political coverage in the US and Australia.' Rosen says that journalists 'are identifying with the wrong people'.[5] It's part of the co-dependent relationship which positions both journalists and politicians as players in a game where discussion about how a government policy will play out with the public is deemed to be more important than whether the policy is fair or will work at all.

This kind of game-show journalism has another impact. Everyone has a say, but there is no investigation. Opinion passes as revelation. Controversial subjects may be discussed, but there is no resolution. It is the perfect product for the modern mass media: it fills space, it's cheap and no one complains.

Though *Insiders* has produced some good journalism, what the program mainly provides for those who appear is a boost to their all-important profile in the increasingly significant world of the insider as celebrity journalist.

———

Insiders fitted perfectly with what an incoming Liberal government wanted from the ABC.

In 1996 soon after winning the federal election the conservative government appointed Donald McDonald, a former CEO of Opera Australia, as Chairman of the ABC

board. McDonald, generally acknowledged as an accom-
plished arts administrator, had even more alluring credentials.
He was a long-time friend of the new Prime Minister, John
Howard. Two years later McDonald made it known to the
ABC's Managing Director, Brian Johns, the Labor-appointed
amiable former book publisher, that he would not be reap-
pointed for a second five-year term. The problem was that
Johns still had more than a year to go before his first term was
up; he was reduced to operating as a lame duck.

In March 2000 Johns left the ABC. Finding a replacement
was not easy; the corporation had been starved of funds by
both Labor and conservative governments over the previous
decade. A ten-year comparison between government spending
in 1988–89 and 1998–99, showed that while Australia's gross
domestic product had increased by 32.7 per cent and spending
on defence had risen 9.7 per cent, education 16.2 per cent,
health 57.9 per cent and social security 69.6 per cent, spending
on the ABC had declined by 20.3 per cent. Compared to other
public broadcasters, back in 1996 the ABC received less per
head of population than Denmark, Germany, Italy, France,
Canada and the Netherlands. A comparison in funding
between 1986 and 1999 shows a decline in funding of 34.1
per cent. As the former ABC staff-elected Director Quentin
Dempster writes in his book *Death Struggle* (Allen & Unwin,
Sydney, 2000), 'Such a comparison can only indicate an intention by government over the past 15 years to marginalise and
even destroy the ABC.'

The cash-strapped ABC paid its managing directors a paltry
sum compared to commercial competitors. There was no flood
of applications to take over from Johns, even though the job was
not without prestige. On the other hand the quality of the list
of contenders was impressive. It included 'Malcolm Long, who
had wound up his term as managing director of SBS two years
before; Alan Kohler, former editor of *The Age* and *The Australian
Financial Review* and *The 7.30 Report*'s finance and economics
correspondent; Nigel Milan, managing director of SBS'.[6]

The applicant who eventually landed the job had performed badly in the first interview with the board and it was only intervention by McDonald that 'gave him a second chance', a well-connected source close to the decision-making process told me. The person who emerged victorious was short, sandy-haired, pugnacious Jonathan Shier. Although he told waiting media after his appointment was announced that he carried no baggage, that wasn't quite the case. He'd been a Liberal Party staffer – and a member of the party until recently.

Exactly how Shier managed to land the job has never been clarified but at least one member of the ABC board, staff-elected Director Kirsten Garrett, registered disapproval of Shier's appointment. In Ken Inglis's *Whose ABC?: The Australian Broadcasting Corporation, 1983–2006* (Black Inc, Melbourne, 2006), Garrett said she asked that her opposition to Shier taking over be recorded in writing after receiving a call from the ABC chairman Donald McDonald. According to Garrett's memory McDonald told her that Shier 'had come up roses'. Unlike all of the other contenders for the post, Shier who had worked at Thames TV, Scottish TV and France's Canal Plus, had no editorial experience. Yet the position of ABC Managing Director made him editor-in-chief. He had direct editorial control over all the ABC's news and current affairs TV and radio programs.

It didn't take long to discover why he had been appointed. Shier says one of the 'major problems' that had to be addressed was the 'accusation of bias in the ABC News and Current Affairs output.'[7] Jonathan Shier, the former Liberal staffer and ex-Liberal Party member who had triumphed so surprisingly over gold-standard candidates with strong journalistic credentials, soon appeared hell-bent on removing the intellectual heart of the ABC's News and Current Affairs division – and replacing it with more compliant personnel. Three months after taking over, Shier fired the head of News and Current Affairs, Paul Williams, an intelligent and combative defender of fearless journalism. In his place he appointed former news reporter Max Uechtritz, well known for his coverage of the Tiananmen Square uprising and for defending himself in a brawl at an accused Mafia killer's funeral he was covering for the ABC. Onlookers suspected that Uechtritz – although of a similar imposing physical stature to Williams but otherwise very different – had been sent in to clean out the alleged left-wing domination of the ABC's current affairs, the area where governments were put under scrutiny. The allegations of leftist bias were nothing new to the ABC. The right-wing *Quadrant* magazine reported that during the Howard years, when ABC funding was heavily cut, the government fought a 'culture war', because the ABC was 'hostile to conservatives'.[8]

Within 24 hours of being appointed Uechtritz telephoned his friend Barrie Cassidy, the ABC's Europe correspondent, and outlined the idea that had strong support from Shier. By the following year the first *Insiders* program was on air. According to former ABC presenter Tim Bowden, John Howard thought it was a 'terrific program'.[9]

Current affairs reporting was now referred to as 'news analysis'. In a time reminiscent of today's – when the conservatives promised not to cut the ABC's budget but then did, launching an assault from outside – Shier launched an assault from within. His erratic management style, the sackings of talented managers, and the loss of those who grew tired of being bullied caused widespread fear inside the organisation.

As a *Four Corners* reporter I suggested to the program's executive producer, Bruce Belsham, that Shier's credentials might not have matched the résumé he presented to the board and should be investigated. 'Be careful,' Belsham warned. 'I don't want to be the one to preside over the death of *Four Corners* at 40.'[10] Somehow the program did survive to celebrate its 40th anniversary and is still going strong.

What was in doubt was whether Kerry O'Brien, presenter of *The 7.30 Report*, a former *Four Corners* reporter and foundation host of *Lateline*, would survive. O'Brien, feared by both sides of politics as a brilliant interviewer, was loathed by the right wing of the Liberal Party.

Whether or not it was part of the agreement between Shier and Uechtritz, sealed in London as part of Uechtritz's appointment – something Uechtritz denies – what is not disputed by Uechtritz is that Shier had later said, 'O'Brien has to go.'[11] Shier denies having said anything of the sort. However, the targeting of O'Brien was an open secret inside the ABC and soon News Limited newspapers vilified him. One newspaper carried a picture of O'Brien under the headline, 'Dead Man Walking'.[12]

O'Brien wasn't the only person ABC staff believed Shier was angling to remove. On 6 July 2000 another of the extreme right's demons, Phillip Adams, host of ABC Radio's *Late Night Live*, received a visit at his inner-city home from two Radio National executives. The executives wanted to brief Adams on the radical new management regime they were now working under. They also wanted to gauge his reaction to winding back his workload. If Adams took up the offer of less time on air, it would appease the demands from Shier's new management, who wanted Radio National to find 'a right-wing Phillip Adams' and allow Adams to spent more time at his farm, where he already lived half the week. It was a clumsy coupling of ideas. Within hours a story was out that Adams had been threatened with the sack. Adams was quoted as recalling that his visitors warned him, 'If we don't sack you we will get the sack ourselves.'[13] That account of events is vehemently refuted by those with a detailed understanding of what transpired, but it certainly allowed Adams to successfully muster support for a program that Shier's management and the ABC board clearly had in their sights. Whatever the truth about the meeting there was one unambiguous message: those whom the government perceived as enemies were not safe at the ABC.

On 6 November 2000 *Media Watch* presenter Paul Barry, the author and former *Four Corners* and BBC reporter, interviewed ABC Chairman Donald McDonald for *Media Watch*. By any measure it was a robust exchange. Barry posed a number of questions about Shier. 'Can I read you some of the things, some of the headlines, about Mr Shier?' Barry asked with a rhetorical flourish. '"Sheer or Shier Madness" – *The Age*. "Shier's ABC vision still a blur . . ."'

> *McDonald:*   It's a rather tiresome play on words though, isn't it . . .
>
> *Barry:*   Yes, but it's a point of view, isn't it? It's one of our major national papers, calling a managing director mad, essentially. 'Shier's ABC vision still a blur', from *The Oz*. 'Incoherent, embarrassing without substance'. 'Woeful'. Now, doesn't that concern you, that your managing director has provoked that sort of reaction from the critics?'[14]

Three weeks later Barry was sacked. He said he had had reports that the 'managing director was incandescent with rage'[15] about the interview with McDonald. The Head of Television, Gail Jarvis, had told Barry she wasn't renewing his contract because she thought 'someone could do it better'. Though, Barry added, she didn't know who.[16]

McDonald would later be cited as someone who saved the ABC from the excesses of the government that had appointed him. Nothing could be further from the truth. He watched on limp-eyed – 'as cunning as a shit house rat',[17] in the words of the late board member Di Gribble, though she gracefully added that he was 'a nice one'[18] – while the organisation battled for its journalistic independence. Never once did he publicly defend ABC journalism from the ceaseless attacks of the Murdoch press.

—

In 2001 McDonald became the repository of an incendiary allegation against Shier which he kept secret and did not share openly with the board.

Ian Carroll – a member of the ABC executive, a founder of *Lateline* and one-time executive producer of *Four Corners* – terminally ill and speaking at his farewell, described the Shier years as the 'the most destructive period of the ABC' he had ever known.[19] The head of Innovation, in charge of extra TV channels the ABC was now building, Carroll told those assembled on the seventh floor of the ABC's Ultimo headquarters in Sydney – among them program and division heads and Managing Director Mark Scott – 'One of my lovely people working for Kids TV came to my office very early for her, 8.30 on Monday morning, and said, "Look, Ian, something terrible has happened and I need you to meet this woman. I know you never met her before but she's in a terrible mess. I need you to meet her."' Carroll said he did meet her and she told him 'a terrible story of harassment and I was shocked'. With his wife, Geraldine Doogue, an ABC presenter, Carroll's next step was to seek advice about how to handle the situation. 'And this advice was so important,' Carroll said, '. . . when you've got an MD [Shier] involved.'[20]

The advice Carroll was given to pass on to the woman was chilling: 'Firstly, do not talk to or trust anyone in authority at the ABC. You can no longer trust them. Don't talk to anyone without anyone else there. Two: stay out of the public eye. Do whatever you can, do not become a public celebrity. Three: very carefully document what happened. And present it to only one person, the chairman.'[21] That person was of course Donald McDonald.

Carroll said he did not know what happened to the woman in the end but 'certain people have suggested to me that it was the final little bit of the nail in the coffin' of Shier. 'I certainly hope so.'[22] Three weeks before Shier lost his job *The Australian* reported that 'a young female employee of the

ABC had lodged a sexual harassment claim against Mr Shier at the Human Rights & Equal Opportunity Commission'.[23] According to another report in *The Australian*, on 16 October 2001 by media writer Amanda Meade, 'Shier Loses Support of ABC Board', an ABC TV publicist told the commission that Shier behaved in 'an offensive manner' towards her late at night in Mount Isa, Queensland, after the first broadcast in August 2001 of a new TV show *Australia Talks*. Meade reported that Shier and two staff witnesses denied the allegation. Shier told me, in response to a list of written questions, that he would 'never know what motivated a woman who I had never previously met . . . to make an allegation of sexual harassment against me'. He said that the 'woman in question has not pursued any allegations'.

What is strange is that this significant matter involving the allegation of sexual harassment was 'never discussed by the board', according to a member who attended the meetings but asked not to be named.[24] Which means that the dossier containing the allegation appears to have only been known to McDonald, and a few other executives inside the organisation. The board, which had decided to give Shier an AU$20,000 performance bonus in August, now offered him a huge sweetener to leave. If dismissed, he would have collected 18 months' pay of about AU$500,000. But Shier left with more than twice that amount – '$983,000 plus entitlements of $72,000 – in return for a quick departure'.[25]

Shier's tenure had already cost the ABC AU$37.7 million paying out 390 redundancies. Around the ABC they were known as 'Golden Shiers'.

There is no doubt that a decision by the executives of the ABC to withdraw support from the managing director played a role in the board deciding to terminate his contract early. But Shier may not have been removed solely because of his bad management. If the details of the harassment case were as shocking as Carroll suggested, he was about to become an embarrassment, which would cause tremendous political damage to the government and reflect badly upon the reputation of its appointed chairman and Prime Minister Howard. Just ten days away from a federal election the chairman led the Liberal Party's appointed board members in ushering Shier out of his job.

The Communications Minister, Senator Richard Alston, a staunch defender, said, 'Jonathan Shier will leave the ABC a much stronger and more relevant cultural institution than when he took up the reins 18 months ago.'[26] It would not be the last time the ABC would hear from Senator Alston.

Shier's removal did not mark the end of the government attack on the national broadcaster. After the Liberals won the federal election on 10 November 2001, the ABC board appointed the quietly spoken Russell Balding to take over from Shier. Balding had no experience in publishing, broadcasting or journalism. He was an accountant.

Gone were the madcap Shier days but not his central plan. In 2002 Shier said in a newspaper interview, 'The next area that was going to have my attention' was news and current affairs – as though that hadn't already been the case.[27] And as far as ABC reporters were concerned it was as though Shier had never left.

'The ghost walks,' said one journalist. Another, a radio reporter, told me of a conversation he had with an ABC executive about a story the reporter thought was boring. 'Bland is good,' he says the executive told him. In other words, keep your head down. There was even a directive from John Cameron, who had been appointed by Balding to take over from Uechtritz as head of National News when he left, which made it plain what was expected. And it certainly wasn't a rallying call to courageous journalism: Cameron said that departing from style guidelines would 'lead to counselling and formal documentation. This, in turn, can have a major impact on career progression and, eventually, ongoing employment status.'[28]

A clear threat that anyone who stepped out of line could be fired. The style guidelines included a directive not to describe the federal government as 'the Howard government' for fear of being seen to make 'some unspecified editorial point',[29] and they needed to make sure that government comment usually came first in a news bulletin, Opposition second.[30]

For journalists wishing to test out the guidelines in a high-pressure environment, the War on Terror was getting underway. With it there would be a stepping up of the War on Journalism at the ABC. Senator Alston would lead the charge.

—

On Friday 23 March 2003 Linda Mottram, one of the ABC's most experienced broadcasters, slipped on her headphones and relaxed back into her chair. She watched the second hand on the clock sweep up to the top of the hour. The theme tune to the program she hosted played out as the red 'On Air' light glowed in the grey morning light now entering the studio. 'Good morning. I'm Linda Mottram. You're listening to *AM*,' she announced. 'International aid agencies are warning of a humanitarian catastrophe as the war unfolds,' Mottram told her audience. The Iraq War had started three days earlier. 'Hundreds of thousands of Iraqis could soon be streaming out of Iraq.' For the following eight weeks *AM* was a must-listen for anyone with a passing interest in the Iraq War. The program took its listeners on a fact-filled action-packed audio ride, from media briefings at the Pentagon, to Canberra and Whitehall's pronouncements, and to ABC reporters on the war's front line.

As the military action heated up, the Allied casualties began to rise. Mottram, a former ABC Middle East correspondent, asked whether the 'issue of the American dead and captured' had 'disturbed the American public'. On Friday 11 April Mottram told her audience, 'For commanders of the Coalition, the task of advancing the invasion of Iraq is becoming increasingly complicated.' On Monday 14 April, she said,

'. . . there is still no sign of a coherent plan for dealing with transitional issues like security and internecine conflict in the Iraqi community'. All the kind of coverage and questioning you would expect from a first-class radio program. But those comments by Mottram would form the basis of a sustained attack on the ABC, from which it has possibly even today not recovered.

The Iraq War continued without the discovery of WMDs and journalists began taking an increasingly close interest in how governments had reached the conclusion that they existed at all. It was a story nearly every reporter covering the war was chasing.

On 22 May 2003 BBC defence reporter Andrew Gilligan met with Dr Kelly, a government-employed expert in chemical weapons and WMDs, at the four-star Charing Cross Hotel, an ornate Victorian building near Trafalgar Square in Central London. Gilligan had recently spent some time in Baghdad reporting for the BBC and Kelly was keen to hear what was happening as the search for WMDs had still found nothing. As they talked about the progress of the war they also discussed the dire warning by Tony Blair that Iraq was capable of arming and firing a WMD armed missile within 45 minutes – such a missile could hit British troops based in Cyprus. What Kelly told Gilligan was extremely disturbing: the warning – which was the foundation of Blair's decision to go to war – had only come from a single source and the intelligence agencies were against its inclusion in the announcement Blair made committing British troops to the Iraq invasion. Kelly said it had merely been inserted to 'sex up' the threat to Britain.

Throughout the next week, as Gilligan worked on a story about what he'd seen and heard about Britain's participation, many concerns were being voiced about the quality of intelligence used to prosecute the war. It wasn't just journalists who were closely examining the evidence.

Meanwhile Linda Mottram told her audience in Australia, 'Doubts over the US intelligence, upon which the Howard government based its decision to join the invasion of Iraq, have forced the Central Intelligence Agency to begin a review to see if in fact it was wrong.'[31]

A government which had staked so much of its reputation on taking Australia to war, against substantial public opposition, now confronted the possibility of a humiliating admission: the weapons of mass destruction didn't exist.

Out of the blue, on 28 May 2003 Australia's Communications Minister, Senator Richard Alston, sent a blistering complaint to ABC Managing Director Balding, detailing what it said were 68 separate occasions of bias – mainly against its flagship morning current affairs radio program, *AM*, citing prejudice and distortion in its coverage of the war.

What was curious about the timing of Alston's allegations was that every one of the 68 incidents covered the first three weeks of the war. Alston's attack appeared to be triggered – seven weeks after the event – by the realisation that the public might soon find out that *AM*'s reporting of the war had been much more honest than the government's arguments for entering it in the first place.

Twenty-four hours later, on the other side of the world, BBC defence reporter Andrew Gilligan placed a phone call from his apartment in south-west London, using his special broadcast-quality line, into Broadcast House in Central London. It was one of the small benefits of an early start at BBC radio that reporters could sometimes call in from home. A few seconds later, at 6.07 am, Gilligan was live on the breakfast program *Today*. Gilligan reported that he understood that the British government had sexed up a dossier on WMDs to support its case for war and that Tony Blair, the Prime Minister, probably knew that an assertion that Britain would only have a 45-minute warning of a possible attack was false.

It's not recorded how Senator Alston responded when this news reached Australia a few hours later, but it would be true to say, that along with Prime Minister Howard, it ruined what was shaping up to be an otherwise reasonable autumn day.

From that moment on Gilligan became the target of the British government. The inquiry it launched, headed by Justice Hutton, quickly found that the document had not been sexed up and was highly critical of the BBC for letting Gilligan's material go to air. Many newspapers criticised the inquiry as a whitewash and staff at rival Independent Television News described it as a dark day for journalism. Nevertheless the support soon melted away and despite originally having been congratulated on a great story, Gilligan found himself being criticised for his journalism and even lampooned. Kevin Marsh, his editor on BBC's *Today*, said he had probably been 'in his underpants sitting at the end of his bed presumably' when he delivered his broadcast.[32]

As the storm raged, abandoned by his editor and condemned by Justice Hutton, Gilligan stood by the central point of his story: that the threat of a WMD attack had been beaten up by the government.

The subsequent inquiries into how the two sister broadcasting organisations, the BBC and the ABC, were handling the Iraq War could not have been more similar in some regards – or more starkly different in others. In the face of the BBC board's refusal to support Gilligan, the BBC Chairman, Gavyn Davies, and the Director-General, Greg Dyke, both resigned. They remained loyal to their story and to their reporter. Dyke condemned the BBC governors, the equivalent of the ABC board. 'The bulk of them were gutless buggers' who 'pretend they are the great defenders of independent journalism and at any time that it gets tough they are not'.[33]

One year later a review of the intelligence services by Lord Butler vindicated Gilligan. Dyke told *Channel 4 News*, 'If you go back to the very beginning, Dr Kelly told Andrew Gilligan the document had been "sexed up" and one of the examples of it having been "sexed up", the most significant example, was the 45-minute claim.

'Here, we are told today . . . that the 45-minute claim should not have been in the document without a set of caveats, caveats that were there in early drafts and disappeared. The question is who took out the caveats? The BBC was perfectly right to report Dr Kelly's allegations, Dr Kelly's concern.

'That's why I am not at the BBC today, that's why Gavyn Davies is not at the BBC today and I would defend that decision forever.'[34]

In Australia in everything Senator Alston had documented there was not one single complaint about factual errors; what angered the minister was the way questions were framed and the overly sceptical nature of the reporting of purported US victories.

Murray Green of the ABC's senior executive investigated Alston's claims, finding no systemic bias in the reporting. His 130-page reply upheld only two of Senator Alston's specific complaints. Both involved reports from Washington. One covered US President Bush's sensitivity to the bombing campaign, which had caused civilian deaths; Green found *AM*'s reporting of the President's sensitivities 'should have been expressed more tentatively'.[35] The only other criticism of the *AM* coverage of a war being fought on questionable 'evidence' was that one of its reports, according to Green, 'had a tendency towards sarcasm'.[36] You might have thought the overall vindication was a matter for celebration – a 66–2 routing of a political attack on the ABC. But up in his office on the 14th floor of the ABC headquarters, Russell Balding – the ABC's editor-in-chief and Managing Director – made an incredible decision. He did not follow the example of his BBC counterpart Greg Dyke, who had railed against the finding of a judge to support his journalists. Balding took, as one-time *Media Watch* host David Marr later described, 'the bizarre course of appealing against its own victory'.[37] Balding ordered that the Alston dossier be sent to an outside independent panel, explaining that he believed that 'it is in the public interest that this matter be further reviewed by a body that is independent and external to the ABC'.[38] Unlike his BBC peer, Balding felt no necessity to stand by the story. It was weak behaviour by a weak leader. Perfect for the government, however.

In the end the external review found that of the 68 complaints there was no evidence of inaccuracy and no evidence of overall bias. But the review cited 12 cases where there was 'serious bias'.[39] A good example of what 'serious bias' meant to the review was the case where the reporter suggested President George W. Bush might have not watched the bombing attack live on TV because he was sensitive to possible civilian casualties. This was the kind of 'misjudgment' that those who had championed a war which was now being utterly discredited were seizing on.

The behaviour of the ABC board resembled that of the BBC governors, cowardly and silent. Unlike the BBC Chairman however, Donald McDonald never once looked like he would speak up publicly for *AM* and its presenter. What distinguished the organisations was editorial leadership and Greg Dyke's decision to resign in protest at the BBC board's refusal to support one of its reporters.

Seymour Hersh, the US investigative journalist who revealed the My Lai massacre of civilians during the Vietnam War and the torture of Iraqis at Abu Ghraib, has a description for editorial leaders who won't take risks and stand up for strong journalism. He calls them 'chickenshit'[40] editors and he says they're wrecking the industry. Hersh was talking mainly about US editors but if he had cast his net slightly wider he would have found a glowing example elsewhere.

—

In July 2014, at the height of the Gaza invasion, Mike Carlton, one of Australia's most celebrated newspaper columnists, wrote an incisive piece for *The Sydney Morning Herald*. He painted a gruesome scene: 'The images from Gaza are searing, a gallery of death and horror. A dishevelled Palestinian man cries out in agony, his blood-soaked little brother dead in his arms. On a filthy hospital bed a boy of perhaps five or six screams for his father, his head and body lacerated by shrapnel. A teenage girl lies on a torn stretcher, her limbs awry, her face and torso blackened like a burnt steak. Mourners weep over a family of 18 men, women and children laid side by side in bloodied shrouds. Four boys of a fishing family named Bakr, all less than 12 years old, are killed on a beach by rockets from Israeli aircraft.'

Carlton told his readers that as he wrote, just over a week after the Israeli invasion of Gaza, the death toll of Palestinians was climbing towards 1000. Most were civilians, many were children. Assaulting Gaza by land, air and sea, Israel had destroyed homes and reduced entire city blocks to rubble. There were 'desperate shortages of food and water, of medical and surgical supplies'.[41]

It was a powerful narrative with a strong argument against Israel's strategy at its core: 'In defiance of the laws of war and the norms of civilised behaviour, it is waging its own war of terror on the entire Gaza population of about 1.7 million people. Call it genocide, call it ethnic cleansing: the aim is to kill Arabs.'[42]

Carlton pointed out that Hamas was also trying to kill Israelis but they were protected by Israel's anti-missile screen – and only three civilians had died. 'The Israeli response has been out of all proportion, a monstrous distortion of the much-vaunted right of self defence.'[43]

Carlton added that this was 'a new and brutal Israel dominated by the hardline, right-wing Likud Party of Prime Minister Benjamin Netanyahu and his coalition. As one observer puts it: "All the seeds of the incitement of the past few years, all the nationalistic, racist legislation and the

incendiary propaganda, the scare campaigns and the subver-
sion of democracy by the right-wing camp – all these have
borne fruit, and that fruit is rank and rotten. The national-
ist right has now sunk to a new level, with almost the whole
country following in its wake. The word 'fascism', which I try
to use as little as possible, finally has its deserved place in the
Israeli political discourse.'"[44]

Fascism in Israel? Carlton revealed the source of the quote:
'In fact, that paragraph within the quotation marks was
written by an Israeli. Gideon Levy is a columnist and editorial
board member of the daily newspaper *Ha'aretz*. Born in Tel
Aviv to parents who fled the Nazi occupation of Czechoslova-
kia in 1939, he despairs of what his country has become and
the catastrophe its armed forces are visiting upon Gaza.'[45]

Carlton cited the West Bank occupation and the fact that
Israel had been founded by a terrorist group – and then drove the
Palestinians out of their own land. He added that he expected
there would be 'the customary torrent of abusive emails calling
me a Nazi, an anti-Semite, a Holocaust denier, an ignoramus.
As usual they will demand my resignation, my sacking. As it's
been before, some of this will be pornographic or threatening
violence.'[46] He was right. 'I got a fortnight of abuse, of threats of
violence. "You filthy piece of Jew-hating Nazi slime, people like
you started World War II, Catholic Jew-baiter", and so on. And
there was just torrents of this, this filth. And once or twice I
snapped and hit back. We do that in this country. Occasionally
you, you go and tell people to go and get effed.'[47]

Carlton told one reader, 'How arrogant and foolish you
are',[48] while telling another, 'Looking forward to hearing from
you after you have joined the IDF [Israel Defense Forces] and
gone off to kill some kids. Reluctantly, of course. Until then,
fuck off.'[49]

He wrote to another reader, 'You are a vulgar and stupid
bigot.'[50] To another he said, 'What a ridiculous little wanker
you are. Fuck off.'[51]

The Sydney Morning Herald Editor-in-Chef, Darren Goodsir, told Carlton to apologise for the way he had treated readers but Goodsir was overruled by a senior Fairfax executive who decided Carlton should be suspended. Carlton resigned and tweeted, 'Confirming I have quit the SMH, sad that once great newspaper has buckled to the bullies. Thank you for your support. Maintain the rage.'[52]

The Sydney Morning Herald denied that the original column was an issue, but it was clear that editorial independence had a price. And it wasn't just happening on the left-leaning papers like *The Sydney Morning Herald*. The right was censoring its journalists too.

—

What happened at a plush London hotel not far from Buckingham Palace in September 2010 should have been comforting for the journalists who work at the London *Daily Telegraph*. Its chief political correspondent, Peter Oborne, had been invited to lunch by the newspaper's chief executive, Murdoch MacLennan. With circulation spiralling down, the *Telegraph* had engaged in cutting costs by sacking staff and trying to boost its internet presence with click-bait. Among those gems would be 'The Three Breasted Woman', a story Oborne says he was told wasn't true even before it went online.

Oborne had been growing increasingly anxious about the direction of *The Daily Telegraph* and he asked MacLennan not to 'take the newspaper for granted' with its lower-brow editorial innovations, pointing out it still had a 'healthy circulation of more than half a million'. He told MacLennan the *Telegraph* readers were loyal, that the paper was still very profitable and that 'the owners had no right to destroy it'.[53]

Oborne had put his case clearly and he hoped that the management was listening. He felt a personal family connection with the paper. His grandfather, Lt Col. Tom Oborne DSO, had been a *Telegraph* reader. He was also a churchwarden and played a role in the local Conservative Association. Oborne was proud that his grandfather had a special rack on the breakfast table and would read *The Daily Telegraph* carefully over his bacon and eggs, devoting special attention to the leaders. 'I often thought about my grandfather when I wrote my *Telegraph* columns,' Oborne said.[54]

A few weeks later Oborne happened to meet MacLennan in a queue outside the funeral of former Prime Minister Lady Thatcher. Once again Oborne pressed MacLennan not to take the readers for granted. Whether it was the spiritual presence of Lady Thatcher or something more personal, according to Oborne, MacLennan told him, 'You don't know what you are fucking talking about.'[55]

It was a rude awakening for Oborne. In a world of postmodernism and 'comparative' truth, he believed that the pursuit of the truth was a noble journalistic ambition. Only now was he beginning to realise the impact the owners, billionaire twins David and Frederick Barclay, might be having on his beloved *Telegraph*. Once described as working-class Tories who made good, they bought the newspaper in 2004 from Conrad Black's Hollinger group and own, among other things, the Ritz Hotel in London's Piccadilly and a castle on the island of Sark.

Oborne's first troubling experience was the way one of his stories was treated. Well-known British Muslims had received letters from the HSBC bank informing them that their accounts had been closed. No reason was given, and it was made plain that there was no possibility of appeal. 'It's like having your water cut off,' Oborne says one victim told him.[56]

When he submitted the story for publication, he says he was 'fobbed off with excuses' then told there was a 'legal problem'.[57] When he questioned further, 'an executive took me aside and said that "there is a bit of an issue" with HSBC'[58] – the Hong Kong and Shanghai Banking Corporation was a major advertiser with *The Daily Telegraph*.

In November 2014, the *Telegraph* barely touched a story
on HSBC which revealed the bank had set aside more than
£1 billion for customer compensation and an investigation
into the rigging of currency markets. This story was the city
splash in *The Times*, *Guardian* and *Mail*, making a page lead in
The Independent. 'There was no avoiding the impression that
something had gone awry with the *Telegraph*'s news judgment,'
says Oborne.[59]

He went to see MacLennan again, resolved to effect some
kind of change in editorial policy or leave as a matter of principle. MacLennan served Oborne tea and asked him to take off
his jacket, Oborne recalls – an exercise in British civility, but
it could have been taken as an invitation to a brawl. Oborne
laid out his concerns and says MacLennan told him he was a
valued writer and he wanted him to stay. Oborne responded
that he was 'resigning as a matter of conscience'.[60]

As Oborne prepared a graceful exit from the newspaper,
events overtook him. The BBC's flagship investigative
program, *Panorama*, ran a story about HSBC and its Swiss
banking arm, alleging a widescale tax evasion scheme, while
The Guardian and the International Consortium of Investigative Journalists published their 'HSBC Files'. The stories
were splashed across the front pages of the *Financial Times*;
The Times and the *Daily Mail* spread it across several pages.

'You needed a microscope to find the *Telegraph* coverage:
nothing on Monday, six slim paragraphs at the bottom left of
page two on Tuesday, seven paragraphs deep in the business
pages on Wednesday,'[61] said Oborne. The *Telegraph*'s reporting
only picked up when the possibility arose of tax irregularities
with people connected to the Labour Party.

Oborne made another discovery. Three years earlier the
Telegraph investigations team had produced a number of stories
on HSBC, but the investigation had suddenly stopped for no
apparent reason. Reporters were ordered to destroy all emails,
reports and documents related to the HSBC investigation,

Oborne was told. But that wasn't good enough for the bank. It suspended its advertising with the *Telegraph*.

Executives say that Murdoch MacLennan was determined not to allow any criticism of the international bank. 'He would express concern about headlines even on minor stories,' says one former *Telegraph* journalist. 'Anything that mentioned money-laundering was just banned, even though the bank was on a final warning from the US authorities.'[62] Oborne says HSBC finally returned its advertising to the *Telegraph* after approximately one year.

Angry and alarmed, instead of going quietly, Oborne decided to tell the public. He became one of a rare breed – a journalist as whistleblower.

When Oborne questioned the *Telegraph* about its connections with advertisers, the paper responded that his 'questions are full of inaccuracies, and we do not therefore intend to respond to them' but was adamant that 'The distinction between advertising and our award-winning editorial operation has always been fundamental to our business. We utterly refute any allegation to the contrary.'[63]

The readers of the London *Daily Telegraph* may well have wondered idly why HSBC was getting such little editorial space but would never have known what was going on without the decision of Peter Oborne to switch from being an insider to an outsider. The fact that he told his story in an online blog reveals as much about the shifting power in the media as the events traumatising journalists at *The Daily Telegraph*. Giving up its independence – and all the power that provided – to hang on to advertising was what happened in a provincial weekly newspaper, not one of the grand bastions of the British Establishment.

We were heading for the last hurrah of the fourth estate's media barons.

CHAPTER 13
The Last Hurrah

The two-storey stone cottage in a remote part of Britain's West Country seemed just the place to plot a dirty deed. Set back off the road, it had that haunted look suggesting it had seen better days and happier times. Its former occupant, computer hacker Lee Gibling, certainly used to have a sense of humour. Naming it The House of Ill Compute (THOIC), Gibling stuffed it with every electrical gadget imaginable to delight the hacker, including the obligatory bank of computers. The House of Ill Compute would live up to its name. Gibling lived on the edge of legality. His little enterprise in the late 1990s became a virtual one-stop shop for hackers exchanging information about web vulnerabilities.

Gibling found British TV a bit dull and decided to hack into international broadcasters. 'Late night adult, nothing too risqué, but something a bit better than just the boring channels that we had in the UK,' he says.[1] But it was closer to home that he ran into trouble when he hacked into Murdoch's Sky TV and began watching it for free. A security unit working inside Sky tracked Gibling down – but instead of prosecuting him, they discreetly hired him. Gibling says he wondered why Sky wanted THOIC, which was 'principally evolved as a hacking site' to become 'part of their portfolio'.[2] He was about to become enmeshed in a brutal battle for supremacy at the dawn of the digital age. The field was open for all-comers: the foolhardy, the brave and the adventurous. Welcome to the world of the power-hungry media mogul.

During the 1990s, the media industry had been unscrambling itself from the economic crash of 1987 – which, like the recession two decades later, wiped billions off stock-market values. Around the world there was a recalibrating of media power after the profligacy of the 1980s. The Canadian media baron Conrad Black and his company Hollinger International had already snapped up the London *Daily Telegraph* and added the *Chicago Sun-Times* and *The Jerusalem Post* to its portfolio. In the early 1990s Black began stalking the Fairfax group in Australia, which had 20 per cent of the newspaper market. He found an ally in Australia's richest man, Kerry Packer, owner of the Nine TV Network. Packer was cashed up and keen to control Fairfax, both to get bigger and to match his old competitor, Rupert Murdoch. Both had inherited media interests from their fathers, and both were desperate to be winners.

Of the three media titans Murdoch and Black appeared to have most in common. Though both used their newspapers to exhort sometimes strident nationalism, they were both willing to give up their citizenship for personal gain. For the rather pompous, self-important Black it was a matter of prestige. A Canadian, he became British to take up a baronetcy offered by British Prime Minister Margaret Thatcher, in recognition of his support of the Conservative Party. For Murdoch it was simply about commerce. He had renounced his Australian citizenship to become a US citizen – an act which allowed him to buy several TV networks in America, the first steps to establishing Fox News.

Once again Murdoch, with his hunger for expansion, set his sights on the United Kingdom, where he'd first built up his international newspaper empire. Now he wanted to dominate in pay TV via his company Sky. Murdoch would utilise his acclaimed commercial dexterity plus a heavy dose of naked political power to achieve his aim. As the biggest mass-circulation newspapers in the country, *The Sun* and *The News of the World* delivered the raw power; *The Times*, which he'd bought in 1981, conferred a fig leaf of decency. Yet even the acquisition of *The Times* had been crooked, mired in political dealing. Murdoch, who already owned 40 per cent of the British press, should have faced a monopoly inquiry to take it over but Margaret Thatcher – after a secret meeting with Murdoch, denied for 30 years and only revealed in 2012 – waved it through. It guaranteed Thatcher, as former *Times* editor Harold Evans wrote, 'sunshine headlines for herself in the Murdoch press (especially when it was raining)'.[3]

Over the next few years the three media barons would reach the zenith of their influence. How they used it to benefit their commercial interests would harshly reveal the level of danger they posed to the democratic process. Labour MP Tom Watson explained it to the House of Commons as follows:

> The barons of the media, with their red-topped assassins, are the biggest beasts in the modern jungle. They have no predators. They are untouchable. They laugh at the law. They sneer at Parliament. They have the power to hurt us, and they do, with gusto and precision, with joy and criminality. Prime ministers quail before them, and that is how they like it. That indeed becomes how they insist upon it, and we are powerless in the face of them. We are afraid. That is the tawdry secret that dare not speak its name . . . We allow it because we allow narrow party advantage to dominate our thinking, above the long-term health of our democracy.[4]

Murdoch had spent a long time building up the power to intimidate governments and have MPs quivering in their boots. No one's private life was safe from public exposure if they stood in his way. But while he quickly built a newspaper empire, which for a long time continued to run with the rivers of gold, pay TV proved to be wholly different. Unlike selling newspapers – often a straight over-the-counter cash transaction in the local newsagent's – television relied on sophisticated technology to bring in the money. It was its greatest vulnerability.

In the early days consumers bought a smart card which gave them access to the station's signal through a set-top box. But if the smart card was hacked and the encryption unscrambled, anyone could watch the programs for free. There would be no revenue stream. What made life even more problematic from a business perspective was the extreme difficulty of tracking down those who were using phoney smart cards.

News Corp set about to do all it could to protect its investment. For eight years Sky ruled the roost in the United Kingdom as the sole pay TV broadcaster but in 1998 Independent Television (ITV) launched a rival, OnDigital. If anyone managed to break the access codes for OnDigital's smart card, the company's life expectancy would be very limited. In Jerusalem, an Israeli company owned by News Corp – News Datacom Services (NDS) – did exactly that. Finding out how a competitor's system works is perfectly legal. But the OnDigital codes somehow got out onto the internet – launched from THOIC.

Now anyone could download the codes and produce pirated smart cards. And watch OnDigital for free. That's exactly what tens of thousands of people in Britain did. With its income stream fast drying up, OnDigital went broke.

When whispers of dark dealings began circulating, News Corp and NDS claimed they had nothing to do with the release of OnDigital's access codes and that they only became involved in hacking so they could learn how to protect their own pay TV smart cards from piracy. Yet internal emails proved otherwise, linking News Corp's Israeli company to THOIC and the work it had done breaking the OnDigital access codes. In 2008 a Californian district court judge issued a permanent injunction against NDS to stop its 'piracy and an anti-competitive practice'.[5] Though the judge only ordered NDS to pay US$1500 damages, it was a legal finding that NDS were pirates.[6]

On 26 March 2012 the BBC's *Panorama* program broke open the story of THOIC with a 30-minute documentary entitled *Murdoch's TV Pirates*. From the opening titles, which announced the 'biggest Murdoch hacking scandal of all', to the end, it plotted out how NDS had 'hacked down the opposition' which stood in the way of its own Sky channel. The program, based on the assiduous work of *Australian Financial Review* investigative journalist Neil Chenoweth, said News Corp wasn't just hacking telephones to produce stories, it was involved in industrial espionage and sabotage on a grand scale.

As might be expected, News Corp dismissed the program and angrily demanded a retraction. When none was forthcoming News Corp fell silent. Murdoch had other plans for the BBC and they had nothing to do with getting even with *Panorama* and far more to do with attacking what he saw as a commercial competitor: the BBC's innovative 24-hour news, launched in November 1997. In comparison with the easily dispatched OnDigital – which even after changing its name to ITV Digital had not staved off bankruptcy – the government-funded BBC News 24 was proving to be a far more resilient opponent. By August 2004 the BBC was boasting it was beating Sky News in the ratings. For eight out of the previous ten weeks, the BBC's rolling news station had been ahead with a total of 1.99 million viewers compared to Sky's 1.97 million.[7]

Sky proceeded to spend up big but after buying exclusive rights to broadcast the English league football in an attempt to expand its audience base, its profits plummeted. For the 12 months to the end of June 2008 it made a paltry £60 million profit, down from £724 million in the previous year. Then Murdoch changed gear.

His objective was to weaken the national broadcaster and literally shut it out of large sections of the market. At the same time he wanted to increase his holding in Sky from 39 per cent to effectively full control, which was going to be difficult to achieve, given the Labour government's embrace of media plurality. Murdoch launched an audacious twin-pronged plan which involved vicious personal attacks on the British Labour Prime Minister, Gordon Brown, who stood in his way, and a sudden outpouring of admiration for the Opposition leader, David Cameron, who promised to give Murdoch what he wanted. He would later use the same tactics of degrading personal attacks on Australian Prime Minister Kevin Rudd as part of a concerted campaign to kill competition for his Foxtel cable TV network in Australia. In both cases the prime ministers were already politically wounded, easy and soft targets.

According to sources talking to Nick Davies, James Murdoch persuaded his father that a Cameron Government would be less likely to cause problems with their furtively planned bid to buy all of Sky, the most important move on News Corp's horizon.

What happened to Gordon Brown over several months in 2009 unfolded like a halfpenny thriller. From the opening line you understood the plot and where it would end up.

As for the other objective, the key to undermining the BBC involved reducing its funding. Murdoch had long complained about the BBC's licence fee, paid by anyone who owned a radio or TV, whether or not they tuned in to the BBC's programs. In March 2009 David Cameron suddenly declared that the BBC licence fee should be frozen. *The Sun* trumpeted, 'Mr Cameron wants to curb the BBC's bloated bureaucracy and waste of cash. He plans to choke off the taxpayer funding that gives it an advantage over rivals such as Sky.'[8]

News was also keen to scrap Ofcom – the Office of Communications – the independent communications authority which would adjudicate on whether Murdoch could increase his stake in Sky. On 6 July 2009 David Cameron announced that, if elected, he would abolish Ofcom. On 9 July *The Times* ran a story accusing Ofcom executives of having disproportionately high salaries and expense accounts.

On 15 July James Murdoch and Rebekah Brooks met another Cameron ally, Oliver Letwin,[9] who was in charge of drawing up the Conservative manifesto for the coming general election, specifically to discuss the future of Ofcom, the communications regulator.

On 23 July *The Sun* ran a column by Kelvin MacKenzie which accused the Ofcom Chief Executive, Ed Richards, of 'brown-nosing' and described the Ofcom Chair, Colette Bowe, as 'an elderly has-been'.[10]

Gordon Brown explained to the House of Commons what the battering was about as he saw it: 'Their aim was to cut the BBC licence fee, to force BBC Online to charge for its content, for the BBC to sell off its commercial activities, to open up more national sporting events to bids from Sky and move them away from the BBC, to open up the cable and satellite infrastructure market, and to reduce the power of their regulator, Ofcom. I rejected those policies.'[11]

Just in case anyone had missed the News Corp message, on 29 August 2009 James Murdoch delivered the prestigious MacTaggart lecture at the Edinburgh International Television Festival. There he extolled the virtues of the 'free market' and told an incredulous audience that 'The only reliable, durable, and perpetual guarantor of independence is profit.'

Immediately after the lecture the Shadow Minister for Culture, Jeremy Hunt, travelled to New York where, according to the House of Commons register of interests, he had meetings with 'representatives of News Corp'.[12]

Now the pro-Cameron onslaught began in earnest. *The Sun* showed the Conservatives in a good light. Like a press-gang recruiting for a pirate voyage it fooled its readers and misled them with tales filled with trash and distortion. *The Sun* began a concentrated attack on the Prime Minister. When Brown announced free childcare for a quarter of a million impoverished children, *The Sun* howled that the program 'began to unravel immediately as middle-class parents reacted with fury'.[13]

Brown said tests for cancer would be completed within a week, but this 'appeared to be unfunded', according to *The Sun*; he promised tighter controls on immigration, but this was done in 'only 83 words'.[14]

Shortly before Cameron made his speech to the Conservative Party conference in October 2009 *The Sun* editor, Rebekah Brooks, sent him an extraordinarily cringing text – 'I am so rooting for you, not just as a personal friend but because professionally we are in this together. Speech of your life? Yes he Cam!' – in a cross between a sweetheart's billet-doux and a call to arms. Brooks wrote the following day, 'Brilliant speech. I cried twice. Will love "working together".'[15]

The Sun reported that Cameron had 'the strength to get battered Britain back on its feet' and that he had made 'a power-packed speech'.[16]

By early spring of 2010 it was apparent that Brown would announce a general election for a few months' time, at the start of May. Though 52 per cent of the vote went to the main non-Conservative parties, in Britain's first-past-the-post electoral system Cameron became Prime Minister in a deal with the left-of-centre Liberal Democrats.

Thirty-four days later James Murdoch announced that News Corp was bidding to take over Sky. It all seemed to have gone so swimmingly to plan. Only the *News of the World* phone-hacking story brought the whole deal undone. Cross-party opposition in the House of Commons forced Murdoch to drop his aspirations to completely take over Sky.

But all was not lost. News Corp did have one win which slowed the BBC's advances into the digital world. Cameron froze the BBC licence fee and added a list of extra expenditure which the corporation would have to bear: the rollout of rural broadband, the cost of running the BBC World Service, the

Welsh-speaking channel, BBC Monitoring, even the subsidy of new local TV stations. On top of that Cameron announced he would cut money for BBC Online by 25 per cent. It amounted to a 16 per cent across-the-board reduction in total funding. Director-General Tony Hall said the BBC risked becoming 'stuck in an analogue cul-de-sac'.[17]

The cuts clipped the BBC's expansion plans, which greatly favoured Sky. They also effectively reduced the competition for Murdoch's other investments, *The Sun* and *The Times*. Whereas in pre-digital times government-funded national broadcasters like the BBC operated in a separate realm from print newspapers, now TV, radio and newspapers are all competing in the same online space.

Of course Murdoch is underwhelmed about sharing that space and is especially disparaging about what he sees as state-subsidised news dumping. He has an unusual ally in Julian Assange: he and Murdoch have some libertarian views in common. Assange argues that the distribution of huge amounts of free online content makes it difficult for other purveyors of content to compete. 'As much I might disagree with the way his corporation runs, otherwise I agree with his economic argument,' he told me.[18] The problem of a severely limited public broadcaster is that Murdoch would be even more dominant – a frightening vision, even for Julian Assange, who has no belief in the state as saviour.

Yet Murdoch is contradictory on private-sector competition. There are fewer better examples of how Murdoch extols the virtue of competition when it suits him, and gets himself in a muddle when it doesn't, than the 2007 plans of the Australian Labor Party to build a super-fast national broadband network (NBN).

Describing the policy as a contribution to 'nation building for the future',[19] the then Opposition leader Kevin Rudd said broadband infrastructure was on a par with railway construction in the 19th century. The idea was big but quite straightforward. The government would put up AU$4.7 billion and the rest, approximately AU$39 billion, would come from private investors. What was so extraordinary about the NBN was that it would link fibre-optic cable, the fastest form of delivery, straight into the home.

Forty times faster than existing networks, the NBN would be run by an independent operator, renting out space to any company which wanted to use it. It was direct competition to the Telstra–News Corp–Foxtel cable system. The super-highway would be able to carry high-definition movie channels in real time and multi-channel sports events.

As could be expected News Corp, along with the Liberal Party, took an instant dislike to the proposal. The plan received a pounding in the Murdoch press. *The Daily Telegraph* was forced to issue an apology for so-called errors in three stories it published denigrating the NBN. During the 2013 federal election Kevin Rudd, who had just won back the Prime Minister's job he'd been dumped from by his own party three years earlier and was now fighting an unwinnable election, was subjected to a sustained attack by the Murdoch press. From Brisbane's *Courier-Mail*: 'Send in the Clowns' – a story about a former popular Queens-land premier joining the Labor campaign trail – to a blunt 'Kick This Mob Out' from the Sydney *Daily Telegraph*.

Rudd, like Brown a wounded leader, blamed the attacks in part on the NBN proposal. But why did the Murdoch press bother to attack Rudd when the Labor Party, trailing so badly in the opinion polls, would be thrown out of office anyway? The answer is, as in the United Kingdom, to send a clear warning to the Liberal Party that to maintain Murdoch's support they should oppose the NBN if elected.

In the end the NBN did survive but in a neutered form. No more rapid delivery direct to the home, the high-speed fibre-optic stops in the street under the Liberal plan, and from a six-lane superhighway slows to a single track down the existing Telstra connection.

Murdoch insists he has no idea why people believed he was opposed to the NBN. It was no competition for his Foxtel consortium and his newspapers only opposed it because it was a waste of money.

Murdoch appeared to have an unusual capacity for keeping truth at a distance. For his fellow Australian media baron, Kerry Packer, it was a slightly different problem. He seemed to enjoy outright lying.

—

Kerry Packer's performance at a parliamentary inquiry into the Australian print media in 1991 – set up to review potential concentration in Packer's hands of media ownership – is a collector's item. For chutzpah he completely outshone Murdoch 20 years later, when the latter was hauled before a committee of British parliamentarians investigating the phone-hacking scandal. There was none of the effete manoeuvring so typical of press barons like Cecil King, who had tried to overthrow British PM Harold Wilson's Labour government in the 1960s. Packer's style was bare-knuckle brawling – a mauling of parliamentarians who dared question him about his media business. Even today Packer's admirers fondly recall the way he faced down the politicians who challenged him. Their comments praise his blunt speaking but ignore the narcissistic display of greed, money and power which Packer represented. If nothing else his performance revealed in clear sight what other media barons do in private, albeit with slightly less piggishness, but with probably similar effect.

He openly intimidated the young chairman, Michael Lee. His bulky frame hunched forward on a plain wooden table, Packer demanded a cup of tea from the usher and stared down the committee.

Packer had come under scrutiny because of his efforts to buy into the iconic Fairfax newspaper group. His intentions were suspected to be dark. It was no secret that he had scores to settle with the Fairfax press because its journalists had taken a close interest in his business affairs and had published juicy stories with enthusiasm. Packer received scant adverse coverage in Murdoch's newspapers. Though the two men could be business rivals they were friends as well. They also had one very important matter in common: they both detested the Fairfax press with its journalists who demanded their independence.

In September 1984 the now defunct *National Times* had reported an amazing story sourced from a Royal Commission set up to investigate possible corruption in the Federated Ship Painters and Dockers Union. There's no doubt the dockers union had some questions to answer since some of its members had ended up being shot dead at close range or otherwise disposed of, but as often happens the investigation had not gone according to plan.

Packer was the publisher of the *Bulletin* magazine, which had first raised the corruption issue. But when the investigation expanded to follow up the union's links to drug trafficking, money laundering, tax evasion, murder and pornography, Kerry Packer's name bobbed up; it appeared he had been mixing in bad company. The *Bulletin* story had boomeranged on its own proprietor.

When the 1980 Royal Commission – headed by QC Frank Costigan, noted for his fairness and fearlessness – began investigating Packer, it disguised his identity, calling him 'The Squirrel'. The *National Times* replaced it with the reptilian name 'The Goanna' but otherwise it published the Royal Commission documents in full.

Several days after the *National Times* story appeared, anyone driving into the city from what was then the increasingly yuppified suburb of Balmain in Sydney's inner west could see a big painted sign. 'The Goanna = Kerry Packer' it said in metre-high white lettering. It wasn't long before Packer's lawyer, the brilliant and often unpredictable Malcolm Turnbull, was threatening legal action, not against the obvious target, Fairfax and the *National Times*, but against Douglas Meagher, counsel assisting the Royal Commission. Turnbull claimed defamation on the grounds that 'Meagher and Costigan have conducted themselves most reprehensively in failing to stop an unauthorised and illegal leak of information which was inevitably going to do immense or irreparable damage to the reputation of Kerry Packer.'[20] It was a novel approach but Justice Hunt in the NSW Supreme Court wasn't impressed. His court wasn't going to be party to an attempt to bully a Royal Commission. Justice Hunt was scathing about Turnbull's conduct. 'His dominant motive in commencing the proceedings was to enable him to investigate the conduct of the Royal Commission conducted by Mr Costigan, whom the defendant had been appointed to assist . . .' he said.[21] 'All of these matters lead me to infer that the plaintiff [Packer] never did have a case against the defendant in relation to the allegation . . . there may indeed have been a vindictive desire on the part of the plaintiff to make the defendant as uncomfortable as possible, for as long as possible, by having these proceedings hanging over his head in order to punish him for his part in assisting in the compilation of the report of the Royal Commission.'[22]

Justice Hunt said that Turnbull's statement 'managed effectively thereby to poison the fountain of justice immediately before the commencement of the present proceedings'.[23] Turnbull had overplayed his hand. Justice Hunt struck the case out as an abuse of process.

Lucky for the media tycoon he had close – if somewhat unlikely – mates closing ranks to support him. ABC *Late Night Live* host Phillip Adams, the bête noire of the right, tells how he spent hours with Packer talking him out of suicide, such was the anguish he felt as a result of the Goanna story. And Labor Prime Minister Bob Hawke, who has described Packer as 'a close personal friend' and a 'very great Australian',[24] sent in his attorney-general to ease the pain.

In 1987 Lionel Bowen told parliament Kerry Packer 'is entitled' to be regarded by his fellow citizens as 'unsullied by the allegations and insinuations which have been made against him'.[25] The Costigan Royal Commission was effectively finished.

Much of the Goanna material was, as Packer described it in an 8000-word statement he issued in 1984, 'grotesque, ludicrous and malicious'.[26] But the tax findings were not lightly based, nor easily dismissed. In fact Meagher has revealed that briefs for prosecution were prepared against Packer in relation to tax evasion after the commission was wound up. Costigan had told him three 'very senior counsel'[27] based in Sydney 'each looked at them independently and recommended prosecution',[28] but it didn't occur.

'Packer was a man of great influence,' Meagher said. 'He wasn't cleared. Not at all.'[29]

In 1991 Packer took particular exception to being questioned by the Parliamentary Print Media Inquiry about how much tax his companies paid. Like Murdoch's, they didn't pay much. The money was being squirrelled away through offshore tax havens where creative accountants more than earn their money. But it was no wonder he was so aggressive. Though he'd managed to get the inquiry into his financial affairs shut down, what's since been revealed is that the authorities had been keen to know more about AU$50,000 in cash delivered in 1980 to Packer from a near-bankrupt property developer, Brian Ray.[30]

Packer insisted the money was an interest-free loan. But after hearing evidence from a number of witnesses, Costigan became convinced that the money was Packer's from a complex tax swindle. According to author Paul Barry, 'The Queensland fraud squad would come to a similar conclusion in February 1985' when it reviewed all the documents held by the National Crime Authority that had been passed on to it by the Costigan Royal Commission.[31] Packer had been mixing in bad company. As Costigan wrote in his Royal Commission findings about the activities of the Federated Ship Painters and Dockers Union, 'Violence is the means by which they control the members of their group. They do not hesitate to kill. They care not who takes the public offices of their Union so long as the incumbent obeys their dictates, as all office holders do. They are careless of their reputation, glorying in its infamy, and by that reputation attracting employment by wealthy people outside their ranks who stoop to use their criminal prowess to achieve their own questionable ends.'[32]

Frank Costigan later pointed out: 'Packer was anxious to deny that moneys were used for drugs, as were the others. Their problem was the reluctance to disclose the real purpose of the cash payments, for fear that on exposure they would be prosecuted: thus the half-truth, not the whole . . . Those who purvey half-truths have only themselves to blame for the consequences.'[33]

In November 1991 Packer appeared on his own television station, Channel Nine, in an attempt to calm the growing opposition to his attempt to take over John Fairfax Holdings. Nine's prime time *A Current Affair* had managed to persuade three journalists from the Fairfax group to brave a confrontation with Packer at the station's Willoughby studios on Sydney's lower north shore. In what was a pre-emptive strike against the Parliamentary Print Media Inquiry – the scene of his legendary pugilistic performance – where he would be appearing in a few days' time, Packer repeated the assertion that he did not want to control the Fairfax newspaper group. Packer accused the journalists of conspiring to stop him from exercising his legal rights. He didn't go quite as far as his father, Sir Frank, who in 1972 ordered an 'editorial' to be read on air before the start of *A Current Affair*, accusing Gough Whitlam of having policies inspired by 'marijuana dreams of a Utopian Disneyland',[34] but it wasn't far from it.

In the studio set-up Packer appeared to tower over the three Fairfax journalists, Tom Burton, Ken Davidson and Alan Kennedy, as he gave them a lecture in business and journalism. In what must be one of the more bizarre moments in the history of Australian journalism, after Packer repeatedly harangued a reluctant Burton to read out the first clause of the Journalists' Code of Ethics, Burton eventually buckled, reciting that journalists must 'Report and interpret honestly, striving for accuracy, fairness and disclosure of all essential facts.'[35]

'There you are,' said Packer, 'you are not obeying the first clause of your own ethical code.'[36]

—

The liberal centre of politics, which included a good many journalists, was fearful of Packer and for sound reason. The Packers had a family history of meddling with national affairs. For decades his father, Sir Frank Packer, had run scurrilous campaigns against Labor, his papers stuffed with outright fiction passed off as fact, and it was only after Neville Wran took Labor to power in the mid-1970s in New South Wales that Packer junior shifted his support. The change coincided with a consortium made up of racehorse owner Robert Sangster, Rupert Murdoch and Kerry Packer being awarded franchises for the NSW government betting agency, Lotto. To be fair the government also benefited, receiving a sizeable slice of the income, estimated at AU$1 billion in 1984. But for whatever reason, Packer was now in the Labor camp.

Kerry Packer, himself a big gambler, known as a 'whale' for the size of his bets, found a friend in a fellow punter: the former ACTU president who rose to become Prime Minister, Bob Hawke. Not long after, Packer was handed another win from Labor.

In 1987 the Labor government's Treasurer, Paul Keating, introduced a system which restricted how many newspapers and television stations any one person could own in Australia. Known as the cross-media ownership rules, it allowed media proprietors to make a choice between either controlling a TV station or a newspaper in any given geographical market. In Keating's words, they could either be 'Princes of Print or Queens of the Screen'.[37] The changes to the media laws allowed Rupert Murdoch to gain The Herald and Weekly Times newspaper group in Victoria as its owners, Fairfax – forced to choose between maintaining its print presence or divesting itself of its Channel Seven TV interest in Victoria – chose to stay in television. It also gave Packer the opportunity to sell Channel Nine as a network, including the prime Sydney and Melbourne stations. It's been estimated that if he had sold them separately they'd have fetched around AU$400 million. Together they were worth more than a billion. Packer cashed in a huge windfall profit. What no one foresaw was the bonus that the economic crash of 1987 would deliver Packer. An insolvent Alan Bond, who'd purchased the Nine TV Network from Packer, was forced to sell. Kerry Packer bought it back for a song.

Other business moguls might have rested and enjoyed the win but Packer was a driven man. He still had his nemesis, Fairfax, in his sights. Under the cross-media laws Packer couldn't own the newspaper group outright or even have a controlling interest, but as part of a consortium he might be able to bend the rules. That was when Packer dreamed up the plan he hoped would outsmart the regulators, linking up with Canadian Conrad Black, among others, to form a group called Tourang. Packer's friend and legal adviser Malcolm Turnbull brought along some US junk-bond holders who were hoping to get at least some of their money back after a catastrophic attempt at privatising the Fairfax group by 'Young' Warwick, the headstrong son of the late company owner, Sir Warwick Fairfax. It was the botched financing of the privatisation by the devoted Christian, Oxford and Harvard University-educated

Young Warwick which had forced Fairfax into receivership, making it prey to Packer and his Tourang group.

The fear of Packer having any influence at Fairfax united the then deadliest of enemies, former prime ministers Gough Whitlam and Malcolm Fraser. They appeared on the hustings side by side, warning of the perils of a Packer takeover – which they said would significantly curtail media freedom. Even former National Party luminaries Peter Nixon and Doug Anthony joined the protest. In one afternoon 128 of the 224 federal MPs signed a petition calling for an inquiry. The cross-party support on such a contentious media matter was without precedent; there has been nothing remotely like it since. It had only been three years since the MPs had abandoned their old Parliament House, built in the 1920s, for a grander steel and glass structure dominating Canberra like an above-ground air-raid shelter. Many MPs hankered for the old place, with its history of stirring speeches, dirty deeds and blood on the floor. They thought the new Parliament House antiseptic. The Parliamentary Print Media Inquiry would confer the new edifice with some colourful history of its own.

Inquiry Chairperson Michael Lee was an agreeable and intelligent minister who had graduated in electrical engineering. Aggressive from the start, Packer instructed Lee: 'I think it would be nice if we could get all the photographs done and get serious, rather than have this media circus.'[38]

Packer expressed no sense of irony.

In the same way he conducted much of his business, Australia's wealthiest individual opened his evidence with belligerence: 'Kerry Francis Bullmore Packer. I appear here this afternoon reluctantly.'[39]

Lee tried to conduct the hearing with at least a degree of decorum: 'You have made it clear that it is your intention not to exercise any control over the Tourang bid if it is successful in the John Fairfax bid. Is that correct?'

Packer: Will I not exercise any control? I can't. It's a
              combination of won't, can't and don't want to.[40]

Packer added he didn't want to 'have any contact with the
management. I don't have any access to the editors. I don't
have any method of talking to people. Mr Black on the other
hand as a board member and deputy chairman has the capacity
to talk to the management.'[41]

Packer said he accepted 'from day one' that he could not
have control over both TV and newspaper. 'I have made my
decision. My decision was to stay in news . . . television and I do
not have [an] agreement with anyone that contravenes the law.'[42]

In a fleeting moment of humility he revealed to the committee, 'Last year I suffered a major heart attack and died. I didn't
die for long, but it was long enough for me. I didn't come back
to control John Fairfax. I didn't come back to break the law.'[43]

Nevertheless Packer was treading in dangerous territory.

A few days later, on 15 November 1991, Malcolm Turnbull –
now out of all Packer dealings – arranged to meet the head of
the Australian Broadcasting Authority, Peter Westaway, the
person responsible for overseeing the cross-media ownership provisions. Turnbull took the kind of precautions for
the meeting more akin to a character out of the *Spycatcher*
book he'd defended than one of the country's most celebrated
lawyers. As evening fell Westaway parked his car close to his
office in a North Sydney laneway – and waited. When Turnbull
opened the passenger door and got in he handed him copies
of notes written by one of the consortium members, Trevor
Kennedy. He had kept a record of many of his conversations
with Packer, and what they revealed was the latter's true intention for Fairfax. According to Professor Rodney Tiffen, who
was the first to reveal that Turnbull was the leaker, Kennedy's notes recorded that Packer did intend to exercise control
of Fairfax. Tiffen, from the Department of Government and
International Relations at Sydney University and an acclaimed

expert on the Australian media, said the notes also showed Packer had had 'warehousing arrangements' regarding some shares that would have taken him over the limit prescribed by the cross-media laws.[44]

It was damning evidence against Kerry Packer. It put a lie to Packer's response to committee member John Langmore, Labor MP for Fraser, who had asked him, 'You are saying there is no arrangement formal or informal between you and Mr Black over the control of Fairfax?'

> *Packer:*　It's exactly what I'm saying. It's what I have said ad nauseam in that document. You are either going to have to believe me or call me a liar. I am telling you there is no arrangement and I'm sick of telling people there is no arrangement.[45]

Kennedy's notes proved the opposite. Within a few days Westaway informed the parliamentary committee of his intention to investigate the Tourang bid. He sent the group a demand for specific documents, including Kennedy's diary notes. Two days later Packer withdrew from the Tourang consortium. *The Sydney Morning Herald*, *The Age* and *The Australian Financial Review* would now fall into the hands of Tourang, without Packer.

The motives of Kennedy and Turnbull remain unclear but there had earlier been a falling out with Packer. Kennedy had been told he would not be CEO of the company, and Turnbull was not going to get a place on the board. Professor Rodney Tiffen, who has studied the case closely, maintained that Turnbull 'performed a service for Australian democracy by effectively sinking Packer's bid'.[46]

While he certainly lifted the cloak on a bright shining lie that might never otherwise have been revealed, Turnbull's action also highlighted a deep flaw in the democratic process. Turnbull helped expose the truth, but just like his creative defence of Packer with a defamation case that went nowhere, this too had limited benefits. It could have been far different. The rules governing lying to parliament are explicit: 'A person summoned to appear before a committee but who refuses to attend, or a witness who refuses to answer a question or produce a document, or who lies to or misleads a committee, may be punished for contempt by reprimand, fine or imprisonment.'[47] Yet Packer was never called to account for so grievously misleading parliament. It seemed no one had the stomach for taking him on again.

For anyone who didn't quite understand how the media landscape operated, here was a simple lesson: if you are rich enough, powerful enough and unscrupulous enough you can do and say whatever you like; not the police, not parliament, no one will touch you. The Goanna had been caught in his true colours and once again there was no prosecution. Packer was unstoppable.

Over the next few months he increased his holding in Fairfax to well in excess of 15 per cent, beyond the level which put him in breach of the cross-media laws. Paul Keating would pay a price for turning a blind eye to Packer's brazen flouting of legislation. It seems Keating only became interested in what Packer was up to when rumours started – a few months before the 1996 federal election – that Packer had done a deal with the Liberal Party leader John Howard to relax the cross-media ownership laws.

Packer had witnessed Murdoch expanding his business considerably despite the cross-media laws. In fact in the horse trading of Australian politics the laws were deliberately designed to help Murdoch get ahead, and disadvantage Fairfax, long seen as an enemy of the Labor Party. If Murdoch dominated print – his company had amassed 70 per cent of Australia's newspaper circulation – Packer reasoned he could dominate television. Packer devised what he saw as an original idea. With pay TV a rising force he came up with a plan that would guarantee him at least half of the market. Australia would be divided into two, with half the country cabled by Telstra and the other half controlled by a company he'd teamed up with, Optus. It would create a duopoly not dissimilar from Australia's two-airline policy, which delivered no competition and, for many years, high profits for the airline companies, Ansett and Australian Airlines (now Qantas) – and some of the most expensive air fares in the world. As Prime Minister, Keating knocked back the proposal.

Kerry Packer received the news while playing polo in Argentina. He rang Keating and vented his anger. They were finished. Just in case Keating didn't get the message Packer booked a slot on his *A Current Affair* program. Host Ray Martin delivered up a perfect question to get out a none too subtle message: 'Would John Howard make a good prime minister?'

Kerry Packer: Yes, I think he would.

Martin: Why?

Packer: Because he's been around a long time. I think he's a decent man. I think he's an honest man.[48]

The response was measured, by Keating's standards. Interviewed by Laurie Oakes on the following *Sunday* program, Keating accused Packer of trying to scam the public purse with his Optus–Telstra duopoly plans: The 'last scam I had run past me that was ever this large to transfer seven or eight billion from the Commonwealth public purse' involved former NSW Chief Magistrate 'Murray Farquhar's reported attempts to take the gold reserves from the Philippines National Bank. I mean that is the last scam that large'.[49]

Packer obviously believed he could get whatever he wanted. He had his own TV network where he could appear at will to put his case. He gave jobs to Labor mates, like Peter Barron, who had been Bob Hawke's media adviser, and he even snared the former Transport and Communications Minister

Graham Richardson, who left the government to work for his company. Kerry Packer had reverted to family political form. After a 20-year dalliance with Labor he was now back with the Liberals.

Packer let loose the dogs of war against Keating. It's a story that has never been told before and it shows how ruthless Packer could be and how he patently believed he was above the law. If you were kind, you could say it also showed he hadn't lost his Australian egalitarian streak. Not for him the sordid hacking of the phones of dead schoolgirls and minor royalty, Packer hired a top private investigator to hack the telephone of Paul Keating, the former Australian Prime Minister. The man, whom Packer had flown out secretly from Europe, tried to tap the landline of Keating's home phone in Elizabeth Bay.

A source told me the private investigator unlocked the cover on the telephone switching post in Keating's street and placed crocodile clips on the phone line in an attempt to listen in to conversations. An expert in the art of blagging (impersonating someone to get their bank and other personal details), the investigator was specifically employed by Packer to gather 'dirt on Keating'.[50]

The investigator also travelled to Singapore searching for a bank account that Packer was convinced Keating was using to secretly channel money to Switzerland. When the private investigator returned saying he 'could find nothing',[51] Packer sent him back. When he returned, empty-handed for the second time, Packer terminated the contract.

It was not, however, an isolated attempt at revenge.

In July 1998 Kerry Packer threw a dinner at his rambling residence in Sydney's Bellevue Hill for Treasurer Peter Costello. As Niki Savva, Costello's media adviser, explains to those who don't understand how power works among a nation's leaders, 'James Packer [Packer's son], who had become friendly with Peter, was instrumental in organising it, figuring that Peter and his father should get to know one another better.'[52]

She added that John Howard was 'friendly with both Kerry Packer and Rupert Murdoch; as for Peter, he tried to make sure he kept the fathers on side and was always – quite rightly – very keen to ensure that he had the support of Rupert's son Lachlan and Kerry's son, James'.[53] To impress Costello, Packer had invited not only Channel Nine's CEO, David Leckie, and his head of Current Affairs, Peter Meakin, but his star journalists, Laurie Oakes, Paul Lyneham and Ray Martin.

As the evening was winding up Savva says in her book *So Greek: Confessions of a Conservative Leftie* (Scribe, Melbourne, 2010), Packer 'broke off from bagging us to bag Paul Keating, whom he loathed passionately'. Packer then raised the question of the sale by Paul Keating of his piggery in the Hunter Valley, just north of Sydney, to an Indonesian businessman. The issue had been used by the Liberal Party to attack Keating ever since he disposed of it in 1994. The Liberals said Keating had acted improperly in the sale of the piggery. They obsessively attacked Keating over the issue, using a former arms salesman, John Seyffer, working from the Sydney office of Liberal Senator Bill Heffernan, to gather information on the affair.

On that July evening as the Federal Treasurer, Peter Costello, his media adviser and the stars of Channel Nine milled around preparing to leave Kerry Packer's mansion, there emerged a glowing example of just why hundreds of journalists and two former Australian prime ministers from opposite sides of the political divide had been so concerned about Packer taking over the Fairfax newspapers. Packer began to question Laurie Oakes about the Keating piggery story. According to Savva, Packer knew that Oakes had been 'given certain documents' – which came as a surprise to Oakes. Oakes had not known that Packer knew he had the documents – revealing what a close interest Packer was taking in the whole affair. Oakes was taken even further aback when Packer wanted to know 'why, exactly, he had not produced a piece based on them'. Oakes, one of the most talented and trusted journalists in Australia, replied that he had 'checked out the documents, and had found that they didn't stand up'. Oakes said he had been waiting for a source to come through, but he had 'not delivered'. James Packer said he thought that was fair enough, but it was not good enough for Kerry Packer. As Savva recounts, Packer 'tried to heavy Oakes'. Oakes didn't budge.

At this point Paul Lyneham, the former ABC reporter, who'd recently been hired by Channel Nine, stepped forward, 'literally', and 'volunteered his services'.[54] Eight months later, in March 1999, *60 Minutes* gave its entire program over to Lyneham's report on the piggery issue. The program's executive producer, John Westacott, when asked if Packer ever interfered in any programs, said, 'I never received a directive of how a story should be angled or what story should be pursued.'[55] Packer didn't need to talk to the executive producers. He spoke directly to the reporters and leaned on them to get his own way. The piggery mud failed to stick to Keating and no further action was taken by anyone, least of all the Liberal Party, which now had its own problems with Kerry Packer.

Several attempts had been made by Howard to change the media laws to favour his newfound media friend but they were stopped by a hostile party room whose members, reflecting the interests of their constituents, were none too keen on any larger concentration of media ownership in Australia.

Instead of pursuing Keating *60 Minutes* might have been better served examining the business practices of Conrad Black. He'd fired editors and driven out of town some of the most talented journalists, like Michelle Grattan, as he swung *The Age* to the hard right. Although championed by the Victorian Liberal Premier Jeff Kennett and the Melbourne Establishment, the circulation spiralled down as the white-collar readership abandoned the paper in droves.

After six consecutive periods of increased sales before Black arrived, the circulation slumped by 10 per cent. Black had run Fairfax further into the ground than Young Warwick had.

He was certainly better at spending money than making it. In 2004 a group of Hollinger shareholders accused him of misappropriating US$80 million to foster his lavish lifestyle. Black was arrested, charged with fraud and obstruction of justice, and jailed for three and a half years. Fairfax had for the moment at least survived the Canadian crook in Conrad Black, the Christian dupe in Young Warwick and the thuggish liar in Kerry Packer.

It says much about the way media politics is dealt with in Australia that when Kerry Packer died in 2005, the man he'd helped to power, Prime Minister John Howard, ordered a state funeral and hailed him as a 'great Australian'.[56]

As Rupert Murdoch turned 83, there were a few indications that he had seen the best of his power. The mass media, with its hitherto chummy and frightening relationships with governments and corporations, was being sorely tested. The great rollicking newspaper presses that had sustained both demagogue and democracy for so long were creaking to a halt. What replaced them would both pose a threat and offer an opportunity. The insiders, who had ridden the rivers of gold to untold power and influence, were on notice. The outsiders were here.

CHAPTER 14

The Price of Freedom

As Glenn Greenwald made his way through the streets of the German city of Homburg to collect yet another prize for his revelatory journalism, if he'd happened to research his where-abouts he may have been struck by an unusual occurrence in a Google-dominated world: Street View did not exist. Germany is not among the 50 countries where Google's cameras have captured the streetscape of millions of lanes, roads and highways; in Germany Google had run into trouble. In 2013 the company was fined for gathering wi-fi information about local residents as it began mapping the streets. Then thousands more Germans demanded that Google blur out the pictures of their homes. Without explanation, Google stopped its Street View coverage in Germany. What remains is a Google map of Europe with Germany looking like the missing part of a giant jigsaw puzzle.

While the German nation values individual freedom for a variety of reasons, the inhabitants of Homburg – a medieval town near the French border in southern Germany – are particularly proud of their liberal culture. The prize Greenwald received – honouring the work of local jurist and journalist Philipp Jakob Siebenpfeiffer, a 19th-century campaigner for free speech – celebrates not only the region's individualism but also its contrast to Homburg's often authoritarian Bavarian neighbours.

Presenting Greenwald with his award, Germany's Vice-Chancellor Sigmar Gabriel extolled the virtues of Edward

Snowden's work, highlighting that it had revealed to the nation so much more than the NSA's infamous tapping of Chancellor Angela Merkel's mobile phone. Of particular importance was Snowden's revelation that the United States and the United Kingdom had been jointly running a full-scale spying operation against Germany and its European allies, using GCHQ's interception station at Bude in the UK's West Country. The facility is able to access at least 200 fibre-optic cables, giving it the ability to monitor 600 million communications every day – a huge slice of the transatlantic traffic between Europe and the United States.

As Gabriel spoke, a member of the audience shouted out, asking why Snowden had not been offered asylum in Germany. The question was not properly answered, though it went to the heart of the freedom of speech that the prize was supposedly celebrating. Apart from the humanitarian aspect of his plight, if the Germans were ever to understand exactly what the NSA had been doing in their country, it would be sensible to invite Snowden to travel to Berlin. Yet when a German parliamentary committee set up to investigate the NSA's activities decided it needed to talk to Snowden in person, Chancellor Merkel – concerned about US sensitivities – stepped in and vetoed any invitation for him to travel to Germany.

Merkel's diplomacy was lost on the United States. Heedless of the fragile state of its relations with Germany, the CIA had recruited a member of the Bundesnachrichtendienst (BND) – the German foreign intelligence service – to spy on the parliamentary committee. But the CIA had chosen badly and the BND officer made a number of mistakes which alerted German counter-intelligence. In June 2014 the BND officer was arrested. Three weeks later, in response to the blundering US attempts to spy on the very parliamentary committee investigating the NSA's espionage, Chancellor Merkel ordered the CIA station chief – a declared US agent registered with the German government – to leave the country.

For a second time Washington had been caught spying on one of its closest allies, so while the expulsion might have been embarrassing for the Americans, it seemed – relative to the NSA's activities – a minor and perfectly reasonable rebuke. But the perpetrators were in no mood to hang their heads, as might have been expected. Merkel and the parliamentary committee would soon learn that Washington and its Five-Eyes ally, Britain, had been hugely angered by Berlin's response. BND President Gerhard Schindler told the parliamentary inquiry that he was experiencing 'unusually tense relations with British partner agencies'.[1] This uncomfortable situation would have ramifications for Edward Snowden.

After Greenwald collected his prize, he asked Vice-Chancellor Gabriel in private exactly why Snowden had not been allowed to travel to Germany. The official view, he already knew, was that Germany could not guarantee Snowden would not be onwardly extradited to the United States. But that didn't add up: in granting asylum, Germany would be bound to protect Snowden from any charges he might face as a so-called felon. As he talked quietly to Greenwald, Gabriel – the leader of Germany's leftist Social Democratic Party – broke ranks with his conservative coalition partner, Merkel – head of the Christian Democratic Union – to disclose the real reason for the Snowden ban. The decision not to allow Snowden into Germany had nothing to do with extradition and a lot to do with German's security: the US government 'had aggressively threatened the Germans that if they allowed Snowden into their country they would be "cut off" from all intelligence sharing'.[2] The threat disclosed how deeply worried the United States had become about what Snowden had exposed, underscoring the lengths to which the Five-Eyes allies were prepared to go to stop anyone who questioned them.

But here's the rub. Previously, GCHQ had set up a joint project with the Germans to monitor jihadists travelling from

Germany to Iraq and Syria. Crucially the jihadists would also be tracked when they decided to return home. If the US threat were carried out, the agreement with GCHQ might be in tatters; any information on jihadists or even terrorist attacks on Germany might not be passed on.

Germany would not risk being excised from the biggest intelligence-gathering network in the world. It was a straight-out case of blackmail.

If Snowden ever believed he would be treated fairly should he return home to the United States, what happened in Germany would surely have dissuaded him of such a view. The rule of law had been overridden by the rules of international politics. It was something Snowden had difficulty compre-hending. Though his whistleblowing may appear to have been the actions of a rebel, he is in fact a stickler for the law. His motivation as a whistleblower was to correct the violation of the highest law in the land, the US Constitution.

In an ideal world he could have sought some comfort in the United States from the Whistleblower Protection Act of 1989, which covers 'disclosures of illegality' in all areas of government, including intelligence agencies, but as many have discovered before, it is a flawed piece of legislation.

All the references to possible wrongdoing are first inves-tigated internally by the very organisation against which the complaint has been made. If they don't get satisfaction there the best chance for an airing of their grievances rests with the Senate Select Committee on Intelligence – responsible for oversight of the FBI, the CIA and the NSA.

Acclaimed as a maths genius at the NSA, William Binney, who had worked at the agency for more than 30 years, went to the committee soon after the 2001 terrorist attacks. The story he told them bore a striking resemblance to Snowden's: the NSA was gathering information on American citizens using a system he said was not only unconstitutional but was wasting millions of dollars. What was even more unsettling, the NSA had rejected a system named ThinThread, which he says could have caught the terrorists.

Binney, who resigned from the NSA when the agency refused to listen to him, says two other NSA colleagues tried sounding the alarm with Congressional committees but because they did not have documents to prove their charges, nobody believed them.

Others also tried to work within the system. Computer expert Thomas Drake thought blowing the whistle on what he considered unconstitutional NSA programs would lead to an investigation and changes in the organisation.

'The only person who was investigated, prosecuted, charged in secret, then was indicted, then ended up facing trial and 35 years in prison was myself,' he says.[3]

Like Binney, Drake had taken his case both to the NSA and to Congress. After concluding his complaints were going nowhere, he showed unclassified information from the NSA to a newspaper reporter. For that he was charged with violating the Espionage Act of 1917. The FBI raided his home. Four months earlier the FBI had raided Binney's home after he publicly criticised the NSA. As is so frequently the case with whistleblowers, both Drake and Binney suffered the consequences of challenging the system.

'Your life's never the same,' said Drake. 'All your colleagues and people you used to work with all disappear. You're persona non grata, you're radioactive.'[4]

The chances of holding the intelligence community to account may not have been high beforehand, but in 2015 they reached what many believed to be an historic low when Republican Senator Richard Burr took over as chair of the Senate Select Committee on Intelligence. He replaced Senator Dianne Feinstein, who had consistently defended the CIA's targeted killing campaign and the NSA's mass collection of communication records but nevertheless accused the CIA of lying about the severity of their detention and interrogation programs and illegally searching the computers of Senate staffers. Burr had been critical of Feinstein's position and commented to reporters, 'I personally don't believe that anything that goes on in the intelligence committee should ever be discussed publicly.'[5]

Though Snowden was acutely aware of the experiences of both Drake and Binney, when he first considered blowing the whistle, he came perilously close to following them down the same path. Snowden began raising his concerns with fellow workmates that the NSA was breaking the law – deliberately in the case of bulk records collection, and incidentally when the content of American phone calls and emails was gathered up by the NSA, along with those of foreign targets.

As Snowden drove to work from the single-storey home he shared with his girlfriend in the tiny township of Royal Kunia, north-west of the Hawaiian capital Honolulu – travelling the ruler-straight road cutting through the sugar cane fields – he appeared like any one of the thousands of US military and intelligence workers on the island state. What maybe set Snowden apart from the other intelligence workers living in the Hawaiian tropical paradise was his searing intellect. According to his job description he was a rather lowly systems analyst but he was the can-do fixer many people turned to for help. 'That kid was a genius among geniuses,' said one NSA employee who knew Snowden.[6] The fact that he didn't always have security clearance for the work he was asked to do did not prevent people giving him access to some of the top levels of the NSA system so he could solve their problems.

When he drove past the car park towards the helicopter pad and prepared to walk into the huge black tunnel drilled into the side of a rocky outcrop – a relic of the Second World War but now the Hawaiian home of America's most secret agency – the casual observer may have been surprised at what Snowden was wearing. He sported a black hoodie featuring a parody of the NSA's logo, an American Eagle carrying a huge key in its claws. Emblazoned on Snowden's sweatshirt was an evil-looking eagle wearing headphones and clutching a tangle of AT&T cables. The hoodie kept Snowden warm in the air-conditioning cooling the banks of computers buried deep in the tunnel. It also projected what he felt – that the NSA was out of control. Extraordinarily, no one took much notice. Not even it seems, in October 2012, when Snowden says he raised his concerns with four superiors – two from the NSA's Technology Directorate and two from the NSA Threat Operations Center's regional base in Hawaii.

To illustrate the point that the NSA was breaking the law, Snowden says he opened a system on his computer called Boundless Informant, which used colour-coded 'heat maps' to depict the volume of data ingested by NSA taps. He showed this to his four superiors and 15 other co-workers. Snowden said his colleagues were 'astonished to learn we are collecting more in the United States on Americans than we are on Russians in Russia'. Many of them were troubled, and several said they did not want to know any more.

'I asked these people, "What do you think the public would do if this was on the front page?"' he said.[7]

It's difficult to fathom how an agency whose role it is to predict and analyse threats did not understand the gravity of what Snowden was revealing. To help them comprehend the point he was making, Snowden kept a copy of the US Constitution on his desk, often citing the Fourth Amendment, which specifically forbids random searches of American citizens. It's a broad Constitutional pillar which defends the right to privacy – unless intelligence or police agencies specifically know what they are searching for and have reasonable suspicions that a crime has been, or is about to be committed. There is no precedent under the Constitution for the government to seize the vast amounts of data sucked up by the NSA involving innocent Americans' communications. Such is the strength of the Fourth Amendment that in 2012 the US Supreme Court overturned a guilty finding against a cocaine trafficker because the police fixed a tracking device to the suspect's wife's car. The majority decision found that installing the device breached the Fourth Amendment. And one of the most conservative members of the bench, Justice Samuel Alito, went further, finding that the collection of data impinged on 'expectations of privacy'.[8]

Putting aside all the other Snowden revelations, Boundless Informant alone seemed to point to a major breach of that Constitutional right. Even so, the NSA, which has gathered more data on everyone on the planet than any other organisation in history, says it could find no record of Snowden raising any issues of illegality with its management or other members of staff.

They clearly weren't looking very hard. In December 2012, a full six months before he leaked his NSA cache, Snowden was no longer raising issues with his NSA managers. Having realised his arguments about breaches of the US Constitution were wasted on the government, he was publicly proselytising the benefits of encryption to anyone who would listen. He hosted a 'crypto party' at the back of a Honolulu furniture store to teach members of the public how to set up encrypted communications systems to protect them from NSA intrusion.

In June 2013 the Department of Justice charged Snowden in absentia under the Espionage Act of 1917, a blunt instrument used to punish spies. He was accused of receiving classified information 'with intent or reason to believe' that the information would be used to the 'injury of the United States', or to the 'advantage of any foreign nation'.[9]

Appearing before a secret court, there would be scant value placed on the positive aspects of Snowden's revelations to the American people. He would not be free to convince the jury what he did was to their benefit. So the person who revealed to the Americans that the NSA was snooping on their privacy – 'evidence of what appears to be crimes against the Constitution of the United States'[10] according to Nobel Peace Prize winner and former Vice President Al Gore – now faces jail if the prose-cution can prove that a foreign country may have benefited, even in the slightest, from his disclosures. The fact that Snowden's revelations ignited a serious challenge to the legality of the NSA's activities is unlikely to be enough to clear his name.

As Snowden argues, he hasn't broken any laws. He might have signed a non-disclosure agreement with the NSA but his overarching allegiance is to the oath he swore to uphold the values of the US Constitution. 'The oath of allegiance is not an oath of secrecy,' he said. 'That is an oath to the Constitu-tion. That is the oath that I kept.'[11]

Needless to say, the US Director of National Intelligence, James Clapper, and former NSA Director, Keith Alexander – who both denied the organisation was carrying out bulk collection of American data, when that's exactly what they were doing – are not under investigation. It is the whistle-blower who revealed the crime who is to be punished.

—

With internal investigations of wrongdoing and Congres-sional oversight failing, the question of how to deal with the issues of surveillance and data retention has produced some unusual outcomes.

Of all the countries in the world it is the United States – and nations on the receiving end of its spying régime – which are having the strongest debate about how to handle these matters. On 19 June 2014, the US House of Representa-tives voted to defund two major NSA surveillance programs. The House banned searches of Americans' communications without warrants under the Foreign Intelligence Surveillance Act of 1978 and the mandates for technology companies to facilitate electronic surveillance. Even though the bans were overturned in a later vote, they indicated the cross-party concern that the United States had about the intrusion of the state into the daily lives of US citizens.

Finally, in June 2015, the US Senate passed legislation which all but vindicated Snowden, supporting a bill to end the NSA's bulk collection of phone records of millions of Americans. The phone records will still be collected, but by the phone companies, not the NSA. The US Freedom Act will allow the NSA to search the records, but only with a warrant. Other changes to the now expired Patriot Act are expected to be passed.

What's often missing from an understanding of what is going on is that the law changes only offer protection – albeit limited – to US citizens. The rest of the world, except for the Five-Eyes countries, is still fair game for the NSA. They have to deal with the spying on their citizens by the United States and the other Five-Eyes countries.

Soon after Snowden's disclosures, the Parliamentary Assembly of the Council of Europe – representatives of national parliaments drawn from the Council of Europe's 47 member states – began investigating the NSA's mass surveillance. Snowden appeared twice before the Assembly's Legal Affairs and Human Rights Committee, giving evidence by video link. In January 2015 the draft report of the committee condemned the NSA's mass surveillance practice as a violation of fundamental freedoms, finding the United Kingdom in particular to be in breach of the European Convention on Human Rights.

If the committee had probed a little deeper they may have discovered that the French had been up to no good, too. In the north-east of Paris behind a wall topped with barbed wire, the equivalent of the NSA, the Direction Générale de la Sécurité Extérieure (DGSE), hadn't just been gathering the phone, email and internet metadata on overseas targets; like the NSA, it had been also spying on the French population. The giant computers in the compound's basement, which stored the searchable metadata, generated enough heat to warm the building. The revelations in *Le Monde*, which appeared shortly after the Snowden disclosures, barely raised a shrug of interest in the rest of the French media.

Similar apathy could be seen across the English Channel and in another Five-Eyes country – Australia. Within months the UK and Australian governments began introducing what was described as 'emergency legislation' – laws to formalise the collection of metadata on their own citizens. It was couched in the familiar argument about protecting the nation from terrorism, drug trafficking and paedophilia. What was sorely missing from the whole debate was any mention of abuse of power by the government or the intelligence agencies, or any protection for whistleblowers.

Just like in the United States, complaints about illegal activity inside the intelligence agencies of both countries continued to be dealt with internally. What was more alarming, those responsible for direct parliamentary control of the intelligence community, and keeping them in check, appeared to know little about its activities. In the United Kingdom, Cabinet ministers and members of the National Security Council were told nothing about the existence and scale of the vast data-gathering programs. The former Liberal Democrat MP Chris Huhne, who was in the Cabinet for two years until 2012, said ministers were in 'utter ignorance' of the two biggest covert operations – PRISM, which taps into key text or spoken words, and Tempora, the main surveillance system used by GCHQ to intercept transatlantic communications – until *The Guardian* broke the Snowden story. 'The revelations put a giant question mark into the middle of our surveillance state,' Huhne said. 'The state should not feel itself entitled to know, see and memorise everything that the private citizen communicates. The state is our servant.'[12]

In Australia the situation was even more opaque. No member of the two major political parties publicly questioned the NSA's activities. The bipartisan silence was deafening. New surveillance laws met some resistance from the Opposition

Labor Party but even then the government managed to bluster its way through. Attorney-General George Brandis got muddled over whether the intelligence agencies wanted the authority to track an individual's web browsing. Prime Minister Tony Abbott told an interviewer the data retention laws included tracking 'the sites you're visiting'. They were both wrong: there was no plan to store browsing history. Even so, the tough new data retention laws coupled with restrictions on reporting active ASIO operations – known as Special Intelligence Operations (SIO) – caused a furore in the media, and in the end the government made some concessions about tracking the metadata of journalists. What was missing from the whole debate was any question about providing protection for whistleblowers.

Without the kind of protection provided in the United Kingdom indirectly through the European Convention on Human Rights and in the United States through the First and Fourth amendments, Australia is a tough place to work as a journalist. Journalists tend to end up as collateral damage in the war on whistleblowers.

—

It has fallen to the academic world to help save the lifeblood of good journalism. Whistleblower Eileen Chubb and former investigative journalist Gavin MacFadyen, Director of the Centre for Investigative Journalism at the City University in London, co-founded an organisation in March 2014 to provide 'emotional and legal assistance to those who have or are considering righting a wrong'.[13]

Called The Whistler, it has the support of Annie Machon, former intelligence officer for the United Kingdom's MI5, who blew the whistle on the lack of accountability of British spy agencies, and Ray McGovern, a former CIA senior analyst, who helped expose intelligence corruption to justify the war in Iraq. The Whistler provides a one-stop shop for whistleblowers who need urgent help, a product of the desperation Snowden experienced when he landed in Hong Kong. It was Assange, contacted by Snowden, who stepped in at that time – for which he was criticised in the media – offering among other things legal assistance and trying to arrange asylum for Snowden in Ecuador. While Snowden wasn't without friends, he certainly needed help in a hurry and it was WikiLeaks that provided it. Now the system is on a more formal setting with MacFadyen, a close friend of Assange, ready to assist the next Edward Snowden.

If the truth be known, whereas some investigative journalists of the calibre of Greenwald and Davies might care deeply about whistleblowers, the big media organisations, and the stars they employ, are often lukewarm at best in their support. For them the concept of whistleblowing is a threat. Media companies are no different in their culture from any other business. The whistleblower is the dissenter and, as we have witnessed, championing the status quo, not challenging the norm, is where the mainstream media has been most comfortable. The first question many journalists ask of a whistleblower is: do they have an axe to grind? Not what have they got to say? Whistleblowers are dangerous to any large organisation: the individuals concerned are usually driven by ethics, highly focused and, above all, they are difficult to control.

Yet both Snowden and Manning – though they shied away from the organisations they distrusted – understood they needed help to reveal the wrongdoings they were exposing. They could have dumped their cache of documents on a website – unredacted, for anyone to read – not as they appear in newspapers, with names and some system and collection methods blacked out. That would have been the action of someone who wished to 'harm' the United States. Despite all they had seen about the way journalists behaved in the mass media on national security issues, they both decided their disclosures needed to pass through a journalistic filter.

Each chose their outlets carefully, only handing over the material to journalists they believed were courageous enough to get the story out and at the same time balance the rights of the individual against the sometimes necessary demands of the state. Snowden, in particular, might have been formidably computer literate, but he trusted Greenwald to assess what should be published.

There were other considerations. Though Assange, through his WikiLeaks organisation, had many supporters around the world, he did not command the editorial infrastructure, the finances or the capability to reach a massive audience like *The Guardian*, *The New York Times*, *Der Spiegel* and *Le Monde*, which is where he shared his secrets. In the future even some of these publications may not have the money to do such expensive and time-consuming work.

Greenwald also needed a vehicle to disseminate information although, unlike Assange, he was able to work closely with his source, Snowden, to unpick the intricacies of the story and therefore maintain editorial control.

That both Assange and Greenwald turned to *The Guardian* says much about its history of revelatory and challenging journalism, particularly under editor Alan Rusbridger. But *The Guardian*'s rise to prominence has as much to do with its financial independence as its journalism. The Scott Trust, which funds much of *The Guardian*'s work, has allowed it to embrace the internet, publishing online editions worldwide, in the United States, Australia, Africa and the Middle East, without being as concerned as other newspapers that its first line of income – the rivers of classified advertising gold – was drying up. This financial independence also permits it to stand free of the kind of editorial interference that befell the London *Daily Telegraph* when it began digging into the HSBC tax scandal.

What happened at the *Telegraph* also produced a rare breed of journalist, a chief political correspondent turned whistle-blower. Peter Oborne not only quit in disgust at the censorship he uncovered, he posted his grievances online. It was an elegant demonstration of the problems confronting the old media, coupled with the stark reality of an unstoppable shift in power.

As happened 500 years ago, journalism is following technology: from the hand-written leaflet to the printing press and now from Caxton to Google. More by luck than judgement over the centuries, newspapers found a solid source of funding in classified advertising, which gave them the financial independence to fund investigative and revelatory journalism. This reporting helped educate and inform readers and underpinned the long and sustained rise of democratic governments around the world.

Without this advertising funding, the role of informing and educating falls partly to newspapers like *The Guardian*, but it is equally shared with public broadcasters like the BBC and ABC. Yet they too are fragile, their funding under constant threat from political and commercial opponents.

As journalism reduces to click-bait stories recycled through an internet which does not pay for news and information, there is a desperate struggle to find a model that works. In France *Le Canard Enchaîné*, which breaks many political stories, might be a role model. It's a radical option. The newspaper only publishes print editions and has a scant online presence – revealing only the front page for free on its website. It is apparently highly profitable, and independent, carries no advertising and is funded solely by subscriptions. Magazines such as *The Economist*, which links its snappy print edition to deeper product online, or the *Financial Times*, which has done so well, and is turning a profit, might also be the solution. Unfortunately however, none of them are news outlets that reach the broad population.

The answer to the problem may lie in an unlikely marriage: money made through internet businesses could come to the rescue. Jeff Bezos, the founder of Amazon, has taken over *The Washington Post* and eBay's Pierre Omidyar is funding

Glenn Greenwald's online publication *The Intercept*. The question is are they active or passive investors? Greenwald, for one, will likely be a rabid defender of his independence, but *The Washington Post* has already lost some of its lustre. As the new internet tycoons try to build their information empires, the natural predilection will be to interfere, especially if the business model isn't working, and trade access for influence. It's a practice that worked extremely well in the past: power and patronage helped make Lord Beaverbrook of the *Daily Express*, Lord Northcliffe of the *Daily Mail*, Randolph Hearst, Rupert Murdoch and a host of other lesser luminaries.

But this time in humankind's forward march, the landscape is entirely different. In the anarchy of the internet, reputations – and incomes – can be lost as quickly as fortunes are made. Structures that supported the old information insider trading, whereby positive news coverage was run in exchange for influence, are suddenly worthless. The outsiders – Greenwald, Snowden, Manning and Assange – blew a hole in the side of the comfy containment vessel of vested interests. It's one of the reasons why governments are coming down so hard on whistle-blowers; with all the political strength they can muster they're trying to patch up a leak the size of a football field. Governments are desperate to re-establish control over journalism with draconian laws to prosecute anyone who speaks out. Journalists won't need to worry about protecting their sources; they won't have any is the reasoning.

How the media copes with the move from the old system of news gathering and dissemination to the brave new world of the internet is not simply about an industry in transition. Whether it succeeds or fails will determine what kind of society we live in. Many news outlets have dealt with the challenge so far by becoming hysterical, extreme and titillating. Apart from a few notable examples, they're exhibiting the desperation of a disoriented swimmer, heading for the bottom to catch their breath. Who is to blame for this unmitigated disaster? Firstly, the print newspaper owners must accept some of the responsibility. The arrival of the internet as a new form of communication was not a sudden occurrence. It took years to develop into an existential threat to the old media.

Right from the start, newspapers could have charged subscribers to their paper editions a small fee for access to their internet sites. Instead they held on to the old model until it was too late to save, and then began experimenting with paywalls. What's just as bad is that they arrogantly ignored the warnings, and weren't straight with their public about the trouble they were in. This lack of openness and accountability is a major part of what's been bedevilling the media for decades and has played a significant role in its catastrophic failures. The power at this moment rests in the hands of the public, with their demand to know what is really happening in their world.

News has never been truly free and perhaps only now are we beginning to understand its real price.

NOTES

Chapter 1: Reaching Out

1 Greenwald, Glenn, *No Place to Hide*, Hamish Hamilton, London 2014
2 http://blog.amnestyusa.org/us/inhumane-treatment-of-wikileaks-soldier-bradley-manning/, 24 January 2011
3 Mendez, Juan E., Human Rights Council, Addendum to report to UN General Assembly, A/HRC/19/61/Add.4, 29 February 2012
4 Gellman, Barton, 'Code Name Verax: Snowden in Exchange with *Post* Reporter Made Clear He Knew the Risks', *The Washington Post*, 9 June 2013
5 *Ibid.*
6 'David Miranda is Nobody's Errand Boy', Buzzfeed, 15 November 2013; www.buzzfeed.com/natashavc/david-miranda-is-nobodys-errand-boy#.uaVjR9Yvp
7 Gellman
8 Hersh, Seymour, 'Obama, NSA and "Pathetic" American Media', *The Guardian*, 27 September 2013
9 http://news.bbc.co.uk/2/hi/uk_news/politics/3090681.stm
10 http://mediastandardstrust.org/mst-news/how-newspapers-covered-press-regulation-after-leveson-media-standards-trust-analysis/
11 www.thesun.co.uk/sol/homepage/news/politics/5224182/PM-in-spy-rage-at-Guardian-for-printing-Edward-Snowden-leaks.html
12 www.dailymail.co.uk/news/article-2450237/MI5-chief-Andrew-Parke-The-Guardian-handed-gift-terrorists.html

Chapter 2: Star Chamber

1 Joad, Raymond, *Pamphlets and Pamphleteering in Early Modern Britain*, Cambridge University Press, 2000
2 Brown v Entertainment Merchants Association, US Supreme Court, 27 June 2011
3 *Ibid.*

4   www.nydailynews.com/news/politics/chief-judge-wanted-abolish-grand-juries-article-1.2025208
5   http://law2.umkc.edu/faculty/projects/ftrials/conlaw/sullivan2.html
6   Robertson, Geoffrey, *Dreaming Too Loud*, Vintage Books, Sydney, 2013
7   House of Commons Culture, Media and Sport Committee. News International and Phone Hacking. Eleventh report of sessions 2010-2012 , volume II
8   Author interview with Sarah Harrison, Berlin 2014
9   *Freedom of the Press*, Freedom House, 2013

Chapter 3: The Power of One – Plot and Plunder
1   Higham, Charles, *The Duchess of Windsor: The Secret Life*, John Wiley & Sons, Hoboken, New Jersey, 2005
2   BBC, 24 May 1968, http://news.bbc.co.uk/onthisday/hi/dates/stories/may/24/newsid_2988000/2988263.stm
3   Edwards, Ruth Dudley, *Newspapermen*, Martin Secker & Warburg, Great Britain, 2003
4   Horrie, Chris, 11 November 2003, *The Independent*
5   *Ibid.*
6   Edwards
7   *Ibid.*
8   Goodman, Geoffrey, cited in 'The two men who gave news to the proletariat', *Camden New Journal*, 4 November 2004
9   'The Earl of Cromer is Dead at 72', *The New York Times*, 19 March 1991
10   Gapper, John & Denton, Nicholas, *All That Glitters: The Fall of Barings*, Penguin, London, 1997
11   Hansard, House of Commons, 5th series, vol. 560, col. 579
12   Edwards
13   *Ibid.*
14   *Ibid.*
15   *Ibid.*
16   *Ibid.*
17   *Ibid.*
18   Hubert 'Hugh' Cudlipp, *Walking on the Water*, The Bodley Head Ltd, London, 4 November 1976
19   Edwards
20   *Ibid.*
21   Price, Lance, *Where Power Lies: Prime Ministers v The Media*, Simon & Schuster, London, 2010

22 *The New York Times*, 30 May 1968

23 King, Cecil, *The Cecil King Diary, 1965–70*, Jonathan Cape Ltd, London, 1972

24 Response to author's FOI request from CIA Information and Privacy Coordinator Michele Meeks, 18 September 2014

25 Peter Wright with Paul Greengrass, *Spycatcher: The Candid Autobiography of a Senior Intelligence Officer*, Viking Books, New York, 1987

26 Andrew, Christopher & Mitrokin, Vasily, *The Sword and the Shield*, Basic Books, New York, 1999

27 *Ibid.*

28 Wright

29 Andrew, Christopher, *Defence of the Realm: The Authorized History of MI5*, Penguin, London, 2010

30 www.theguardian.com/books/2009/oct/10/defence-of-the-realm-mi5

31 www.telegraph.co.uk/news/obituaries/1487412/Jenifer-Hart.html

32 Wright

33 Chapman Pincher: Obituary, BBC News UK, 6 August 2014

34 *Ibid.*

35 'Harry Chapman Pincher: Ex-*Daily Express* journalist turns 100', BBC news, 28 March 2014

36 'Wallace Clippings Planted on Chapman Pincher', www.lobstermagazine.co.uk/intro/search.cgi?zoom_query=My+inquiries+have+established+this+memo+is+a+fake&zoom_and=

37 *Ibid.*

38 Burnett, Thom (ed.), *Conspiracy Encyclopedia*, Franz Steiner Verlag, Stuttgart, 2006, pp. 158–159

39 *The Plot against Harold Wilson*, BBC TV, 2006

40 *Ibid.*

41 Pincher, Chapman, *Treachery: Betrayals, Blunders and Cover-ups*, Mainstream Publishing, Edinburgh, 2012

42 Leigh, David, 'An official history of MI5 can't bury the truth about the plot against Harold Wilson', *The Guardian*, 10 October 2009

43 'Secret Cables Reveal Murdoch Insights', *The Sydney Morning Herald*, 20 May 2013

44 *Ibid.*

45 *Ibid.*

46 Author source

47 Tiffen, Rodney, *Rupert Murdoch: A Reassessment*, NewSouth
    Publishing, Sydney 2014

48 Kwitny, Jonathan, *The Crimes of Patriots: A True Tale of Dope,
    Dirty Money, and the CIA*, W C Norton & Company, New
    York, 1987

49 Pilger, John, *A Secret Country*, Vintage, Sydney, 1992

50 Richard Hall, *The Secret State*, Cassell Australia, Sydney, 1978

51 *Mother Jones* Magazine, February 1984, March 1987

52 http://johnpilger.com/articles/the-forgotten-coup-how-america-
    and-britain-crushed-the-government-of-their-ally-australia

53 Kwitney

54 Mark Davis, *Dateline*, SBS, 18 February 2014, www.sbs.com.au/
    news/dateline/story/falcon-lands

55 Hocking, Jenny, *Gough Whitlam*, *His Time*, Melbourne
    University Press, 2012

56 *Ibid.*

57 *Ibid.*

Chapter 4: Rise of the Internet

 1 'Forty Years Later Looking Back at the Internet's Birth',
    All Things Considered, NPR, 1 November 2009

 2 *Ibid.*

 3 *Ibid.*

 4 www.academia.edu/1416892/Getting_Started_Computing_at_
    the_AI_Lab

 5 *Ibid.*

 6 Lowen, Rebecca S, *Creating the Cold War University:
    The Transformation of Stanford*, University of California Press,
    Berkeley and Los Angeles, 1997

 7 http://exploredegrees.stanford.edu/stanfordsmission/#text

 8 *Encyclopedia Britannica*, 2014: www.britannica.com/
    EBchecked/topic/264529/Hewlett-Packard-Company
    #toc92971

 9 http://web.archive.org/web/20120708201732/http://www.hp.
    com/retiree/memoriam/hp/2011.html

10 http://steveblank.com/2009/08/17/stanford-crosses-the-
    rubicon/

11 Facts on File History Database, 2014: www.fofweb.com/
    History/MainPrintPage.asp?iPin=TNFY230&DataType=
    AmericanHistory&WinType=Free

12 www.sourcewatch.org/index.php?title=Committee_on_the_
    Present_Danger

13 www.hpmuseum.net/pdf/HPAnnualReport_1988_52pages_
    OCR.pdf

14 *Wired* magazine, December 2000: http://archive.wired.com/
    wired/archive/8.12/mustread.html?pg=11

15 'In Search of Google', *Time* magazine, 13 August 2000

16 McEachern, William, *Contemporary Economics*, South Western
    Publishing, Florence, February 2012

17 *Lost in the Cloud: Google and the US Government*, published by
    Consumer Watchdog, California, 2011

18 Tenet, George, *At The Center Of The Storm: My Years at the
    CIA*, HarperCollins, New York, 2007

19 *Ibid.*

20 www.linkedin.com/in/ripainter

21 www.threadwatch.org/node/9612

22 *Ibid.*

23 *Ibid.*

24 *Ibid.*

25 *Ibid.*

26 http://pages.cs.wisc.edu/~shavlik/ICDM_2003_Schedule.pdf

27 http://battellemedia.com /archives/2006/10/just_in_case.php

28 https://www.mattcutts.com/blog/debunking-google-in-bed-
    with-cia/

29 www.siliconbeat.com/entries/2004/10/27/spooks_and_google.
    html

30 Google official blog, http://googleblog.blogspot.com.au/
    2006/02/response-to-doj-motion.html

31 Copy of court document held by author

32 www.wired.com/2010/07/exclusive-google-cia/

33 18 March 2010, CNBC

34 www.spaceref.com/news/viewsr.html?pid=25413

35 'Lost in the Cloud: Google and the US Government',
    Consumer Watchdog, California, 2011

36 'U.S. spy network's successes, failures and objectives detailed in
    "black budget" summary', viewed at www.washingtonpost.com/
    world/national-security/black-budget-summary-details-us-spy-
    networks-successes-failures-and-objectives/2013/08/29/7e57bb78-
    10ab-11e3-8cdd-bcdc09410972_print.html

37 www.eisenhowerproject.org

Chapter 5: Race to the Bottom

1 www.smh.com.au/news/national/rising-after-the-fall/2008/
   11/01/1224956397578.html

2   *The Monthly*, July 2013

3   *Ibid.*

4   *Ibid.*

5   *Ibid.*

6   *Ibid.*

7   *Ibid.*

8   Crikey, August 2014

9   News Centre 4, San Francisco, 1981 Youtube archived TV report viewed at www.wamp.com/theinternet/#close

10   Philip Myer, 'Learning to Love Lower Profits', *American Journalism Review*, December 1995

11   www.theguardian.com/media/greenslade+music/elton-john

12   *The Wall Street Journal*, June 1997, viewed at www.wsj.com/articles/SB852688850493222500

13   *Ibid.*

14   'Letter from the Publisher', *The Wall Street Journal*, January 2007

15   *Ibid.*

16   *Ibid.*

17   'Can Newspapers End the Free Ride Online?', *The New York Times*, 14 March 2005

18   *Ibid.*

19   *Ibid.*

20   'Online Newspaper Ads Gaining Ground on Print', *The New York Times*, 6 June 2006

21   *Ibid.*

22   Response to author questions

23   'Times of London Paywall Paying off Already!' *Forbes* magazine, 12 March 2010

24   *Ibid.*

25   *The Guardian*, 2 July 2013

26   *Ibid.*

27   www.theguardian.com/media/greenslade/2014/oct/10/abc-figures-show-papers-efforts-to-stem-circulation-decline

28   Year 2008 figures from Australian Press Council site: www.presscouncil.org.au/uploads/52321/state-of-the-news-print-media-2008.pdf; Year 2014 figures from Audited Media Association of Australia site: www.auditedmedia.org.au

29   Audited Media Association of Australia site: www.auditedmedia.org.au

30   http://newscorp.com/2014/09/17/news-corp-opposed-googles-european-commission-settlement-offer-welcomed-competition-commission-reconsideration/

31 *Ibid.*

32 *Columbia Journalism Review*, volume 18, number 5 Jan/Feb
    1980

33 'The Fight to Get Google to Pay for News Continues in
    Europe', NiemanLab, 2 December 2014

34 http://newscorp.com/2014/09/17/news-corp-opposed-
    googles-european-commission-settlement-offer-welcomed-
    competition-commission-reconsideration/

35 *Ibid.*

36 http://googlepolicyeurope.blogspot.com.au/2014/09/dear-
    rupert_25.html

Chapter 6: Trash Sells

1   http://news.bbc.co.uk/2/hi/6301243.stm

2   *Ibid.*

3   www.theguardian.com/media/2009/jul/08/murdoch-
    newspapers-phone-hacking

4   Leveson Inquiry: www.levesoninquiry.org.uk/wp-content/
    uploads/2011/11/Transcript-of-Morning-Hearing-24-
    November-2011.pdf

5   www.publications.parliament.uk/pa/cm201012/cmselect/
    cmcumeds/903/90304.htm

6   www.publications.parliament.uk/pa/cm201012/cmselect/
    cmcumeds/903/90304.htm

7   www.pcc.org.uk/newsarchive/index.html?article=NjAyOA==

8   www.thewire.com/business/2011/08/news-corp-best-friends-
    us-attorney-investigating-them/41111/

9   www.telegraph.co.uk/news/uknews/leveson-inquiry/9072308/
    Leveson-Inquiry-the-truth-behind-Freddie-Starr-ate-my-
    hamster.html

10 House of Commons Culture, Media and Sports Committee

11 www.publications.parliament.uk/pa/cm201012/cmselect/
    cmcumeds/903/90313.htm

12 *Ibid.*

13 *Ibid.*

14 House of Commons Culture, Media and Sports Committee,
    News International and Phone Hacking, Eleventh Report of
    Session, 2010–12 Volume II

15 *Ibid.*

16 www.independent.co.uk/news/people/profiles/lord-
    justice-leveson-grand-inquisitor-of-the-press-2328682.
    html

17   See for example, www.huffingtonpost.co.uk/2012/11/22/
      leveson-inquiry-publication-date_n_2174910.html
18   House of Commons Culture, Media and Sports Committee

Chapter 7: Source for the Goose
 1   The Commission on the Intelligence Capabilities of the United
      States Regarding Weapons of Mass Destruction. Report to the
      President of the United States, 31 March 2005
 2   Blix, Hans (Dr), UN Security Council Update, 23 January 2003
 3   Goetz, John & Drogin, Bob, '"Curveball" speaks, and a
      reputation as a disinformation agent remains intact', *Los Angeles
      Times*, 18 June 2008
 4   *Ibid.*
 5   The Commission on the Intelligence Capabilities of the United
      States Regarding Weapons of Mass Destruction Report to the
      President of the United States, 31 March 2005
 6   'Lie By Lie: A Timeline of How We Got into Iraq', *Mother
      Jones*, September/October 2000
 7   Clarke, Richard, *Against All Enemies*, Thorndike Press,
      Waterville, 2004
 8   *Ibid.*
 9   *Ibid.*
10   *Ibid.*
11   Drogin, Bob & Goetz, John, 'How US Fell Under Spell of
      Curveball', *Los Angeles, Times*, 20 November 2005
12   Foer, Franklin, 'Flacks Americana, John Rendon's Shallow PR
      War on Terrorism', *New Republic*, 20 May 2002
13   Davis, John (ed.) *Presidential Policies and the Road to the Second
      Iraq War*, Ashgate Publishing Company, Aldershot, 2006
14   Jennings, Peter, 'Unfinished Business: the CIA and Saddam
      Hussein', ABC News America, 1997
15   Foer
16   *Ibid.*
17   www.sourcewatch.org/index.php/Rendon_Group
18   Foer
19   Ricks, Thomas E., *Fiasco: The American Military Adventure in
      Iraq*, Penguin, New York, 2006
20   Duthel, Heinz, *Global Secrets and Intelligence Services II*, Books
      on Demand Norderstd, Germany 2006
21   *Ibid.*
22   Hersh, Seymour, 'Selective Intelligence', *New Yorker*,
      12 May 2003

23 *Dateline*, 23 July 2003, SBS TV

24 Author interview, Sydney, 2015

25 Author interview, Sydney, 2015

26 www.abc.net.au/corp/memorial/

27 www.sbs.com.au/news/article/2003/07/23/paul-moran-story

28 Anderson, Fay, & Trembath, Richard, 'Witness to War: The History of Conflict Reporting', Melbourne University Press, Melbourne, 2011

29 Bush, George W., State of the Union Address, 29 January 2002, http://georgewbush-whitehouse.archives.gov/stateoftheunion/2002/

30 http://pmtranscripts.dpmc.gov.au/preview.php?did=12764

31 *Ibid.*

32 'The Case Against Saddam', BBC *Panorama*, 23 September 2002

33 'Spinning the Tubes', *Four Corners*, ABC TV, October 2003

34 US Presidential Commission, March 2005

35 'Interview With CIA's Former Europe Director: We Probably Gave Powell the Wrong Speech', *Der Spiegel*, 29 January 2007

36 *Ibid.*

37 *The Washington Post*, 25 June 2006

38 *Sunday Herald* (Scotland), 10 August 2003, Wayback Machine

39 Author interview, 2015

40 *Ibid.*

41 Risen, James & Lichtblau, Eric, 'Bush Lets US Spy on Callers without Courts', *The New York Times*, 16 December 2005

42 *Ibid.*

43 *The Sydney Morning Herald*, 12 March 2003

44 www.pbs.org/newshour/bb/middle_east-jan-june03-search_04-22/

45 *Ibid.*

46 www.nytimes.com/2003/04/21/international/worldspecial/21CHEM.html

47 www.nytimes.com/2003/04/21/world/aftereffects-prohibited-weapons-illicit-arms-kept-till-eve-war-iraqi-scientist.html

48 www.nytimes.com/2003/04/23/world/aftereffects-the-search-focus-shifts-from-weapons-to-the-people-behind-them.html

49 www.nytimes.com/2003/04/24/international/worldspecial/24CHEM.html

50 www.nytimes.com/2005/10/16/national/16miller.html?pagewanted=all

51 Friel, Howard & Falk, Richard A., *The Record of the Paper: How The New York Times Misreports US Foreign Policy*, Verso, London, 2004

52 www.salon.com/2004/05/27/times_10/

53 *The Sun*, 27 February 2004

54 Author note

55 www.latrobe.edu.au/news/articles/2014/opinion/the-iraq-wars-coalition-of-the-shilling

56 *Ibid.*

57 www.smh.com.au/news/Anti-Terror-Watch/Downers-office-asked-for-copy-of-leaked-report/2004/06/18/1087245110202.html

58 'Mortality in Iraq Associated with the 2003–2011 War', was published in the journal *PLOS Medicine*, a weekly peer-reviewed medical journal, 15 October 2013

59 *The New York Times*, 26 May 2004

60 www.editorandpublisher.com/Article/-The-New-York-Times-in-Editors-Note-Admits-Fault-in-Iraq-WMD-Coverage

61 www.salon.com/2004/05/27/times_10/

62 Moore, James C., www.theguardian.com/world/2004/may/29/iraq.usa1

63 Calame, Byron, 'Eavesdropping and the Election', *The New York Times*, 13 August 2006

64 Greenwald, Glenn, *No Place to Hide*, Hamish Hamilton, London, 2014

65 Jackson, William E. (Jr.), 'Miller's Star Fades (Slightly) at *NY Times*', *Editor and Publisher*, 2 October 2003

66 *The New York Times*, www.nytimes.com/packages/pdf/national/nat_MILLER_051001.pdf.

67 Salon, 28 May 2004

Chapter 8: WikiLeaks

1 https://cpj.org/2012/02/despite-pardon-correa-does-lasting-damage-to-press.php

2 Assange, Julian, author interview, Melbourne, May 2010

3 *Ibid.*

4 Internal WikiLeaks emails published by Cryptome, http://cryptome.org

5 http://home.comcast.net/%7Eantaylor1/counterpunchnonfict.html

6 IQ.org 31 December 2006

7 *Ibid.*

8 ABC TV *Foreign Correspondent*, May 2010
9 Keller, Bill, 'Dealing with Assange and the WikiLeaks Secrets',
   The New York Times, 26 January 2011.
10 *Ibid.*
11 *Ibid.*
12 'Leaked Reports Paint an Unvarnished and Grim Look at the
   Afghan War', NPR.org, 26 July 2010
13 'The Story Behind the Publication of WikiLeaks' Afghanistan
   Logs', *Columbia Journalism Review*, 28 July 2010.
14 www.cjr.org/campaign_desk/the_story_behind_the_publicati.php
15 *Ibid.*
16 *Ibid.*
17 www.nytimes.com/2010/07/30/world/asia/30wiki.html?_r=0
18 http://edition.cnn.com/2010/US/07/29/wikileaks.mullen.gates/
19 Keller
20 Fowler, Andrew, *The Most Dangerous Man in the World*,
   Melbourne University Press, Melbourne, 2011
21 Greenwald, Glenn, *No Place to Hide*, Hamish Hamilton, United
   Kingdom, 2014
22 Assange, Julian, author interview, December 2010
23 'WikiLeaks Founder on the Run, Chased by Turmoil', *The New
   York Times*, 23 October 2010
24 *Wired* magazine, September 2010
25 Ellsberg, Daniel, author interview, January 2011
26 'An Inside Look at Difficult Negotiations with Julian Assange',
   Der Spiegel, 28 January 2011
27 *Ibid.*
28 Assange
29 Leigh, David, & Harding, Luke, *WikiLeaks: Inside Julian
   Assange's War on Secrecy*, Guardian Books, London, 2011
30 Assange
31 *Ibid.*
32 Author informant
33 Assange
34 Ellsberg
35 *Ibid.*
36 Greenwald
37 www.reuters.com/article/2010/12/10/uk-wikileaks-indictment-
   report-idUKTRE6B94I620101210
38 'Leader should be executed', 30 November 2010,
   politico.com
39 *Insiders*, ABC TV, 24 June 2012

40 Letter from Australia's attorney-general to Assange's lawyers;
www.ag.gov.au/RightsAndProtections/FOI/Documents/
(Publicly%20Available)%20-%20Letter%20from%20AG%20
to%20JR.pdf

41 *Ibid.*

42 Assange

43 http://cancilleria.gob.ec/ecuador-reaffirms-its-commitment-
in-defense-of-human-rights-freedom-and-the-life-of-julian-
assange/?lang=en

44 *Ibid.*

45 *Ibid.*

46 www.theguardian.com/uk-news/2014/oct/28/assange-sweden-
prosecutor-marianne-ny-uk-embassy-ruling

47 *Ibid.*

48 www.wired.com/2014/11/sweden-rejects-assange-appeal/

49 Assange, Julian, author interview, August 2014

50 *Ibid.*

Chapter 9: iSpy

1 'Found: The Beatles tape one man wishes he'd never heard.
Original audition reel REJECTED by Decca records
50 years ago', *Daily Mail*, 23 November 2012

2 Greenwald, Glenn, *No Place to Hide*, Hamish Hamilton,
London, 2014

3 *Ibid.*

4 *Ibid.*

5 *Ibid.*

6 *Ibid.*

7 *Ibid.*

8 *Ibid.*

9 www.washingtontimes.com/news/2013/may/24/eric-holder-
signed-doj-affidavit-fox-reporter-repo/?page=all

10 Greenwald

11 *Ibid.*

12 *Ibid.*

13 *Ibid.*

14 *Ibid.*

15 *Ibid.*

16 *Ibid.*

17 *Ibid.*

18 *Ibid.*

19 *Ibid.*

20 *Ibid.*
21 *Ibid.*
22 *Ibid.*
23 *Ibid.*
24 *Ibid.*
25 *Ibid.*
26 *Ibid.*
27 Greenwald, Glenn, with additional reporting by Ewen MacAskill & Spencer Ackerman, www.guardian.com, 6 June 2014
28 www.nytimes.com/2013/06/07/opinion/president-obamas-dragnet.html?_r=0
29 Greenwald, Glenn, *No Place to Hide*
30 www.nytimes.com/2013/06/08/technology/tech-companies-bristling-concede-to-government-surveillance-efforts.html
31 *Ibid.*
32 www.microsoft.com/security/online-privacy/onedrive.aspx
33 Greenwald, Glenn, *No Place to Hide*
34 www.pcworld.com/article/2044164/report-microsoft-helped-nsa-circumvent-its-own-encryption.html
35 Greenwald, Glenn, *No Place to Hide*
36 Author informant
37 Bamford, James, 'A terabyte of data can now be stored on a flash drive the size of a man's pinky': www.wired.com/2012/03/ff_nsadatacenter/
38 Snowden, Edward, interview by Glenn Greenwald & Laura Poitras, Hong Kong, 6 June 2013
39 www.theguardian.com/world/2013/jun/09/edward-snowden-nsa-whistleblower-surveillance
40 www.washingtonpost.com/world/national-security/us-charges-snowden-with-espionage/2013/06/21/507497d8-dab1-11e2-a016-92547bf094cc_story.htm
41 Reuters, London, 24 June 2013
42 www.theguardian.com/world/2013/jun/09/edward-snowden-nsa-whistleblower-surveillance
43 www.youtube.com/watch?v=QwiUVUJmGjs&spfreload=10
44 *Ibid.*
45 www.theguardian.com/world/2013/jun/09/edward-snowden-nsa-whistleblower-surveillance

Chapter 10: Hide-and-Seek

1 'US Pressing Its Crackdown Against Leaks', *The New York Times*, 17 June 2009

2 Woodward, Bob, & Bernstein, Carl, *All the President's Men*, Simon and Schuster, New York, 1974
3 www.dcd.uscourts.gov/dcd/sites/dcd/files/10-291MRedacted OrderToUnseal.pdf
4 *Ibid.*
5 *Ibid.*
6 *Ibid.*
7 *Ibid.*
8 *Ibid.*
9 *Ibid.*
10 *Ibid.*
11 Fox News, www.foxnews.com/politics/2009/06/11/nk-post-un-sanctions-plans-revealed
12 *Ibid.*
13 www.dcd.uscourts.gov/dcd/sites/dcd/files/10-291MRedacted OrderToUnseal.pdf
14 *Ibid.*
15 *Ibid.*
16 *Ibid.*
17 *Ibid.*
18 Fowler, Andrew, *The Most Dangerous Man in the World*, Melbourne University Press, Melbourne, 2011
19 *Ibid.*
20 *Ibid.*
21 Harrison, Sarah, author interview, Berlin, 16 September 2014
22 www.laquadrature.net
23 *Le Monde*, 21 September 2012
24 'More State Power not Free Speech the Likeliest We-Are-Charlie Result', Canadian Broadcasting Corporation, 15 January 2015

Chapter 11: Press One for Jingoism
1 Hastings, Max, 'Why the liberals who defended traitors like Snowden and Assange should look at this photo and admit: We were deluded fools', 10 January 2015, www.dailymail.co.uk/news/article-2904237/MAX-HASTINGS-liberals-defended-traitors-like-Snowden-Assange-look-photo-admit-deluded-fools.html
2 *Ibid.*
3 *Ibid.*
4 'My Vote', *The Guardian*, 11 April 2010
5 'Edward Snowden Leaks Mean it Takes Three Times as Long to Track Terrorists', *The Daily Telegraph*, London, 11 October 2014

6   *Ibid.*

7   *Ibid.*

8   *The Sun*, 10 October 2013

9   *The Sun*, 13 October 2013

10   www.dnotice.org.uk

11   The Defence Press and Broadcasting Advisory Committee, minutes, 7 November 2013

12   *Ibid.*

13   *Ibid.*

14   www.theguardian.com/world/2013/oct/28/david-cameron-nsa-threat-newspapers-guardian-snowdenline.

15   The Defence Press and Broadcasting Advisory Committee, minutes, 7 November 2013

16   *Ibid.*

17   *The 7.30 Report*, ABC 1, 17 February 2013

18   'Australia Spied on Indonesian President Bangbang Yudhoyono Leaked Snowden Documents Reveal', ABC, 18 November 2013

19   *Ibid.*

20   *Ibid.*

21   'Tony Abbott Blasts ABC judgment on Indonesia Spying Story', *The Australian*, 4 December 2013

22   'Malcolm Turnbull Slams ABC boss Mark Scott', *The Daily Telegraph*, Sydney, 3 December 2013

23   *Ibid.*

24   'Tony Abbott Blasts ABC judgment on Indonesia Spying Story'

25   'ABC's Mark Scott defends publishing spy story, hits back at News Corp', ABC TV, 2 December 2013

26   *SBS News*, 6 September 2013

27   'Crazy Act of Will: *The Guardian Australia* Turns One', http://mumbrella.com.au/bold-adventure-guardian-australia-228790

28   www.telegraph.co.uk/news/politics/10418823/GCHQ-revelations-may-be-treasonous-MP-claims.html

29   'David Miranda, Schedule 7 and the Dangers all Reporters Must now Face', *The Guardian*, 19 August 2013

30   www.theguardian.com/commentisfree/2013/aug/19/david-miranda-schedule7-danger-reporters

31   'GCHQ Intercepted Foreign Politicians Communications at G20 Summits', *The Guardian*, 17 June 2013

32   www.theguardian.com/commentisfree/2013/aug/19/david-miranda-schedule7-danger-reporters

33   'David Miranda, Schedule 7 and the Dangers all Reporters Must now Face'

34 *Ibid.*
35 www.theguardian.com/media/2013/dec/03/keith-vaz-alan-rusbridger-love-country-nsa
36 'MPs Question Alan Rusbridger's Patriotism Over Edward Snowden, Leaks', *The Independent*, 3 December 2013
37 House of Commons Home Affairs Committee Counter Terrorism, 17th Report of Session 2013-14
38 *Daily Mail*, 4 December 2013
39 *The Guardian*, 19 August 2013
40 *Le Parisien*, 10 January 2015

Chapter 12: Chickenshit Editors

1   http://archives.nbclearn.com/portal/site/k-12/flatview?cuecard=1419
2   www.wsj.com/articles/edward-kosner-the-temptation-of-the-celebrity-journalist-1423527690
3   'When the Post Banned Anonymous Sources', *American Journalism Review*, http://ajrarchive.org/Article.asp?id=3946
4   www.abc.net.au/lateline/content/2010/s2981595.htm
5   www.abc.net.au/news/2011-08-30/rosen---why-political-coverage-is-broken/2862328
6   Dempster, Quentin, *Death Struggle*, Allen & Unwin, Sydney, 2000
7   Response to author questions
8   http://quadrant.org.au/magazine/2011/11/how-tony-abbott-should-fight-the-culture-wars/
9   'Surviving the ABC's Survival', *The Sydney Morning Herald*, 16 July 2002
10 Author note, Sydney, 2000
11 Inglis, Ken, *Whose ABC?: The Australian Broadcasting Corporation, 1983–2006*, Black Inc., Melbourne, 2006, p. 509
12 www.crikey.com.au/2010/11/05/former-abc-chief-says-laws-on-board-appointments-are-offensive/?wpmp_switcher=mobile
13 'Senate to look into ABC threat to sack Adams', *The Sydney Morning Herald*, 11 September 2000
14 www.abc.net.au/mediawatch/transcripts/s208677.htm
15 www.abc.net.au/pm/stories/s218786.htm
16 *Ibid.*
17 Simons, Margaret, 'Fear and Loathing at the ABC', *The Monthly*, May 2005
18 *Ibid.*
19 Author note, 5 August 2011
20 *Ibid.*
21 *Ibid.*

22 *Ibid.*
23 www.fabcnsw.org.au/Update/update_2001-2/update2001_11.pdf
24 Author note, 2 February 2015, Sydney
25 www.theage.com.au/articles/2002/05/24/1022038479432.html
26 'ABC Head Resigns', *Lateline*, ABC TV, 31 October 2001
27 'Calm After the Storm', *The Sydney Morning Herald*,
   23 September 2002
28 Simons
29 *Ibid.*
30 *Ibid.*
31 www.abc.net.au/am/content/2003/s861872.htm
32 Marsh, Kevin, *The Independent*, 4 April 2013
33 'Hutton Inquiry: Alistair Campbell, Andrew Gilligan and Greg
   Dyke Look Back 10 Years On', *The Independent*, 27 April 2013
34 Morris, Nigel, 'BBC report on Sexed-Up Dossier is Vindicated,
   says Dyke', *The Independent*, 15 July 2004
35 Complaints Review Executive Report, ABC, July 2003, copy
   held by author
36 *Ibid.*
37 www.abc.net.au/mediawatch/transcripts/s981335.htm
38 *Ibid.*
39 www.abc.net.au/pm/content/2003/s964566.htm
40 www.thewire.com/politics/2013/09/sy-hershs-plan-fix-
   journalism-first-fire-all-editors/69945/
41 www.smh.com.au/comment/israels-rank-and-rotten-fruit-is-
   being-called-fascism-20140725-zwd2t.html
42 *Ibid.*
43 *Ibid.*
44 *Ibid.*
45 *Ibid.*
46 *Ibid.*
47 *ABC Radio 702*, 6 August 2014
48 www.theaustralian.com.au/business/media/jewish-bigot-
   pissant-likudnik-mike-carlton-ordered-to-apologise-for-
   torrent-of-abuse/story-e6frg996-
49 http://resources.news.com.au/files/2014/08/05/1227014/
   706878-140806carlton.pdf
50 https://twitter.com/mikecarlton01/status/493257798264688640
51 https://twitter.com/yorka1/status/493671873209569281
52 https://twitter.com/mikecarlton01/status/496864619646816256
53 www.opendemocracy.net/ourkingdom/peter-oborne/why-
   i-have-resigned-from-telegraph

54 *Ibid.*
55 *Ibid.*
56 *Ibid.*
57 *Ibid.*
58 *Ibid.*
59 *Ibid.*
60 *Ibid.*
61 *Ibid.*
62 *Ibid.*
63 *Ibid.*

Chapter 13: The Last Hurrah

1   www.sbs.com.au/news/datelin/story/murdochs-tv-pirates
2   'Murdoch's TV Pirates', *Panorama*, BBC One
3   www.theguardian.com/uk-news/2015/apr/28/how-margaret-thatcher-and-rupert-murdoch-made-secret-deal
4   www.publications.parliament.uk/pa/cm201011/cmhansrd/cm100909/debtext/100909-0002.htm
5   www.murdochspirates.com/Pirates/Echostar/court/injunction.pdf
6   *Ibid.*
7   www.digitalspy.com.au/media/news/a15400/bbc-news-24-edging-ahead-of-sky-news.html#~p3zG8sQDAEkUOL#ixzz3R10aZCL3
8   Davies, Nick, *Hack Attack*, Chatto & Windus, London, 2014
9   *Ibid.*
10 *Ibid.*
11 www.publications.parliament.uk/pa/cm201011/cmhansrd/cm110713/debtext/110713-0003.htm#11071379000002
12 Davies
13 *Ibid.*
14 *Ibid.*
15 *Ibid.*
16 *Ibid.*
17 www.bbc.com/news/entertainment-arts-30817270
18 Assange, Julian, author interview, London, August 2014
19 www.smh.com.au/news/wireless--broadband/labors-47-billion-broadband-plan/2007/03/21/1174153131586.html
20 www.smh.com.au/articles/2003/10/16/1065917548326.html?from=storyrhs
21 https://newmatilda.com/2009/06/24/turnbull-plays-hard-ball
22 *Turnbull v Meagher* (1984) 3 NSWLR

23 Ackland, Richard, 'A Sureness that Weakens Turnbull's Case',
    The Sydney Morning Herald, 17 October 2003

24 Barry, Paul, *The Rise and Rise of Kerry Packer*, Bantam, 1993

25 'Kerry Packer wasn't cleared on Taxes', *The Australian*,
    1 January 2011

26 'Crime Fighters Tax War on big Shots', *The Sydney Morning
    Herald*, 15 April 2009

27 'Kerry Packer Wasn't Cleared on Taxes'

28 *Ibid.*

29 *Ibid.*

30 *Ibid.*

31 Barry

32 Costigan Royal Commission Vol. III, 1984; www.parliament.vic.
    gov.au/papers/govpub/VPARL1982-85No177.pdf

33 *Ibid.*

34 Tiffen, Rod, 'The Packer–Labor Alliance 1978–79: RIP', *Media
    International Australia*, August 1995

35 www.youtube.com/watch?v=ueoJdaCTsy8

36 *Ibid.*

37 Print Media Inquiry, Parliament House, 1991; www.youtube.
    com/watch?v=xOLbbkC1qqo

38 *Ibid.*

39 *Ibid.*

40 *Ibid.*

41 *Ibid.*

42 *Ibid.*

43 'Australian media tycoon whose World Series changed the face of
    international cricket', *The Independent*, 28 December 2005

44 http://apo.org.au/commentary/how-packer-slipped-fairfax-
    help-malcolm-turnbull

45 'House of Representatives Print Media Inquiry, November
    1991', www.youtube.com/watch?v=xOLbbkC1qqo

46 Tiffen, Rod, 'How Packer slipped on Fairfax – with help from
    Malcolm Turnbull', *Australian Policy Online*, 26 August 2008

47 www.aph.gov.au/about_parliament/house_of_representatives/
    powers_practice_and_procedure/oo_-_infosheets/infosheet_
    4_-_committees

48 Ramsay, Alan, *The Way They Were*, University of New South
    Wales Press, Sydney, 2011

49 *Sunday*, Channel Nine, 19 February 1995

50 Author source

51 *Ibid.*

52 Savva, Niki, *So Greek: Confessions of a Conservative Leftie*, Scribe Publications Ltd, Melbourne, 2010

53 *Ibid.*

54 *Ibid.*

55 'Packer Wobbled on Whether to run Keating Piggery Story', *The Australian*, 15 June 2009

56 'Packer A Great Australian: Howard', *The Sydney Morning Herald*, 27 December 2005

Chapter 14: The Price of Freedom

1 www.theage.com.au/world/snowden-fallout-uk-threatens-to-stop-intelligencesharing-with-germany-20150206-137i77.html?skin=text-only

2 https://firstlook.org/theintercept/2015/03/19/us-threatened-germany-snowden-vice-chancellor-says/

3 *Ibid.*

4 www.npr.org/2014/07/22/333741495/before-snowden-the-whistleblowers-who-tried-to-lift-the-veil

5 www.newrepublic.com/article/120154/cia-ally-burr-will-chair-senate-select-committee-intelligence

6 'An NSA Coworker Remembers The Real Edward Snowden: "A Genius Among Geniuses"', *Forbes*, 16 December 2013

7 www.washingtonpost.com/world/national-security/edward-snowden-after-months-of-nsa-revelations-says-his-missions-accomplished/2013/12/23/49fc36de-6c1c-11e3-a523-fe73f0ff6b8d_story.html

8 www.supremecourt.gov/opinions/11pdf/10-1259.pdf

9 www.google.com.au/url?sa=t&rct=j&q=&esrc=s&source=web&cd=1&cad=rja&uact=8&ved=0CB4QFjAA&url=http%3A%2F%2Fwww.law.cornell.edu%2Fuscode%2Ftext%2F18%2F793&ei=hfwpVbrJBMG8mgW22IDYBQ&usg=AFQjCNHemmlYoqVlvoKn3gx-WQ66bkzhrw&sig2=xnI5ghMJUykK1132IDhZMg&bvm=bv.90491159,d.dGY

10 www.theguardian.com/world/2013/nov/06/al-gore-snowden-revealed-evidence-crimes-nsa/

11 www.washingtonpost.com/world/national-security/edward-snowden-after-months-of-nsa-revelations-says-his-missions-accomplished/2013/12/23/49fc36de-6c1c-11e3-a523-fe73f0ff6b8d_story.html

12 www.theguardian.com/uk-news/2013/oct/06/cabinet-gchq-surveillance-spying-huhne

13 www.thewhistler.org/tag/gavin-macfadyen/

ACKNOWLEDGEMENTS

Thanks firstly to my wife, Pamela Clark-Pearman, and our daughters, Elouise and Sophia, for their support while I wrote the book. Also for their encouragement and often insightful assistance with the manuscript.

To everyone at Penguin Random House Australia, particularly the book's brilliant editor, Anne Reilly, and Alison Urquhart, every author's dream publisher, who recognised there was an important story to tell here.

To my wonderful agent Jane Burridge, for all her guidance and support.

Thanks too for the insights and assistance of Heather Forbes, Quentin Dempster, Peter Cronau, Wayne Harley, Jeremie Zimmermann, and hosts of others still working in the media, who perhaps quite sensibly prefer not to be named.

Finally to Di and Graham Morris, Thierry and Florence Beauge, and the staff at Archives diplomatiques du ministère des Affaires étrangères et du Développement international, Paris. They variously provided shelter, encouragement and assistance in making this book a reality.

INDEX

350